NEW BLACK PLAYWRIGHTS

NEW
BLACK
PLAYWRIGHTS

An Anthology EDITED
AND WITH AN INTRODUCTION BY
William Couch, Jr.

LOUISIANA STATE UNIVERSITY PRESS · BATON ROUGE

CAUTION

ISBN 0-8071-0409-4
Library of Congress Catalog Card Number 68-31137

Manufactured in the United States of America
Designed by J. Barney McKee

To the Memory of W. E. B. D.

Contents

Introduction   *ix*

Happy Ending   DOUGLAS TURNER WARD   *3*

Day of Absence   DOUGLAS TURNER WARD   *25*

A Rat's Mass   ADRIENNE KENNEDY   *61*

Tabernacle   PAUL CARTER HARRISON   *71*

Goin' a Buffalo   ED BULLINS   *153*

Family Meeting   WILLIAM WELLINGTON MACKEY   *215*

Contributors   *253*

Introduction

It has been more than fifty years since W. E. B. Du Bois appealed to his fellow Negro writers to "set the black man before the world as both a creative artist and a strong subject for artistic treatment." And it has been several decades since Langston Hughes, at the height of the Harlem Renaissance, formulated his challenge echoing Du Bois: "We young Negro artists who are creating now intend to express our individual dark-skinned selves without fear or shame. If white people are pleased we are glad. If they are not, it does not matter . . . if colored people are pleased we are glad. If they are not, their displeasure does not matter either. We build our temples for tomorrow." Although today's black militants and revolutionaries were not born when Hughes and Du Bois (who now is one of the patron saints of the Black Left) proclaimed their independence, the spirit of their manifestoes is renascent.

As in most endeavor, assertion preceded the act. Langston Hughes's "temples for tomorrow" were built slowly, book by book, as gifted Negro writers arrived on the scene: Jean Toomer, Richard Wright, Chester Himes, Willard Motley, Ralph Ellison, James Baldwin. The list of sterling literary achievements in which these writers "set the black man before the world"—and the list could be extended—shows at a glance the mounting success of the Negro writer as novelist. An equally impressive roster could be made of Negro poets. Three years before Ralph Ellison received the 1953 National Book Award for *Invisible Man*, Gwendolyn Brooks—coming out of a tradition that dates from Jupiter Hammond, whose poems were published in 1760, and continuing through Phyllis Wheatley, Paul Lawrence Dunbar, Georgia Douglas Johnson, Countee Cullen, and Robert Hayden—became the first Negro to be awarded the Pulitzer Prize for poetry.

When we turn to the Negro as playwright, however, there is a noticeable difference. Very few plays written by Negroes have received major or even serious production, and fewer still have enjoyed a good run on Broadway—a neglect which appears all the more strange when we consider how closely Negroes have been allied with the major fields of entertainment in this country.

As early as the mid-eighteenth century, Negro minstrel companies like the Congo Melodists, the Ethiopian Serenaders, and the Georgia Minstrels were delighting American audiences. Bob Cole's *A Trip to Coontown* (1898) was probably the first show to be organized, produced, and managed by Negroes. By the turn of the century Paul Lawrence Dunbar, in collaboration with Will Marion Cook, was producing such successful Broadway theatricals as *Clorindy—the Origin of the Cakewalk* and *Jes Lak White Folks*, titles which clearly bespeak the era. The 1920's saw a spurt in the Negro's success in the field of musical comedy, with Broadway productions of Noble Sissle's *Chocolate Dandies* and Miller and Lyle's *Shuffle Along*, *Runnin' Wild*, and *The Black Birds*. That same period saw the rise to fame of such authentic stars of vaudeville as Bert

Williams, Florence Mills, Miller and Lyle, Sissle and Blake, and Bill "Bojangles" Robinson. Though discriminated against, black theatrical entertainers nevertheless found it possible to participate in a sector of the American theater, where they gained considerable prominence and acclaim.

This of course does not mean that Negroes did not desire to bring to the more serious side of the theater the same talents that they have demonstrated in the novel, in poetry, and in the lighter side of the theater. In fact, there is a considerable amount of history to attest to the black man's determination to establish himself in the great world of the theater. As early as 1821 an actor named James Hewlett formed the African Company in New York, where he became famous for his performances in Shakespearean roles. In 1833 Ira Aldridge, who entered the theater in this country as a handyman, was appearing on the London stage as Othello opposite Ellen Terry.

Charles Gilpin, who made drama history in 1920 playing the title role of Eugene O'Neill's *The Emperor Jones*, was selected by the New York Drama League, along with David Belasco and Eugene O'Neill, as one of the ten persons who contributed most to the American theater during the year. Paul Robeson, Rutgers University's four-letter man, a member of Phi Beta Kappa, and a graduate of the Columbia University Law School, later won fame in the Gilpin-created role and in O'Neill's *All God's Chillun*. "The Negro is a born actor," wrote George Jean Nathan, and "Robeson, with relatively little experience, and with no training to speak of, is one of the most thoroughly eloquent, impressive, and convincing actors that I have looked at and listened to in the past twenty years of theater going."

Similar accolades went to Leigh Whipper for his Broadway successes in John Steinbeck's *Of Mice and Men* and in George Sklar and Paul Peters' *Stevedore*, to Frank Wilson for his role in Paul Green's Pulitzer Prize–winning drama *In Abraham's Bosom*, and to Richard B. Harrison for his masterful portrayal of De Lawd in Marc Connelly's *Green Pastures.* Today the stage artistry of Robert Hooks, Sidney Poitier, and James Earl Jones forms a link with the accomplishments of the great Negro performers of the past.

Alain Locke, who in 1927 published an anthology entitled *Plays of Negro Life,* was optimistic about the rise of a national Negro theater "where the black playwright and the black actor will interpret the soul of their people in a way to win the attention and admiration of the world." Through the 1920's and 1930's Negroes, in the spirit of Langston Hughes, did seem to redouble their efforts to "build temples." In 1921 the Howard Players at Howard University in Washington, D. C., were organized, with the hope of establishing a basis for a Little Theater movement among Negroes. The Morgan College Players in Baltimore, Maryland, formed by playwright-teacher Randolph Edmonds in 1930, became a distinguished theatrical group. Edmonds also founded a Negro Intercollegiate Dramatic Association which included such predominately Negro schools as Morgan College, Howard University, Virginia State College, Shaw University, North Carolina College at Durham, Lincoln University in Pennsylvania, and A & T College at Greensboro, North Carolina. At the same time Fannin Belcher, drama coach at West Virginia State College, was organizing play tournaments among Negro high schools in the state "to cultivate in our students a more genuine enthusiasm for drama."

The contagion to perform and write for, to become an integral part of, the theater spread from black college campuses to black communities across the nation. Drama groups began to spring up—the Gilpin Players in Cleveland; the Krigwa Players with ensembles in Washington, in New York, and on the West Coast; Langston Hughes's Suitcase Theater in New York; the Rose McClendon Players; the Little Theater of Columbus, Ohio; The Neighborhood Players in Atlantic City, New Jersey, under the direction of Montgomery Gregory, who with Alain Locke founded the Howard University Players; and, currently, LeRoi Jones's Spirit House in Newark, New Jersey; and the Robert Hooks Negro Ensemble Company which operates in the Village on New York's Lower East Side under a $100,000 Ford Foundation grant. All such enterprises, despite their sometimes phoenix existence, provided Negroes with the opportunity for apprenticeship and expression in the field of drama.

But, as the Chicago *Defender* observed in 1930, the lot of the Negro in the theater continued to be "hard and the path more than unusually difficult. Work was uncertain, and wages more so." And the reality of the present, unfortunately, is that Negro actors have difficulty finding nonracial parts. A Negro actor cannot look forward to playing a lead role in a university theatrical production, where some of our best actors are receiving their training today; he still finds himself cast in plays written by white writers whose perception of Negro life, however sympathetic, often strikes one as false and superficial. Frederick O'Neal, Negro president of Actor's Equity Association, notes that there has been some improvement in the employment of Negro actors, but admits that the situation is far from acceptable. There was, in fact, a slight decrease between 1964 and 1965 in the number of Negroes employed in Broadway and off-Broadway shows. Also there is only a small handful of Negro producers and directors, and very few stage managers (Charles Blackwell, who was formerly with David Merrick Productions and now works with Harry Belafonte; James Wall, who works in television; and one or two others). Among theater talent agents the list is even shorter, probably the only successful one being Ernestine McClendon, whose clientele is integrated and who holds franchises from the major performer unions. An accurate estimate of the black actor's achievement must fall somewhere between, on the one hand, Locke's hopeful predictions and the brilliant instances that seem to bear out his judgment, and, on the other hand, the sobering comment recently made by James Baldwin: "It is a sad fact that I have rarely seen a Negro actor really well used on the American stage and screen, or on television."

As for black playwrights, it is possible that George Jean Nathan, in acclaiming Negroes as "born actors" and praising Paul Robeson for his ability to act without any training, inadvertently put his finger on the source of the problem. Actors, perhaps, may be "born," but the experience and craftsmanship necessary for successful playwrighting is more likely to come through close contact with the stage. Denied access to the full ambience of the theater, yet driven by an understandable urgency to make public their protests, Negro playwrights too often have suffered from the twin disasters of racial discrimination and hastily done work. Moreover, the relative preeminence of the black actor over the black playwright is in some degree the result of the public's tendency to regard actors as entertainers, a role traditionally "acceptable" for Negroes. Certainly it could be speculated that the kinds of social involvement attending the function of the playwright, the various contacts in the steps to Opening Night—the whole sociology of the theater world—restrict the opportunities of a black man. Poets and novelists work in solitude, their task being accomplished when they have had their say; but in the world of the theater, which demands relationships and interaction, the national ritual of race predominates.

From the start Negro writers have resisted the restrictions forced on black men. William Wells Brown's *The Escape, or a Leap to Freedom* (1858), the first play written in America by a Negro, satirized slavery. This play is not known to have been produced, although Brown did give numerous lyceum readings from it. Significantly, while Brown's plays (it is difficult to say how many he wrote, but he read from at least three in his lectures) languished unproduced in America, Victor Séjour, a Negro who was born in New Orleans in 1817, achieved a notable success in Europe as playwright and actor.

Le Théâtre Français presented Séjour's first play, *Diegarias,* in 1844, and it is believed that the theaters of Paris presented in all some twenty-one of this black expatriate's works.

Apparently the first successful drama written by a Negro and interpreted on the stage by Negro actors was Angeline Grimke's *Rachel,* a play in three acts dealing with the lynching of a girl's father, which was produced in 1916 by the Drama Committee of the NAACP in Washington, D.C. The tendentious character of the play was evident from the program announcement: "This is the first attempt to use the stage for race propaganda in order to enlighten the American people relative to the lamentable condition of ten millions of colored citizens in this free republic." In April, 1917, on the day of America's entrance into World War I, Broadway for the first time witnessed Negro actors performing in serious drama, when at the Garden City Theater the all-Negro Hapgood Players presented Ridgley Torrence's three one-act plays "written for the Negro theatre" (*Granny Maumee, The Rider of Dreams,* and *Simon the Cyrenian*). The event marked the beginning of public interest in the legitimate drama of Negro life as interpreted by Negroes. Five years later, in May, 1923, the Colored Folk Theatre, later known as the Ethiopian Art Theater, was organized by Raymond O'Neil in cooperation with Mrs. Sherwood Anderson. It offered such varied theater fare as Oscar Wilde's *Salome,* a jazz interpretation of Shakespeare's *A Comedy of Errors,* and *The Chip Woman's Fortune,* by Willis Richardson, a Negro government clerk who between 1921 and 1927 wrote six plays which were produced.

One of the most talented writers associated with the Harlem Renaissance was Jean Toomer, best known as a writer of fiction (*Cane*), whose almost tragic attempts to turn playwright were frustrated because the techniques he used were regarded as too advanced for the times. *Kabnis* (1923), a play that demonstrates his modernist methods, found no producer. *Balo, A Sketch of Negro Life* (1922), a less mature work dealing with

Negro peasants in Georgia, was performed by the Howard Players during the 1923–24 season.

Drama contests sponsored in the twenties by *Opportunity, A Journal of Negro Life* brought to light several new Negro playwrights: Frank Wilson, already well-known as an actor, who won first prize in 1925 with *Sugar Cane*; John Matheus, a promising literary talent who later turned to college teaching, who won first prize in 1926 with *'Cruiter*, a play which dealt with migrant Negro labor from the South after the First World War; and Georgia Douglas Johnson, the poet, whose *Plumes* won first prize in 1927.

Almost half the plays contributed to Alain Locke's *Plays of Negro Life* in 1927 were written by Negroes. That most of the white authors in the anthology (Eugene O'Neill, Paul Green, Ridgley Torrence) were better known than their Negro counterparts (Willis Richardson, Frank Wilson, or even Jean Toomer) neither obscured the Negroes' determination to succeed as playwrights nor concealed the progress these black writers had been making in spite of discouraging obstacles. Their achievement could be measured in light years from the days of minstrelsy and coon shows not too many decades before.

The following year, 1928, audiences at the Princess Theater on Broadway were captivated by Frank Wilson's *Meek Mose*, a serious study of Negro life. It had been a long journey for Wilson, from postal clerk to the *Opportunity* contests to Broadway as both playwright and actor. In 1929 Wallace Thurman's *Harlem* (written with assistance from William Rapp), which attempted to give an actual reproduction of the average Negro's existence in New York City, enjoyed a short run on Broadway before moving to Canada. In 1933 Hall Johnson's *Run Little Chillun* opened on Broadway. A folk play, it was a mixture of fantasy and realism, music and drama, and it revealed Johnson, whose reputation was already high as a composer and choir director, as a dramatist of genuine promise. In spite of weaknesses of plot and the overuse of melodramatic effects, *Run Little Chillun* is still probably one of the best theater works by an American Negro.

Creation of a Federal Theater Project in 1935 gave Negroes a laboratory for experiment in all areas of the theater. Plays of varying degrees of success devoted to the plight of the Negro were numerous and enjoyed a popularity which was reinforced by the general preoccupation with proletarian art in the thirties. Project productions of *The Hot Mikado, Haiti,* and *Macbeth* with black casts are still exciting memories. Of the contributions by Negro playwrights, perhaps the most notable in retrospect were Frank Wilson's *Walk Together Children* (1936), which focused on the race riots and friction that develop when southern Negro laborers come North, and Augustus Smith and Peter Morrell's powerful depiction in *Turpentine* (1936) of the struggles of workmen, black and white, in the Florida pines. When the Federal Theater Project ended in 1939, it had already served the purposes of revitalizing the interest of Negro communities in plays, especially in the larger cities, and had increased the knowledge and interest of black writers and actors in the techniques of the theater.

But it is not until we come to Langston Hughes that we find what, without any doubt, has been the most successful and enduring career of any Negro playwright. Hughes's *Mulatto,* a study of illicit relationships in the South which centers on the conflict between a mulatto son and his white father, is the first (and only) long-run Broadway hit by a Negro dramatist. Opening at the Vanderbilt Theatre on October 24, 1935, *Mulatto* played continuously until December 9, 1937. Encouraged by this success and loyal to a creative bent which embraced drama, poetry, and the novel, Hughes, unlike many of his contemporaries who after a few militant forays in the theater succumbed to what can only be described as the almost insurmountable difficulties of being a black playwright, continued to write plays for the rest of his life. Thirty years after his first Broadway success, and two years before his death in 1967,

Hughes's play *Tambourines to Glory* was running on Broadway. During the intervening years he had courageously accepted the writer's risk of never letting his pen remain idle, and he had steadfastly lived up to his credo that Negro artists should express themselves "without fear or shame." The results, in terms of artistry, were not always even. But the passionate confirmation of black life in America in such plays as *Trouble Island, Scottsboro Limited, Angela Herndon Jones,* and *Don't You Want to Be Free?,* not to mention dozens of lesser plays, comprises an honorable legacy to the proletarian drama of this country. Few American playwrights have surpassed the total achievement of Langston Hughes.

Ossie Davis, author of *Purlie Victorious* and an astute commentator on the theater, recently remarked that "No one can deny that integration has come to Broadway . . . that the Negro is now included, meaningfully, in more aspects of Broadway life." *Anna Lucasta* still remains one of the all-time record-holders for Broadway runs of straight plays, and Paul Robeson's *Othello* holds the record for the Broadway run of a Shakespearean play. Yet Mr. Davis is quick to confess "that while there are no impediments to plays about the truth of Negro experiences being produced on Broadway, such productions so far have not succeeded—have not been 'hits' in the sense that *Anna Lucasta* was." The hope that Negroes would be included in the mainstream of American theater, Mr. Davis confesses, "has been realized in form, but defeated in substance." Mr. Davis discloses that his own play, *Purlie Victorious,* which is a stunning comedy-satire on race nonrelations, was kept on Broadway for seven and one-half months with money out of his own pocket and that of his sympathetic producer. Lorraine Hansberry's *A Raisin in the Sun* did make money, but her *The Sign in Sidney Brustein's Window* was a financial failure. James Baldwin's much talked about, and little supported, *Blues for Mister Charlie* drained the author's friends and financial backers in the unsuccessful attempt to keep it in production.

The conclusion seems inescapable: Plays about Negroes, especially plays that deal candidly with the harsher realities of the Negro's existence in America, are not attractive to the general theater audience, and the bulk of the theatergoing audience is white.

Juxtaposed with this discouraging fact of our cultural life is the Negro's growing insistence that his story be told, and told in terms compatible with his own experience and self-awareness, told like it is. This conflict may force more and more Negro playwrights into an alliance with a revolutionary theater which already finds its expression in such plays as LeRoi Jones's *Dutchman*, *The Slave*, and *The Toilet*. "It is a political theatre," Mr. Jones has written, "a weapon to help in the slaughter of these dim-witted fat-bellied white guys who somehow believe that the rest of the world is here for them to slobber on." Mr. Jones goes on to claim for the revolutionary theater the task of "taking dreams" and "giving them a reality." It must "isolate the ritual and historical cycles of reality." Here he is on solid ground; a criticism of American life for its chronic and destructive necessity to substitute ritual for reality, and in far more areas than race, is entirely relevant and is indeed very hard to refute.

Ed Bullins, whose work is represented in this anthology, is similarly motivated by a consciousness of the "new roles, new themes and new definitions" that are waiting to be created and explored by the black writer. In fact, for men like Jones, Bullins, and William Wellington Mackey, this is the arresting and inescapable vocation of the black playwright today.

Such writers are, of course, aware of the problems facing them in the immediate future. Mr. Bullins, for instance, foresees a time when the black playwright may be told that his work is too "experimental" and "obscene" if it uses too much of the idiom of the black ghetto. Even where black theater groups are concerned we should not be surprised "when Negroes of flesh and blood are depicted on the stage, that this is verging upon revolution and is too drastic." Such groups, Mr. Bullins reflects, like their white counterparts, will perhaps for some time to come prefer the classics or the work of proven Negro writers like Langston Hughes to that of the "revolutionary" playwright. But the net result of the new black playwright's estrangement, in spite of a certain amount of confusion and vituperation which in the circumstances probably cannot be avoided, could be the emergence, in time, of a more sharply defined, and badly needed, sense of the white and the black dramatist's true function in this society. After all, the revolutionary's urgency to bring into being a theater where, as LeRoi Jones claims, "the nakedness of the human spirit is paraded" is certainly in accord with the profoundest requirements of dramatic art and is open very little to challenge in good faith. When we consider the vacuum that exists in the American theater today, which is largely the result of a nearly wholesale rejection of the vital uses of the theater by most established American playwrights, the current dispute of black playwrights with a public which seems to insist upon regarding the theater as a Fun House gains a better perspective, and we are inclined to believe that those playwrights who come forth with legitimate claims, however "revolutionary" they may be, ought to be warmly encouraged.

The plays in this book are a good sample of the concerns, in subject matter and treatment, of modern black consciousness. Douglas Turner Ward's *Day of Absence* and *Happy Ending* superbly combine thesis with theater farce, establishing a real, and sometimes half surreal, world in which whites get their comeuppance from black folks whose sardonic cunning is mordant proof that they, like people in general, though less than angels are far more than fools. Mr. Ward's effects derive chiefly from his access to a brand of realism that is geared to the tempo and style of the absurd theater.

Adrienne Kennedy's *The Owl Answers* (not included) and *A Rat's Mass*, on the other hand, are richly symbolic, poetic pieces. Her plays, structured in interplays of lights and shadows of meaning, achieve a delicately muted resonance. Images like shapes beneath a surface transform the black man's social and moral tragedies into an iconography of the universal quest for selfhood and identity. Satiric wit crackles like live current through Mr. Ward's plays, but in the plays of Miss Kennedy there is an evocative and mystical sense of being.

"Black people have a natural instinct for spontaneous creativity," writes Paul Harrison. "It is this gift, with its ritualistic overtones, that I'd like to investigate in order to discover a new standard for theatre arts." Mr. Harrison's *Tabernacle,* based on the Harlem riots of Summer, 1964, is an attempt to articulate black experience through a synthesis of all elements of the stage—plasticity of set design, dance movement, music (African and jazz), masks, choral chants, verse, and improvisation. The commanding theme is justice, probed with classical range and austerity, but the net effect, which entails both lyric poetry and *dozen playing,* is a beautiful exemplum of black theater experience. Employing a language that is rich, authentic, and full of tantalizing ambiguities, *Tabernacle* is a form which, eschewing both American theatrical tradition and the "formlessness" of European contemporary theater, reaches for "a new unity of Black creative expression." It is a fantasy, it is a musical, it is an opera, it is a play. It is Black.

In *Goin' a Buffalo* Ed Bullins brings us fully into the revolutionary theater or, as Mr. Bullins prefers to call it, "the theatre of reality." "The revolutionary nature of this theater is not of style and technique but of theme and character." Honesty, Mr. Bullins writes, "is what the writer should be after." The black playwright performs his function "by uncovering the reality of his art, his humanity, his existence as an intelligent and moral entity in the universe, and makes the entire universe an audience of this transformation of the psyche and spirit." Mr. Bullins, who could be called "an angry young man," is gifted with extraordinary imagination and ability. His play reflects the dramaturgy of Antonin Artaud yet brandishes the ideology of the current Black Left. Mama Too Tight, one of the main characters, displays an amazing element of the comic and pathetic, the sacred and profane. One of society's New Waifs, she is surely one of the least forgettable creatures likely to be encountered in contemporary plays. *Goin' a Buffalo* (the title is deceptive) must be seen, or read, to be believed.

The pursuit of new ideology, and a redefinition of social roles, preoccupies all thoughtful black Americans today. The result is a proliferation of viewpoints that mirrors the circumstances enjoyed, or endured, by black men and women across the nation. The conflict that exists between the middle-class, successful Negro and his numerous less fortunate brothers is a subject that interests William Wellington Mackey. Mr. Mackey has written one play (*Requiem for Brother X, A Homage to Malcolm X*) to be "a spit at the black middle class for turning their backs on the black masses still in bondage." Indeed Mr. Mackey shares a rapidly growing belief among the black masses that the cynicism of white Americans toward black Americans is total and intransigent, and has infected the minds of many Negroes themselves. In this conviction Mr. Mackey has found the matrix of his reality—namely, that black people must, through supreme acts of self-reevaluation and efforts of the will, rescue themselves from a malignant history, and through their own energy and genius must recover their stolen humanity. It is precisely this fiery protest and affirmation, joined with a perfect grasp of the black idiom and a superb use of irony, that elevates Mr. Mackey's *Family Meeting* to a level at which his polemics become irresistible.

Other black writers today would include Woodie King, Jr., Alice Childress, William Branch, Loftin Mitchell, Errol John, Abram Hill, Irving Burgie, Ann Flagg, Louis Peterson, and William Hairston.

Black writers, of course, differ among themselves in their

outlook on the world and society, as well as in their views on the purposes of drama. Out of such diversity come many of the instances of beauty and honesty to be found in this collection. Because there are vast tracts of unrecorded American experience, uncharted regions of the heart, we are fortunate that black playwrights today with renewed strength are undertaking to reveal us to ourselves more clearly than we have been able to perceive in our troubled history.

WILLIAM COUCH, JR.

NEW BLACK PLAYWRIGHTS

Happy Ending

Short One-Act Play

DOUGLAS TURNER WARD

Cast of Characters (in order of appearance)

ELLIE

VI

JUNIE

ARTHUR

TIME: The present; an early weekday evening around 5 or 6 P.M.

PLACE: The spotless kitchen of a Harlem tenement apartment. At stage left is a closed door providing entry to the outside hallway. On the opposite side of the stage is another door leading into the interior of the railroad flat. Sandwiched between this door and a window facing the brick walls of the apartment's inner shaft is a giant, dazzling white refrigerator. Positioned center stage is a gleaming, porcelain-topped oval table. Directly behind is a modern stove. To the left of the

3

stove, another window looks out upon a backyard court. The window is flanked on its left by a kitchen sink. Adjacent to the sink, upstage left, a bathroom door completes the setting.

As curtain rises, waning rays of daylight can be seen streaming through the courtyard window. Two handsome women, both in their late thirties or early forties, are sitting at opposite ends of the kitchen table. They are dressed as if recently entered from work. Hats and coats are still worn; handbags lie on floor propped against legs of respective chairs. They remain in dejected poses, weeping noiselessly.

ELLIE. Let me have your handkerchief, Vi . . .

(VI *hands it to her absently.* ELLIE *daubs eyes, then rests hankie on table. It lies there until* VI *motions for it to be handed back.*)

VI. What we gon do, Ellie?

ELLIE. Don' know . . . Don't seem like there's much more we kin do . . .

VI. This time it really might happen . . .

ELLIE. I know . . .

ELLIE. Lord, this may be the limit . . .

VI. End of the line . . .

VI. Persons kin go but just so far . . .

ELLIE. Hear us, Savior!

VI. Think it might help if I prayed a novena to him first thing tomorrow morning?

ELLIE. Certainly couldn't do no harm . . . .

(*They lapse into silence once again, passing hankie back and forth on request. Suddenly* JUNIE, *a tall, slender, sharply handsome, tastefully dressed youth in his early twenties, bursts upon the scene, rushing through hallway door.*)

JUNIE (*rapidly crossing, shedding coat in transit*). Hey Vi, Ellie . . . (*Exits through interior door, talking offstage*)

Ellie, do I have any more pleated shirts clean . . . ? Gotta make fast impression on new chick tonight . . . . (*Thrusting head back into view*) One of them foxy, black "Four Hundred" debutantes, you dig! All class and manners, but nothing underneath but a luscious, V-8 chassis!—which is a-o-reeet wit me since that's all I'm after. You hear me talking to ya! Now, tell me what I say! Hah, hah, hah! (*Withdraws head back offstage*) Sure got them petty tyrants straight at the unemployment office today. (*Dripping contempt*) Wanted me to snatch up one of them jive jobs they try to palm off on ya. I told 'em no thanks!—Shove it! (*Re-entering, busily buttoning elegantly pleated shirt*) If they can't find me something in my field, up to my standards, forget it! . . . Damn, act like they payin you money out their own pockets . . . Whatcha got to eat, Ellie? . . . I'm scarfy as a bear. In fact—with a little salt 'n pepper, I could devour one of you—or both between a double-decker! (*Descends upon them to illustrate playfully. Pulls up short on noticing their tears for the first time*) Hey? . . . What'sa matter . . . ? What's up? (*They fail to respond.*) Is it the kids? (*They shake heads negatively.*) Somebody sick down home? (*Fearfully*) Nothing's wrong wit mother? (*They shake heads again.*) Roy or Jim in jail? . . . Arthur or Ben lose their jobs? (*Another double headshake.*) Tell me, I wanta know! Everything was fine this morning. Somp'um musta happened since. Come on, what is it?

ELLIE. Should we tell him, Vi?

VI. I don't know . . . No use gitting him worried and upset . . .

ELLIE (*Sighing heavily*). Maybe we better. He's got to find out sooner or later.

JUNIE. What are you crying for?

ELLIE. Our bosses—Mr. and Mrs. Harrison, Junie . . .

JUNIE. Mr. and Mrs. Harrison . . . ? (*Suddenly relieved; amused and sardonic*) What happened? They escape from a car wreck—UNHURT?

ELLIE (*failing to grasp sarcasm*). No.

JUNIE (*returning to shirt-buttoning*). Did you just git disappointing news flashes they gon live forever?

VI (*also misreading him*). No, Junie.

JUNIE. Well, what then? . . . I don't get it.

ELLIE. They's getting a divorce . . .

JUNIE. A what—?

VI. A divorce.

JUNIE. Why?

ELLIE. 'Cause Mr. Harrison caught her wit a man.

JUNIE. Well, it's not the first time 'cording to you.

ELLIE. The other times wasn't wit his best friend.

JUNIE. His best friend? Wheeee! Boy, she really did it up this time . . . Her previous excursions were restricted to his casual acquaintances! . . . But why the hell should he be so upset? He's put up wit all the rest. This only means she's gitting closer to home. Maybe next time it'll be him, ha, ha, ha . . .

ELLIE (*reprimandingly*). It's no joke, Junie.

JUNIE (*exiting into bathroom*). How'd it happen?

ELLIE. (*flaring at the memory*). Just walked in and caught 'em in his own bedroom!

VI. (*even more outraged*). Was that dirty dog, Mr. Heller, lives on the nineteenth floor of the same building!

ELLIE (*anger mounting*). I warned her to be careful when she first started messing with him. I told her Mr. Harrison was really gon kick her out if he found out, but she'd have the snake sneak in sometimes soon as Mr. Harrison left! Even had nerve to invite him to chaperone his wife back later in the evening for a lil after-dinner snack!

JUNIE (*re-entering*). What's a little exchange of pleasantries among rich friends, bosom buddies? Now, all Harrison has to do is return the favor and even things up.

VI. She really cooked her goose this time.

JUNIE. Good for her.

ELLIE. Good . . . ?

JUNIE. Sure—What'd she 'spect? To wait 'till she hauled some cat into bed right next to her old man befo' he got the message?

VI. They is gitting a *divorce*, Junie!

JUNIE (*sauntering over to fruit bowl atop refrigerator*). That's all? . . . I'm surprised I didn't read headlines 'bout a double murder and one suicide . . . But I forgot!—that's our soul folk's method of clearing up little gummy problems like that—that is, *minus* the suicide bit.

ELLIE. *They's breaking up their home, Junie!*

JUNIE (*biting into apple selected from bowl*). They'll learn to live wit it . . . Might even git to like the idea.

VI. And the chillun?

JUNIE. Delicate lil boobies will receive nice fat allowances to ease the pain until they grow up to take over the world.

ELLIE. Is that all you feel at a time like this, boy?

VI. Disastrous, that's what it is!

ELLIE. Tragicull 'n unfair!

JUNIE. Is this what you boohooing 'bout?

ELLIE. Could you think of anything worser?

JUNIE. But, why?

ELLIE. 'Cause this time we *know he means business, Junie!* Ain't no false alarm like them other times. We were there, right there! . . . Had a feeling somp'um was gon happen soon as I answered the door and let Mr. Heller in! Like chilly pneumonia on top a breeze . . . Miss Harrison tole me she didn't wanta be disturbed for the rest of the afternoon. Well, she was disturbed all right! They musta fell asleep 'cause Mr. Harrison even got home late and still caught 'em . . .

JUNIE. Couldn't you have interrupted their togetherness and sounded a timely danger warning?

ELLIE. We didn't hear him. I was in the kitchen, Vi down

in the basement ironing. I didn't know Mr. Harrison had come in 'till I heard screaming from the bedroom. But soon as I did, I called Vi and me and her tipped down the hall and heard Mr. Harrison order Mr. Heller to put his clothes back on and stop considering hisself a friend for the rest of his life! " 'N you—slut! Pack up and git out soon as you find a suitable apartment." . . . Then he invited me and Vi into the room and told us he was divorcing her . . . That man was hurt, Junie, hurt deep! Could see it in his eyes . . . Like a little boy, so sad he made you wanta grab hold his head and rock him in your arms like a baby.

VI. Miss Harrison looked a sight herself, po' thing! Like a lil girl caught stealing crackers out the cookie jar.

ELLIE. I almost crowned ole back-stabber Heller! Brushing 'gainst me on his way out!

JUNIE. Shoulda pinned a medal on him as he flew by. Escaping wit head still on shoulder and no bullet holes dotting his chest.

ELLIE. The skunk really left us all too high and dry for that, Junie . . . Oh, don't think it wouldn't broke your heart, too, nephew . . . Sneaky rascal gone, rest of us in sorrow, tears pouring down our faces 'n me and Vi jist begging and begging . . . "Y'all please think twice befo' you act rash and do anything you'll be sorry for. You love each other—and who's in better position than Vi and me to know how much you love each other—"

VI. 'Course she love him, just can't help herself.

ELLIE. "—When two hearts love each other as much as we know y'all do, they better take whole lots of time befo' doing something so awful as breaking up a marriage—even if it ain't hunert-percent perfect. Think about your reputation and the scandal this will cause Mr. Harrison. Jist 'bout kill your po' mother—her wit her blood pressure, arthritis, gout, heart tickle 'n everything. But most of all, don't orphan the kids! Kids come first. Dear lil angels! Just innocents looking on gitting hurt in ways they can't understand."

JUNIE. You told 'em this, Ellie?

ELLIE. Love conquers all, Junie.

JUNIE. Wit your assistance, Vi?

VI. As much as I could deliver, Junie.

JUNIE. And what impression did your tender concern have on the bereaved couple?

ELLIE. Mr. Harrison said he understood 'n appreciated our feelings and was very grateful for our kindly advice—but he was sorry, his mind was made up. She'd gone too far and he couldn't forgive her—not EVER! . . . We might judge him a harsh, vindicty man, he said, but he couldn't bring hisself to do it. Even apologized to us for being so cruel.

JUNIE (*continuing his slow boil*). You accepted his apology, Vi?

VI. I should say not. I pleaded wit him agin to think it over for sake of home, family and good name!

JUNIE. Well of all the goddamn things I ever heard!

ELLIE. (*heartened by his support*). I'm telling ya!

VI. I knew it was gon happen if she kept on like she did!

ELLIE. Just wouldn't listen!

JUNIE. It's a disgrace!

ELLIE. Ain't the word!

VI. Lot worse than that!

JUNIE. Did you both plop to your knees begging him to give her another chance?

VI. NO!—but we woulda if we'd thought about it! Why didn't we, Ellie?

ELLIE. Things happened so fast—

JUNIE. Never have I been so humiliated in all my life—!

VI. (*self-disgusted by their glaring omission*). No excuse not thinking 'bout it, Ellie!

ELLIE. Certainly ain't

JUNIE. What about your pride—?

VI. You right! Musta been false pride kept us from dropping to our knees!

JUNIE. Acting like imbeciles! Crying your heart out 'cause Massa and Mistress are gon break up housekeeping! Maybe I oughta go beat up the adulterous rat crawling in between the sheets! (*Pacing up and down in angry indignation as they sit stunned*) Here we are—Africa rising to its place in the sun wit prime ministers and other dignitaries taking seats around the international conference table—us here fighting for our rights like never before, changing the whole image, dumping stereotypes behind us and replacing 'em wit new images of dignity and dimension—and I come home and find my own aunts, sisters of my mother, daughters of my grandpa who never took crap off no cracker even though he did live on a plantation—drowning themselves in tears jist 'cause boss man is gonna kick boss lady out on her nose! Maybe *Gone With the Wind* was accurate! Maybe we jist can't help "Miss Scarrrrrrlet-ing" and "Oh Lawdying" every time mistress white gets a splinter in her pinky. That's what *I'm* talking about.

VI. Ain't you got no feelings, boy?

JUNIE. Feelings? . . . So you work every day in their kitchen, Ellie, and every Thursday you wash their stinky clothes, Vi. But that don't mean they're paying you to bleed from their scratches! . . . Look—don't get me wrong—I'm not blaming you for being domestics. It's an honorable job. It's the only kind available sometimes, and it carries no stigma in itself—but that's all it is, *a job!* An exchange of work for pay! *Bad pay at that!* Which is all the more reason why you shouldn't give a damn whether the Harrisons kick, kill or mangle each other!

ELLIE. You gotta care, Junie—

JUNIE. "Breaking up home and family!"—Why I've seen both of you ditch two husbands apiece and itching to send third ones packing if they don't toe the line. You don't even cry over that!

ELLIE. Don't have time to—

JUNIE. Boy, if some gray cat was peeping in on you, he'da sprinted back home and wrote five *Uncle Tom's Cabins* and ten "Old Black Joes"!

ELLIE. Wait a minute, now—

JUNIE. I never heard you shedding such tragic tears when your own lil crumb-crushers suffered through fatherless periods! All you grumbled was "good riddance, they better off wit'out the sonsabitches!" . . . Maybe Harrisons' tots will make out just as well. They got puny lil advantages of millions of dollars and slightly less parched skins!

VI. Show some tenderness, boy. Ain't human not to trouble over our bosses' sorrows—

JUNIE. That's what shames me. I gave you credit for more integrity. Didn't figger you had chalk streaks in ya. You oughta be shamed for *yourselves*!

ELLIE. And done what?

JUNIE. NOTHING!—Shoulda told 'em their sticky mess is their own mud puddle. You neutrals. Just work there. Aren't interested in what they do!

ELLIE. That wouldn't be expressing our deepest sentiments—

JUNIE. I'm ashamed you even had any "sentiments"! . . . Look, it's hopeless, I'm not getting anywhere trying to make you understand . . . I'm going out for a whiff of fresh air! (*Rushes to exit.*)

ELLIE. Come back here, boy!

JUNIE (*stopping at door*). What? To watch you blubber over Massa? No thanks!

ELLIE. I said come here, you hear me talking to you!

VI. You still ain't too big to git yourself slapped down!

ELLIE. Your ma gave us right any time we saw fit!

(*He returns reluctantly. An uneasy silence prevails.*)

ELLIE. Better git yourself somp'um to eat. (*rises, taking off coat.*)

JUNIE (*sulking*). I lost my appetite.

ELLIE (*hanging coat up*). What you want?

JUNIE. I told you I'm not hungry anymore.

VI. *We* made you lose your appetite . . . ?

(*He doesn't reply.*)

ELLIE. What did you crave befo' you lost it?

JUNIE. Anything you had cooked. Didn't have anything special in mind . . .

ELLIE (*offhandedly*). Steak? . . . T-Bone? . . . Porterhouse? . . . Filet . . . ?

JUNIE. No . . . I didn't particularly have steak in mind.

VI. Been eating too many lately, huh?

JUNIE. Just kinda tired of 'em, that's all.

ELLIE. How bout some chicken then . . . ? Roast beef? . . . Lobster? . . . Squab? Duck, or something?

JUNIE (*nettled*). All I wanted was some food, Ellie! . . . In fact, I really had a hankering for some plain ole collard greens, neck bones or ham hocks . . .

ELLIE. Good eatin', boy. Glad to hear that. Means that high-class digestion hasn't spoiled your taste buds yet . . . But if you want that rich, choice food, you welcome to it—

JUNIE. I know that, Ellie!

ELLIE. It's in the freezer for you, go and look.

JUNIE. I don't hafta, Ellie, I know—

ELLIE. Go look anyway.

JUNIE (*goes and opens refrigerator door*). It's there, Ellie, I didn't need to look.

VI. Come here for a second, Junie, got something on your pants leg. (*He obeys. She picks a piece of lint off trousers, then rubs material admiringly.*) Pants to your suit, ain't they? . . . Sure is a fine suit to be trotting off to the unemployment office . . . Which one-r the other you gon wear tonight when you try to con that girl outa her virginity—if she still got it?—The gray one? Brown one? The tweed? Or maybe you gon git sporty and strut that snazzy plaid jacket and them tight light pants? If not—which jacket and which pants?

ELLIE. Slept good last night, nephew? Or maybe you gitting tired of that foam rubber mattress and sheep fur blanket?

VI. How do them fine college queens and snooty office girls like the furniture they half see when you sneak 'em in here late at night? Surprised to see such fancy stuff in a beat-up ole flat, ain't they? But it helps you put 'em at ease, don't it? I bet even those sweet lil white ones are impressed by your class?

JUNIE (*indignantly*). That's not fair, Vi—

ELLIE. When last time you bought any food in this house, boy?

JUNIE. Ellie, you know—

ELLIE. When, Junie?

JUNIE. Not since I been here, but—

VI. And your last piece of clothes?

JUNIE (*more indignant*). I bought some underwear last week, Vi!

VI. I mean clothes you wear on top, Junie. Shirts, pants, jackets, coats?

JUNIE (*squirming*). You—you know I haven't, Vi—

ELLIE. Buy anything else in your room besides that tiny, midget frame for your mama's picture?

JUNIE. All right. I know I'm indebted to ya. You don't have to rub it in. I'll make it up to you when I git on my feet and *fulfill* my potential . . . But that's not the point!

ELLIE. You ain't indebted to us, Junie.

JUNIE. Yes, I am, I know it, I thank you for it.

ELLIE. Don't hafta thank us—

JUNIE. But that's not the issue! Despite your benevolence, I refuse to let you blackmail my principle, slapping me in the face wit how good you been to me during my temporary outta work period! I'm talking to you now, 'bout something above our personal relationship. Pride—Race—Dignity—

ELLIE. What's gon happen to me and Vi's dignity if Mr. Harrison throws Mrs. Harrison out on her nose as you put it?

JUNIE. Git another job! You not dependent on them. You young, healthy, in the prime of life . . . In fact—I've always wondered why you stagnate as domestics when you're trained and qualified to do something better and more dignified.

ELLIE. Glad you brought that up. Know why I'm not breaking my back as a practical nurse and Vi's not frying hair—'cept on the side? . . . Cause the work's too hard, the money ain't worth it and there's not much room for advancement—

JUNIE. Where kin you advance as a domestic? From kitchen to closet?

ELLIE (*refusing to be provoked, continuing evenly*). Besides, when I started working for the Harrisons, Junie, Mr. Harrison vowed that he would support me for life if I stayed with 'em until his daughter Sandy, his oldest child, reached ten years old.

JUNIE. Bully for him! He'll build ya a little cottage backa the penthouse garage!

ELLIE (*still unruffled*). Mr. Harrison is strictly a man of his word, Junie. Which means that even if I left one day after Sandy made ten, he owes me some money every week or every month as long as I live . . . . Sandy is *nine*, Junie, N-I-N-E! If I don't last another year, the deal is off.

JUNIE. Don't need no handouts! Even hearing you say you want any makes me shame!

ELLIE. Done used that word quite a lot, boy. You shamed of us? . . . Well, git slapped in the face wit this! How shame you gon be when you hafta git outta here and hustle yourself a job?—*any job*?

JUNIE. Huh?

ELLIE. How shame you gon be when you start getting raggedy and all them foxy girls are no longer impressed bout how slick, smooth and pretty you look? When you stop being one-r the best dressed black boys in New York City?

JUNIE. Don't get you, Ellie.

ELLIE. I know you went to college for a coupler years, boy, but I thought you still had some sense, or I woulda told you . . .

VI. Every time you bite into one of them big tender juicy steaks and chaw it down into your belly, ever think where it's coming from?

ELLIE. The Harrisons.

VI. Every time you lay one of them young gals down in that plush soft bed of yours and hear her sigh in luxury, ever think 'bout who you owe it to?

ELLIE. The Harrisons.

VI. When you swoop down home to that run-down house your ma and pa rent, latch eyes on all that fine furniture there, you ever think who's responsible?

ELLIE. The Harrisons.

VI. You ain't bought a suit or piece of clothes in five years and none of the other four men in this family have . . . . Why not?

ELLIE. Mr. Harrison

VI. Junie, you is a fine, choice hunk of chocolate pigmeat, pretty as a new-minted penny and slick 'nuff to suck sugar outta gingerbread wit'out it losing its flavor—but the Harrisons ain't hardly elected you no favorite pinup boy to introduce to Santa Claus. Took a heap of pow'ful coaxing to win you such splendid sponsorship and wealthy commissions, 'cause waiting for the Harrisons to voluntarily *donate* their Christian charity is one sure way of landing headfirst in the poorhouse dungeon . . . Who runs the Harrison's house, Junie?

JUNIE. Ellie . . . I guess . . . ?

ELLIE. From top to bottom. I cook the food, scrub the floor, open the doors, serve the tables, answer the phones, dust the furniture, raise the children, lay out the clothes, greet the guests, fix the drinks and dump the garbage—all for bad pay as you said . . . You right, Junie, money I git in my envelope ain't worth the time 'n the headache. . . . *But—God Helps Those Who Help Themselves* . . . I also *order* the food, estimate the credit, *pay* the bills and *balance* the budget. Which means that each steak I order for them, befo' butcher carves cow, I done reserved *two* for myself. Miss Harrison wouldn't know how much steak cost and Mr. Harrison so loaded, he writes me a check wit'out even looking . . . Every once in a full moon they git so good-hearted and tell me take some leftovers home, but by that time my freezer and pantry is already fuller than theirs . . . Every one of them high-price suits I lay on you haven't been worn more than once and some of 'em not at all. You lucky to be same size as Mr. Harrison, Junie. He don't know how much clothes he got in his wardrobe, which is why *yours* is as big as *his*. Jim, Roy, Arthur and Ben can't even fit into the man's clothes, but that still don't stop 'em from cutting, shortening, altering and stretching 'em to fit. Roy almost ruined his feet trying to wear the man's shoes . . . Now, I've had a perfect record keeping y'all elegantly dressed and stylishly fashion-plated—'cept that time Mr. Harrison caught me off guard asking: "Ellie, where's my brown suit?" "In the cleaners," I told him and had to snatch it off your hanger and smuggle it back—temporarily.

VI. If y'all warn't so lucky and *Mrs.* Harrison so skinny and tacky-flashy, Ellie and I would also be best dressed domestics of the year.

ELLIE. Which, if you didn't notice, is what your Aunt Doris was—rest her soul—when we laid her in her grave, decked out in the costliest, ritziest, most expensest nightgown the good Lord ever waited to feast his eyes on . . . As for furniture, we could move out his whole house in one day if we had to.

VI. Which is what we did when they moved from the old penthouse and we hired us a moving van to haul 'nuff pieces to furnish both our own apartments and still had enough to ship a living room set down home to your ma. Mr. Harrison told us to donate the stuff to charity. We did—US!

ELLIE. And all our bills I add on to their bills—Jim even tried to git me to sneak in his car note, but that was going too far—all the deluxe plane tickets your ma jet up here on every year, weekly prescriptions filled on their tab, tons of laundry cleaned along wit theirs and a thousand other services and I'm earning me quite a bonus along with my bad pay. It's the BONUS that counts, Junie. Total it up for nine years and I'd be losing money on any other job. Now Vi and I, after cutting cane, picking rice and shucking corn befo' we could braid our hair in pigtails, figure we just gitting back what's owed us . . . But, if Mr. Harrison boots Mrs. Harrison out on her tocus, the party's over. He's not gon need us. Miss Harrison ain't got a copper cent of her own. Anyway, the setup won't be as ripe for picking. My bonus is suddenly cut off and out the window go my pension.

VI. Suppose we did git us another job wit one-r them penny-pinching old misers hiding behind cupboards watching whether you stealing sugar cubes? Wit our fringe benefits choked off, we'd fall down so quick to a style of living we ain't been used to for a long time, it would make your head swim. I don't think we could stand it . . . Could you?

ELLIE. So when me and Vi saw our pigeons scampering out the window for good today, tears started flowing like rain. The first tear trickle out my eyes had a roast in it.

VI. Mine was a chicken.

ELLIE. Second had a crate of eggs.

VI. Mine a whole pig.

ELLIE. Third an oriental rug.

VI. A continental couch.

ELLIE. Fourth an overcoat for Arthur.

VI. A bathrobe for Ben.

ELLIE. The fifth one had my gas, electric and telephone bills in it.

VI. Three months' rent, Lord!

ELLIE. The faster the stream started gushing, the faster them nightmares crowded my eyes until I coulda flooded 'em 'nuff water to swim in. Every time I pleaded "Think of your love!"—

VI. She meant think 'bout our bills.

ELLIE. Every time I begged "Don't crack up the home!"—

VI. It meant please keep *ours* cemented together!

ELLIE. "Don't victim the chillun!"—

VI. By all means insure the happiness of *our* lil darlings!

ELLIE. They didn't know 'bout these eyeball visions—they only see what they see 'n hear what they hear—and that's okey-dokey wit me—but I was gitting these watery pictures in my mind 'n feeling a giant-size sickness in my gut! Few seconds longer and I woulda been down on my knees witout even thinking 'bout it.

VI. If I didn't beat ya to the floor!

ELLIE. Junie—maybe we shoulda given a little more thought to that—whatchamacallit?—"image" of yours. Maybe we did dishonor Africa, embarrass the NAACP, are hopelessly behind time and scandalously outdated. But we didn't have too much time to think . . . Now that you know the whole truth, you have a right to disown us. We hardly worthy of your respect . . . But when I thought 'bout that new topcoat wit the velvet-trimmed collar I jest packed to bring you (*tears begin to reform.*) . . . coupler new cashmere sweaters, brand new slacks, a shiny new attaché case for your appointments, and a scrumptious new collapsible swimming pool I promised your ma for her backyard—I couldn't help but cry.

(VI *has joined her in a double torrent.*)

JUNIE (*back turned to audience*). Vi?

VI. What?

JUNIE. Pass me the handkerchief . . .

(*He receives it and joins the table—a moist-faced trio.* AR-THUR, ELLIE's *husband, walks in finding them thus.*)

ARTHUR (*beelining for bathroom*). Even' everybody . . . (*Hearing no response, stops before entering john*) Hey, what's the matter? What you three looking like somebody died for?

ELLIE. It's the Harrisons, Arthur. Mr. Harrison getting a divorce.

ARTHUR. Aww, not agin!

VI. He really means it this time, Arthur.

ARTHUR. He does?

ELLIE. Yes, Jesus.

ARTHUR. You sure?

VI. Caught her dead to rights.

ARTHUR (*indignant*). But he can't do that!

VI. He is.

ARTHUR. What 'bout us?

JUNIE. What you think we grieving bout?

ARTHUR. Well, just don't sit there! What we gon do?

ELLIE. Done it, didn't work.

ARTHUR. Not at all?

ELLIE. Nope.

ARTHUR. Not even a little bit?

ELLIE. Not one lousy inch.

ARTHUR (*crestfallen*). Make room for me.

(*They provide space. He sits, completing the depressed quartet.*)

JUNIE (*suddenly jolted with an idea*). Ellie! Wait! Why don't you tell him to take her on a private ocean cruise, just the two of 'em, so they kin recapture the thrill for one another!

ELLIE. He did that already, until somebody told him she was cuddling up with the ship stoker in the engine room.

JUNIE (*undaunted*). Advise him to spend less time wit his business and more with her. She wouldn't need to look outside for satisfaction!

ELLIE. Tried that too, but his business like to fell apart and he caught her making eyes at the messenger bringing him the news.

JUNIE (*desperate*). Convince him she's sick! It's not her fault, he should send her to a psychiatrist!

ELLIE. Already did . . . till he found out she was doing more than talking on the couch.

JUNIE. What 'bout a twenty-four hour guard on her? That won't give her so many opportunities!

ELLIE. What about guards? They men too.

JUNIE (*in angry frustration*). Well, damn, git her a chastity belt and lock her up!

ELLIE. Locks, also, have been known to be picked.

ARTHUR (*inspired by a brilliant solution*). Wait! I got it! I got it! . . . Tell him you know of some steady-ready goofer dust . . . or jooger-mooger saltpeter to cool her down. And you'll slip it in her food every day!

ELLIE. Wouldn't work . . . Way her glands function, probably jazz her up like a spanish fly.

VI. Let's face it, it's all over. We just gotta tuck in our belts, stare the future square in the eye and git ready for depression. It's not gon do us no good to whine over spilt clabber . . . . You jist better start scrounging 'round for that job, Junie. Befo' you git chance to sneeze, we will have had it. And call up—No! Write your ma and tell her not to come up this year.

ELLIE. Arthur, best you scrape up another job to moonlight wit the one you got. We facing some scuffling days 'head us.

VI. Well . . . I better git out of here and go warn my own crew bout Satan's retribution . . . Well . . . it was good while it lasted, Ellie . . .

ELLIE. Real good.

(*They glance at each other and another deluge starts. The phone interrupts, but no one bothers to answer. Finally,* AR-

THUR *rises and exits in the direction of peals. During his absence, the disconsolate trio remains silent.*)

ARTHUR (*re-entering slowly, treading each step with the deliberateness of a man fearful of cracking eggs*). That—was—Mr. Harrison—He said—thank both of you for desperately trying to —shock him to his senses—pry open his eyes to the light—and rescue his house from collapsing—He and Mrs. Harrison, after stren'ous consideration, are gonna stick it out together! (*A stunned moment of absolute silence prevails, finally broken by an earsplitting, exultant whoop which erupts simultaneously from each member of the quartet. They spring to their feet, embracing and prancing around the room, crying through laughter.* ARTHUR *simmers down first, tries to recapture their attention.*) *Ellie* . . . Ellie, Mr. Harrison requests if it's not too much trouble, he'd like for you to come over and stay wit Sandy and Snookie while he and Mrs. Harrison go out and celebrate their reunion, and it's too late to git a baby-sitter.

ELLIE. If it's all right? . . . Tell him I'm climbing on a broomstick, then shuttling to a jet! (ARTHUR *starts to exit.*) Wait a minute! Waaaait a minute! Hold on!—I must be crazy! Don't tell him that . . . Tell him he knows very well it's after my working hours and I'm not paid to baby-sit and since I've already made plans for the evening, I'll be glad to do it for double overtime, two extra days' pay and triple time off to recuperate from the imposition . . . . And, Arthur! . . . Kinda suggest that *you* is a little peeved 'cause he's interrupting me from taking care of something important for you. He might toss in a day for your suffering.

ARTHUR. He'll swear he was snatching you away from my deathbed, guarding my door 'gainst Lucifer busting through! (*Exits.*)

ELLIE. I'd better throw on some more clothes. (*Exits.*)

JUNIE. Vi, what you s'pose granpa would say bout his chillun if he got a breathing spell in between dodging pitchforks and sidestepping the fiery flames?

VI. Shame on you, boy, Papa ain't near 'bouts doing no ducking 'n dodging. Why he's right up there plunked down safe, snuggled up tight besides the good Lord's righteous throne.

ARTHUR (*re-entering*). He was real sorry. 'If it wasn't such a special occasion, he wouldn't bother us!' (*They guffaw heartily.*)

JUNIE. This IS a special occasion! . . . (*Grandly*) Arthur, break out a flagon of the latest champagne Ellie brought us.

ARTHUR. At your service, Massa Junie.

JUNIE. The 1947! That was a good year. Not the fifty, which was bad! (ARTHUR *moves to refrigerator.* ELLIE *returns, ready to depart.*) Wait for a drink, auntie. We've gotta celebrate *our* resurrection. A toast of deliverance. (ARTHUR *presents* JUNIE *with champagne, points out 1947 label, then gets goblets from shelf.* JUNIE *pours. They lift goblets.*) First! . . . To the victors and the vanquished, the top dog and the bottom dog! Sometimes it's hard to tell which is which . . . !

VI. If nothing else, boy, education did teach you how to sling around some choice conversation.

ARTHUR. Ain't hardly the way I heard the slinging described. (*They all laugh.*)

JUNIE. Second! . . . To my two cagey aunts. May they continue to prevail in times of distress! . . . Third! . . . To the Harrisons . . . . May they endure forever in marital bliss! Cheers to 'em! (*After finishing drink,* ELLIE *moves to exit through hallway door.* JUNIE *stops her.*) Oh, Ellie . . . Why don't you start fattening Mr. Harrison up. Please slip some more potatoes and starch into his menu. I've gained a few pounds and the clothes are gitting a little tight. Don't you think it's time for him to plumpen up a bit, stick on a little weight? . . .

ELLIE. Would ten pounds do?

JUNIE. Perfect! (*Again she moves to exit.*) And Ellie! . . .

Kinda hint 'round to him that fashions is changing. I wouldn't want him to fall behind in the latest styles . . .

VI (*lifting goblet, along with* ARTHUR *and* ELLIE, *in a final toast*). There's hope, Junie. You'll make it, boy, you'll make it . . .

CURTAIN

Day of Absence

A Satirical Fantasy

DOUGLAS TURNER WARD

The time is now.

*Play opens in unnamed Southern town of medium popula-
tion on a somnolent cracker morning—meaning no matter the
early temperature, it's gonna get hot. The hamlet is just beginning to rouse itself from the sleepy lassitude of night.*

*NOTES ON PRODUCTION: No scenery is necessary—only
actors shifting in and out on an almost bare stage and freezing
into immobility as focuses change or blackouts occur.*

*Play is conceived for performance by a Negro cast, a reverse
minstrel show done in white face. Logically, it might also be
performed by whites—at their own risk. If any producer is faced
with choosing between opposite hues, author strongly suggests:
"Go 'long wit the blacks—besides all else, they need the work
more."*

*If acted by the latter, race members are urged to go for
broke, yet cautioned not to ham it up too broadly. In fact—it*

25

just might be more effective if they aspire to serious tragedy. Only qualification needed for Caucasian casting is that the company fit a uniform pattern—insipid white.

Before any horrifying discrimination doubts arise, I hasten to add that a bona fide white actor should be cast as the ANNOUNCER *in all productions, likewise a Negro thespian in pure native black as* RASTUS. *This will truly subvert any charge that the production is unintegrated.*

All props, except essential items (chairs, brooms, rags, mop, debris) should be imaginary (phones, switchboard, mikes, eating utensils, food, etc.). Actors should indicate their presence through mime.

The cast of characters develops as the play progresses. In the interest of economical casting, actors should double or triple in roles wherever possible

PRODUCTION CONCEPT: *This is a red-white-and-blue play—meaning that the entire production should be designed around the basic color scheme of our patriotic trinity. Lighting should illustrate, highlight, and detail time, action, and mood—opening scenes stage-lit with white rays of morning, transforming to panic reds of afternoon, flowing into ominous blues of evening. Costuming should be orchestrated around the same color scheme. In addition, subsidiary usage of grays, khakis, yellows, pinks, and patterns of stars and bars should be employed. All actors (*ANNOUNCERS *and* RASTUS *excepted, of course) should wear white shoes or sneakers, and all women characters clothed in knee-length frocks should wear white stockings. Blond wigs, both for males and females, can be used in selected instances. Makeup should have uniform consistency, with individual touches thrown in to enhance personal identity.*

SAMPLE MODELS OF MAKEUP AND COSTUMING:

MARY: *Kewpie-doll face, ruby-red lips painted to valentine pursing, moon-shaped rough circles implanted on each cheek, blond wig of fat flowing ringlets, dazzling ankle-length snow-white nightie.*

MAYOR:*Seersucker white ensemble, ten-gallon hat, red string tie, and blue belt.*

CLEM: *Khaki pants, bareheaded, and blond.*

LUKE: *Blue work jeans, strawhatted.*

CLUB WOMAN: *Yellow dress patterned with symbols of Dixie, gray hat.*

CLAN: *A veritable, riotous advertisement of red-white-and-blue combinations with stars and bars tossed in.*

PIOUS: *White ministerial garb with black cleric's color topping his snow-white shirt.*

OPERATORS: *All in red with different color wigs.*

All other characters should be carefully defined through costuming which typifies their identity.

SCENE: Street.

TIME: Early morning.

CLEM (*sitting under a sign suspended by invisible wires and bold-printed with the lettering:*"STORE"). Morning, Luke . . .

LUKE (*sitting a few paces away under an identical sign*). Morning, Clem . . .

CLEM. Gon be a hot day.

LUKE. Looks that way . . .

CLEM. Might rain though . . .

LUKE. Might.

CLEM. Hope it does . . .

LUKE. Me too . . .

CLEM. Farmers could use a little wet spell for a change . . . How's the Missis?

LUKE. Same.

CLEM. 'N the kids?

LUKE. Them too . . . How's yourns?

CLEM. Fine, thank you . . . (*They both lapse into drowsy silence, waving lethargically from time to time at imaginary passersby.*) Hi, Joe . . .

LUKE. Joe . . .

CLEM. How'd it go yesterday, Luke?

LUKE. Fair.

CLEM. Same wit me . . . Business don't seem to git no better or no worse. Guess we in a rut, Luke, don't it 'pear that way to you?—Morning, Ma'm.

LUKE. Morning . . .

CLEM. Tried display, sales, advertisement, stamps—everything —yet merchandising stumbles 'round in the same old groove. . . . But—that's better than plunging downwards, I reckon.

LUKE. Guess it is.

CLEM. Morning, Bret. How's the family? . . . That's good.

LUKE. Bret—

CLEM. Morning, Sue.

LUKE. How do, Sue.

CLEM (*staring after her*). Fine hunk of woman.

LUKE. Sure is.

CLEM. Wonder if it's any good?

LUKE. Bet it is.

CLEM. Sure like to find out!

LUKE. So would I.

CLEM. You ever try?

LUKE. Never did . . .

CLEM. Morning, Gus . . .

LUKE. Howdy, Gus.

CLEM. Fine, thank you. (*They lapse into silence again.* CLEM *rouses himself slowly, begins to look around quizzically.*) Luke . . . ?

LUKE. Huh?

CLEM. Do you . . . er, er—feel anything—funny . . . ?

LUKE. Like what?

CLEM. Like . . . er—something—strange?

LUKE. I dunno . . . haven't thought about it.

CLEM. I mean . . . like something's wrong—outta place, unusual?

LUKE. I don't know . . . What you got in mind?

CLEM. Nothing . . . just that—just that—like somp'um's outta kilter. I got a funny feeling somp'um's not up to snuff. Can't figger out what it is . . .

LUKE. Maybe it's in your haid . . .

CLEM. No, not like that . . . Like somp'um's happened—or happening—gone haywire, loony.

LUKE. Well, don't worry 'bout it, it'll pass.

CLEM. Guess you right (*attempts return to somnolence but doesn't succeed*). I'm sorry, Luke, but you sure you don't feel nothing peculiar . . . ?

LUKE (*slightly irked*). Toss it out your mind, Clem! We got a long day ahead of us. If something's wrong, you'll know 'bout it in due time. No use worrying about it 'till it comes and if it's coming, it will. Now, relax!

CLEM. All right, you right . . . Hi, Margie . . .

LUKE. Marge.

CLEM (*unable to control himself*). Luke, I don't give a damn what you say. Somp'um's topsy-turvy, I just know it!

LUKE (*increasingly irritated*). Now look here, Clem—it's a bright day, it looks like it's gon git hotter. You say the wife and kids are fine and the business is no better or no worse? Well, what else could be wrong? . . . If somp'um's gon happen, it's gon happen anyway and there ain't a damn fool thing you kin do to stop it! So you ain't helping me, yourself or nobody else by thinking 'bout it. It's not gon be no better or no worse when it gits here. It'll come to you when it gits ready to come and it's gon be the same whether you worry about it or not. So stop letting it upset you! (LUKE *settles back in his chair.* CLEM *does likewise.* LUKE *shuts his eyes. After a few moments, they reopen. He forces them shut again. They reopen in greater curiosity. Finally, he rises slowly to an upright position in the chair, looks around frowningly. Turns slowly to* CLEM.) Clem? . . . You know something? . . . Somp'um is peculiar . . .

CLEM (*vindicated*). I knew it, Luke! I jist knew it! Ever since we been sitting here, I been having that feeling!

(*Scene is blacked out abruptly. Lights rise on another section of the stage where a young couple lie in bed under an invisible wire-suspension sign lettered "*HOME.*" Loud, insistent sounds of baby yells are heard.* JOHN, *the husband, turns over trying to ignore the cries;* MARY, *the wife, is undisturbed.* JOHN's *efforts are futile; the cries continue until they cannot be denied. He bolts upright, jumps out of bed, and disappears offstage. Returns quickly and tries to rouse* MARY.)

JOHN. Mary . . . (*Nudges her, pushes her, yells into her ear, but she fails to respond*) Mary, get up . . . Get up!

MARY. Ummm . . . (*Shrugs away, still sleeping.*)

JOHN. GET UP!

MARY. Ummmmmmmmm!

JOHN. Don't you hear the baby's bawling? . . . NOW GET UP!

MARY (*mumbling drowsily*). What baby . . . whose baby . . . ?

JOHN. Yours!

MARY. Mine? That's ridiculous . . . what'd you say . . . ? Somebody's baby bawling? . . . How could that be so? (*Hearing screams*) Who's crying? Somebody's crying! . . . What's crying? . . . *Where's Lula?*

JOHN. I don't know. You better get up.

MARY. That's outrageous! . . . What time is it?

JOHN. Late 'nuff! Now rise up!

MARY. You must be joking . . . I'm sure I still have four or five hours' sleep in store—even more after that head-splittin' blowout last night . . . (*Tumbles back under covers.*)

JOHN. Nobody told you to gulp those last six bourbons—

MARY. Don't tell me how many bourbons to swallow, not

after you guzzled the whole stinking bar! . . . Get up? . . . You must be cracked . . . Where's Lula? She must be here, she always is . . .

JOHN. Well, she ain't here yet, so get up and muzzle that brat before she does drive me cuckoo!

MARY (*springing upright, finally realizing gravity of situation*). Whaddaya mean Lula's not here? She's always here, she must be here . . . Where else kin she be? She supposed to be . . . She just can't *not* be here—call her!

(*Blackout as* JOHN *rushes offstage. Scene shifts to a trio of* TELEPHONE OPERATORS *perched on stools before imaginary switchboards. Chaos and bedlam are taking place to the sound of buzzes. Effect of following dialogue should simulate rising pandemonium.*)

FIRST OPERATOR. The line is busy—

SECOND OPERATOR. Line is busy—

THIRD OPERATOR. Is busy—

FIRST OPERATOR. Doing best we can—

SECOND OPERATOR. Having difficulty—

THIRD OPERATOR. Soon as possible—

FIRST OPERATOR. Just one moment—

SECOND OPERATOR. Would you hold on—

THIRD OPERATOR. Awful sorry, madam—

FIRST OPERATOR. Would you hold on, please—

SECOND OPERATOR. Just a second, please—

THIRD OPERATOR. Please hold on, please—

FIRST OPERATOR. The line is busy.

SECOND OPERATOR. The line is busy—

THIRD OPERATOR. The line is busy—

FIRST OPERATOR. Doing best we can—

SECOND OPERATOR. Hold on, please—

THIRD OPERATOR. Can't make connections—

FIRST OPERATOR. Unable to put it in—

SECOND OPERATOR. Won't plug through—

THIRD OPERATOR. Sorry, madam—

FIRST OPERATOR. If you'd wait a moment—
SECOND OPERATOR. Doing best we can—
THIRD OPERATOR. Sorry—
FIRST OPERATOR. One moment—
SECOND OPERATOR. Just a second—
THIRD OPERATOR. Hold on—
FIRST OPERATOR. *Yes*—
SECOND OPERATOR. *Stop it!*—
THIRD OPERATOR. *How do I know*—
FIRST OPERATOR. *You another one!*
SECOND OPERATOR. *Hold on, Dammit!*
THIRD OPERATOR. *Up yours, too!*
FIRST OPERATOR. *The line is busy*—
SECOND OPERATOR. *The line is busy*—
THIRD OPERATOR. *The line is busy*—

(*The switchboard clamors a cacophony of buzzes as* OPERATORS *plug connections with the frenzy of a Chaplin movie. Their replies degenerate into a babble of gibberish. At the height of frenzy, the* SUPERVISOR *appears.*)

SUPERVISOR. *What's the snarl-up?*
FIRST OPERATOR. Everybody calling at the same time, Ma'am!
SECOND OPERATOR. Board can't handle it!
THIRD OPERATOR. Like everybody in big New York City is trying to squeeze a call through to lil ole us!
SUPERVISOR. God! . . . Somp'um terrible musta happened! . . . Buzz the emergency frequency hookup to the Mayor's office and find out what the hell's going on!

(*Scene blacks out quickly to* CLEM *and* LUKE.)

CLEM (*something slowly dawning on him*). Luke . . . ?
LUKE. Yes, Clem?
CLEM (*eyes roving around in puzzlement*). Luke . . . ?
LUKE (*irked*). I said what, Clem!
CLEM. Luke . . . ? Where—where is—the—the—?
LUKE. The *what*?
CLEM. Nigras . . . ?

LUKE. What . . . ?

CLEM. Nigras . . . Where is the Nigras, where is they, Luke . . . ? *All the Nigras!* . . . I don't see no Nigras . . . !

LUKE. Whatcha mean . . . ?

CLEM (*agitatedly*). Luke there ain't a darkey in sight . . . . And if you remember, we ain't seen a nappy hair all morning . . . The Nigras, Luke! We ain't laid eyes on nary a coon this whole morning!

LUKE. You must be crazy or something, Clem!

CLEM. Think about it, Luke, we been sitting here for an hour or more—try and recollect if you remember seeing jist *one* go by!

LUKE (*confused*). I don't recall . . . But . . . but there musta been some . . . The heat musta got you, Clem! How in hell could that be so?

CLEM (*triumphantly*). Just think, Luke! . . . Look around ya . . . Now, every morning mosta people walkin 'long this street is colored. They's strolling by going to work, they's waiting for the buses, they's sweeping sidewalks, cleaning stores, starting to shine shoes and wetting the mops—Right? . . . Well, look around you, Luke—Where is they? (LUKE *paces up and down, checking*.) I told you, Luke, they ain't nowheres to be seen.

LUKE. This . . . this . . . some kind of holiday for 'em—or something?

CLEM. I don't know, Luke . . . but . . . but what I do know is they ain't here'n we haven't seen a solitary one . . . It's scarifying, Luke . . . !

LUKE. Well . . . Maybe they's jist standing 'n walking and shining on other streets—Let's go look!

(*Scene blacks out to* JOHN *and* MARY. *Baby cries are as insistent as ever.*)

MARY (*at end of patience*). Smother it!

JOHN (*beyond his*). That's a hell of a thing to say 'bout your own child! You should know what to do to hush her up!

MARY. Why don't you try?

JOHN. You had her!

MARY. You shared in borning her!

JOHN. Possibly not!

MARY. Why, you lousy—!

JOHN. What good is a mother who can't shut up her own daughter?

MARY. I told you she yells louder every time I try to lay hands on her—Where's Lula? Didn't you call her?

JOHN. I told you I can't get the call through!

MARY. Try agin—

JOHN. It's no use! I tried numerous times and can't even git through to the switchboard. You've got to quiet her down yourself. (*Firmly*) Now, go in there and clam her up 'fore I lose my patience! MARY *exits. Soon, we hear the yells increase. She rushes back in.*)

MARY. She won't let me touch her, just screams louder!

JOHN. Probably wet 'n soppy!

MARY. Yes! Stinks something awful! Phooooey! I can't stand that filth and odor!

JOHN. That's why she's screaming! Needs her didee changed —go change it!

MARY. How you 'spect me to when I don't know how? Suppose I faint?

JOHN. Well let her blast away. I'm getting outta here.

MARY. You can't leave me here like this!

JOHN. Just watch me! . . . See this nice split-level cottage, peachy furniture, multicolored T.V., hi-fi set n' the rest? . . . Well, how you think I scraped 'em together while you curled up on your fat lil fanny? . . . By gitting outta here—not only *on time* . . . but *earlier!*—Beating a frantic crew of nice young executives to the punch—gitting there fustest with the mostest brown-nosing you ever saw! Now if I goof one day—just ONE DAY!—you reckon I'd stay ahead? NO! . . . There'd be a wolf pack trampling over my prostrate body, racing to replace my smiling face against the boss's left rump! . . . *No, mam!* I'm zooming outta here on time, just as I always have, and what's more—you gon fix me some breakfast. *I'm hungry!*

MARY. But—

JOHN. No buts about it! (*Flash blackout as he gags on a mouthful of coffee.*) What you trying to do, STRANGLE ME? (*Jumps up and starts putting on jacket.*)

MARY (*sarcastically*). What did you expect?

JOHN (*in biting fury*). That you could possibly boil a pot of water, toast a few slices of bread and fry a coupler eggs! . . . It was a mistaken assumption!

MARY. So they aren't as good as Lula's!

JOHN. That is an overstatement. Your efforts don't result in anything that could possibly be digested by man, mammal, or insect! . . . When I married you, I thought I was fairly acquainted with your faults and weaknesses—I chalked 'em up to human imperfection . . . But now I know I was being extremely generous, overoptimistic and phenomenally deluded!— You have no idea how useless you really are!

MARY. Then why'd you marry me?

JOHN. Decoration!

MARY. You shoulda married Lula!

JOHN. I might've if it wasn't 'gainst the segregation law! . . . But for the sake of my home, my child and my sanity, I will even take a chance on sacrificing my slippery grip on the status pole and drive by her shanty to find out whether she or someone like her kin come over here and prevent some ultimate disaster. (*Storms toward door, stopping abruptly at exit*) Are you sure you kin make it to the bathroom wit'out Lula backing you up?

(*Blackout.* Scene shifts to MAYOR's *office where a cluttered desk stands center stage amid paper debris.*)

MAYOR (*striding determinedly toward desk; stopping midway, bellowing*). Woodfence! . . . Woodfence! . . . Woodfence!

(*Receiving no reply, completes distance to desk*) Jack-son! . . . Jackson!

JACKSON (*entering worriedly*). Yes, sir . . . ?

MAYOR. Where's Vice-Mayor Woodfence, that no-good brother-in-law of mine?

JACKSON. Hasn't come in yet, sir.

MAYOR. *Hasn't come in?* . . . Damn bastard! Knows we have a crucial conference. Soon as he staggers through that door, tell him to shoot in here! (*Angrily focusing on his disorderly desk and littered surroundings*) And git Mandy here to straighten up this mess—Rufus too! You know he shoulda been waiting to knock dust off my shoes soon as I step in. Get 'em in here! . . . What's the matter wit them lazy Nigras? . . . Already had to dress myself because of J. C., fix my own coffee without May-Belle, drive myself to work 'counta Bubber, feel my old bag's tits after Sapphi—*Never Mind!*—Git 'em in here—*Quick!*

JACKSON (*meekly*). They aren't . . . they aren't here, sir . . .

MAYOR. Whaddaya mean they aren't here? Find out where they at. We got important business, man! You can't run a town wit laxity like this. Can't allow things to git snafued jist because a bunch of lazy Nigras been out gitting drunk and living it up all night! Discipline, man, discipline!

JACKSON. That's what I'm trying to tell you, sir . . . they didn't come in, can't be found . . . none of 'em.

MAYOR. Ridiculous, boy! Scare 'em up and tell 'em scoot here in a hurry befo' I git mad and fire the whole goddamn lot of 'em!

JACKSON. But we can't find 'em, sir.

MAYOR. Hogwash! Can't nobody in this office do anything right? Do I hafta handle every piddling little matter myself? Git me their numbers, I'll have 'em here befo' you kin shout to—

(THREE MEN *burst into room.*)

ONE. Henry—they vanished!

TWO. Disappeared into thin air!

THREE. Gone wit'out a trace!

TWO. Not a one on the street!

THREE. In the house!

ONE. On the job!

MAYOR. Wait a minute! . . . Hold your water! Calm down—!

ONE. But they've gone, Henry—GONE! All of 'em!

MAYOR. What the hell you talking 'bout? Gone? Who's gone—?

ONE. The Nigras, Henry! They gone!

MAYOR. Gone? . . . Gone where?

TWO. That's what we trying to tell ya—they just disappeared! The Nigras have disappeared, swallowed up, vanished! All of 'em! Every last one!

MAYOR. Has everybody 'round here gone batty? . . . That's impossible, how could the Nigras vanish?

THREE. Beats me, but it's happened!

MAYOR. You mean a whole town of Nigras just evaporated like that—poof!—overnight?

ONE. Right!

MAYOR. Y'all must be drunk! Why, half this town is colored. How could they just sneak out?

TWO. Don't ask me, but there ain't one in sight!

MAYOR. Simmer down 'n put it to me easy-like.

ONE. Well . . . I first suspected somp'um smelly when Sarah Jo didn't show up this morning and I couldn't reach her—

TWO. Dorothy Jane didn't 'rive at my house—

THREE. Georgia Mae wasn't at mine neither—and SHE sleeps in!

ONE. When I reached the office, I realized I hadn't seen nary one Nigra all morning! Nobody else had either—Wait a minute —Henry, have you?

MAYOR. Now that you mention it . . . no, I haven't . . .

ONE. They gone, Henry . . . Not a one on the street, not a one in our homes, not a single, last living one to be found no-wheres in town. What we gon' do?

MAYOR (*thinking*). Keep heads on your shoulders 'n put clothes on your back . . . They can't be far . . . Must be 'round somewheres . . . Probably playing hide 'n seek, that's it! . . . *Jackson!*

JACKSON. Yessir?

MAYOR. Immediately mobilize our Citizens Emergency Distress Committee!—order a fleet of sound trucks to patrol streets urging the population to remain calm—situation's not as bad as it looks—everything's under control! Then, have another squadron of squawk buggies drive slowly through all Nigra alleys, ordering them to come out wherever they are. If that don't git 'em, organize a vigilante search squad to flush 'em outta hiding! But most important of all, track down that lazy goldbricker Woodfence and tell him to git on top of the situation! By God, we'll find 'em even if we hafta dig 'em outta the ground!

(*Blackout. Scene shifts back to* JOHN *and* MARY *a few hours later. A funereal solemnity pervades their mood.*)

JOHN. Walked up to the shack, knocked on door, didn't git no answer. Hollered: "Lula? Lula . . . ?—not a thing. Went 'round the side, peeped in window—nobody stirred. Next door —nobody there. Crossed other side of street and banged on five or six other doors—not a colored person could be found! Not a man, neither woman or child—not even a black dog could be seen, smelt or heard for blocks around . . . They've gone, Mary.

MARY. What does it all mean, John?

JOHN. I don't know, Mary . . .

MARY. I always had Lula, John. Never missed a day at my side . . . That's why I couldn't accept your wedding proposal until I was sure you'd welcome me and her together as a package. How am I gonna git through the day? Baby don't know *me*, I ain't acquainted wit *it*. I've never lifted cover off pot, swung a mop or broom, dunked a dish or even pushed a dustrag. I'm lost wit'out Lula, I need her, John, I need her. (*Begins to weep softly.* JOHN *pats her consolingly.*)

JOHN. Courage, honey . . . Everybody in town is facing the same dilemma. We mustn't crack up . . .

(*Blackout. Scene shifts back to* MAYOR's *office later in day. Atmosphere and tone resembles a wartime headquarters at the front.* MAYOR *is perched on ladder checking over huge map.*)

INDUSTRIALIST. Half the day is gone already, Henry. On behalf of the factory owners of this town, you've got to bail us out! Seventy-five percent of all production is paralyzed. With the Nigra absent, men are waiting for machines to be cleaned, floors to be swept, crates lifted, equipment delivered and bathrooms deodorized. Why, restrooms and toilets are so filthy until they not only cannot be sat in, but it's virtually impossible to get within hailing distance because of the stench!

MAYOR. Keep your shirt on, Jeb—

BUSINESSMAN. Business is even in worse condition, Henry. The volume of goods moving 'cross counters has slowed down to a trickle—almost negligible. Customers are not only not purchasing—but the absence of handymen, porters, sweepers, stock-movers, deliverers and miscellaneous dirty-work doers is disrupting the smooth harmony of marketing!

CLUBWOMAN. Food poisoning, severe indigestitis, chronic diarrhea, advanced diaper chafings and a plethora of unsanitary household disasters dangerous to life, limb and property! . . . As a representative of the Federation of Ladies' Clubs, I must sadly report that unless the trend is reversed, a complete breakdown in family unity is imminent . . . Just as homosexuality and debauchery signaled the fall of Greece and Rome, the downgrading of Southern Bellesdom might very well prophesy the collapse of our indigenous institutions . . . . Remember— it has always been pure, delicate, lily-white images of Dixie femininity which provided backbone, inspiration and ideology for our male warriors in their defense against the onrushing black horde. If our gallant men are drained of this worship and idolatry—God knows! The cause won't be worth a Confederate nickel!

MAYOR (*jumping off ladder*). Stop this panicky defeatism, y'all hear me! All machinery at my disposal is being utilized. I assure you wit great confidence the damage will soon repair itself—Cheerful progress reports are expected any moment now —Wait! See, here's Jackson . . . Well, Jackson?

JACKSON. As of now, sir, all efforts are fruitless. Neither hide nor hair of them has been located. We have not unearthed a single one in our shack-to-shack search. Not a single one has heeded our appeal. Scoured every creek and cranny inside their hovels, turning furniture upside down and inside out, breaking down walls and tearing through ceilings. We made determined efforts to discover where'bouts of our faithful Uncle Toms and informers—but even they have vanished without a trace . . . Searching squads are on the verge of panic and hysteria, sir, wit hotheads among 'em campaigning for scorched earth policies. Nigras on a whole lack cellars, but there's rising sentiment favoring burning to find out whether they're underground-dug in!

MAYOR. Absolutely counter such foolhardy suggestions! Suppose they are tombed in? We'd only accelerate the gravity of the situation using incendiary tactics! Besides, when they're rounded up where will we put 'em if we've already burned up their shacks—*in our own bedrooms?*

JACKSON. I agree, sir, but the mood of the crowd is becoming irrational. In anger and frustration, they's forgetting their original purpose was to *find* the Nigras!

MAYOR. At all costs! Stamp out all burning proposals! Must prevent extremist notions from gaining ascendancy. Git wit it . . . Wait—'n for Jehovah's sake, find out where the hell is that trifling slacker, *Woodfence!*

COURIER (*rushing in*). Mr. Mayor! . . . We've found some! We've found some!

MAYOR (*excitedly*). Where?

COURIER. In the—in the—(*Can't catch breath*).

MAYOR (*impatiently*). Where, man? Where?

COURIER. In the colored wing of the city hospital!

MAYOR. The hos—? The hospital! I shoulda known! How could those helpless, crippled, cut and shot Nigras disappear from a hospital? Should thought of that! . . . Tell me more, man!

COURIER. I—I didn't wait, sir . . . I—I ran in to report soon as I heard—

MAYOR. Well git back on the phone, you idiot! Don't you know what this means?

COURIER. Yes, sir. (*Races out*).

MAYOR. Now we gitting somewhere! . . . Gentlemen, if one sole Nigra is among us, we're well on the road to rehabilitation! Those Nigras in the hospital must know somp'um 'bout the others where'bouts . . . Scat back to your colleagues, boost up their morale and inform 'em that things will zip back to normal in a jiffy! (*They start to file out, then pause to observe the* COURIER *re-entering dazedly.*) Well . . . ? Well, man . . . ? What's the matter wit you, ninny? Tell me what else was said!

COURIER. They all . . . they all . . . they all in a—in a—a coma, sir . . .

MAYOR. They all in a what . . . ?

COURIER. In a coma, sir . . .

MAYOR. Talk sense, man! . . . Whaddaya mean, they all in a coma?

COURIER. Doctor says every last one of the Nigras are jist laying in bed . . . *still* . . . not moving . . . neither live or dead . . . laying up there in a coma . . . every last one of 'em . . .

MAYOR (*sputters, then grabs phone*). Get me Confederate Memorial . . . Put me through to the Staff Chief . . . YES, this is the Mayor . . . Sam? . . . What's this I hear? . . . But how could they be in a coma, Sam? . . . You don't know! Well, what the hell you think the city's paying you for! You've got 'nuff damn hacks and quacks there to find out! . . . How could it be somp'um unknown? You mean Nigras know somp'um 'bout drugs your damn butchers don't? . . . Well, what the crap good are they? . . . All right, all right, I'll be calm. . . . Now, tell me . . . Uh huh, uh huh . . . Well, can't you give 'em some injections or somp'um . . . ?—You did . . . uh huh . . . *Did you try a lil rough treatment?—* that too, huh . . . All right, Sam, keep trying . . . (*Puts phone down deliberately, continuing absently.*) Can't wake 'em up. Just lay there. Them that's sick won't git no sicker, them that's half-well won't git no better, babies that's due won't be born and them that's come won't show no life. Nigras wit cuts won't bleed and them which need blood won't be transfused . . . He say dying Nigras is even refusing to pass away! (*Is silently perplexed for a moment, then suddenly breaks into action.*) Jackson? . . . Call up the police—*the jail!* Find out what's going on there! Them Nigras are captives! If there's one place we got darkies under control, it's there! Them sonsabitches too onery to act right either for colored or white! (JACKSON *exits.*) Keep your fingers crossed, citizens, them Nigras in jail are the most important Nigras we got!

(*All hands are raised conspicuously aloft, fingers prominently crossed. Seconds tick by. Soon* JACKSON *returns crestfallen.*)

JACKSON. Sheriff Bull says they don't know whether they still on premises or not. When they went to rouse Nigra jailbirds this morning, cell block doors refused to swing open. Tried everything—even exploded dynamite charges—but it just wouldn't budge . . . Then they hoisted guards up to peep through barred windows, but couldn't see good 'nuff to tell whether Nigras was inside or not. Finally, gitting desperate, they power-hosed the cells wit water but had to cease 'cause Sheriff Bull said he didn't wanta jeopardize drowning the Nigras since it might spoil his chance of shipping a record load of cotton pickers to the State Penitentiary for cotton-snatching jubilee . . . Anyway—they ain't heard a Nigra-squeak all day.

MAYOR. That so . . . ? *What 'bout trains 'n busses passing through?* There must be some dinges riding through?

JACKSON. We checked . . . not a one on board.

MAYOR. Did you hear whether any other towns lost their Nigras?

JACKSON. Things are status quo everywhere else.

MAYOR (*angrily*). Then what they picking on us for?

COURIER (*rushing in*). Mr. Mayor! Your sister jist called—hysterical! She says Vice-Mayor Woodfence went to bed wit her last night, but when she woke up this morning he was gone! Been missing all day!

MAYOR. Could Nigras be holding him hostage?

COURIER. No, sir. Besides him—investigations reveal that dozens or more prominent citizens—two City Council members, the chairman of the Junior Chamber of Commerce, our City College All-Southern halfback, the chairlady of the Daughters of the Confederate Rebellion, Miss Cotton Sack Festival of the Year and numerous other miscellaneous nobodies—are absent wit'out leave. Dangerous evidence points to the conclusion that they been infiltrating!

MAYOR. Infiltrating?

COURIER. Passing all along!

MAYOR. *What?*

COURIER. Secret Nigras all the while!

MAYOR. *Naw!*

(CLUBWOMAN *keels over in faint.* JACKSON, BUSINESSMAN *and* INDUSTRIALIST *begin to eye each other suspiciously.*)

COURIER. Yessir!

MAYOR. *Passing?*

COURIER. Yessir!

MAYOR. *Secret Nig—?*

COURIER. Yessir!

MAYOR (*momentarily stunned to silence*). The dirty mongrelizers! . . . Gentlemen, this is a grave predicament indeed . . . It pains me to surrender priority of our states rights credo, but it is my solemn task and frightening duty to inform you that we have no other recourse but to seek outside help for deliverance.

(*Blackout. Lights rise again on Huntley-Brinkley-Murrow-*

Severeid-Cronkite- Reasoner-type ANNOUNCER *grasping a hand-held microphone [imaginary] a few hours later. He is vigorously, excitedly mouthing his commentary, but no sound escapes his lips. During this dumb, wordless section of his broadcast, a bedraggled assortment of figures marching with picket signs occupies his attention. On their picket signs are inscribed various appeals and slogans.* "CINDY LOU UNFAIR TO BABY JOE" . . . "CAP'N SAM MISS BIG BOY" . . . "RETURN LIL BLUE TO MARS JIM" . . . "INFORMATION REQUESTED BOUT MAMMY GAIL" . . . "BOSS NATHAN PROTEST TO FAST LEROY." *Trailing behind the* MARCHERS, *forcibly isolated, is a* WOMAN *dressed in widow black holding a placard which reads:* "WHY DIDN'T YOU TELL US—YOUR DEFILED WIFE AND 11 ABSENT MONGRELS.")

ANNOUNCER (*who has been silently mouthing his delivery during the picketing procession, is suddenly heard as if caught in the midst of commentary*). Factories standing idle from the loss of nonessential workers. Stores remaining shuttered from the absconding of uncrucial personnel. Fruit, vegetables and other edible foodstuffs rotting in warehouses, with uncollected garbage threatening pestilence and pollution . . . Also, each second somewhere in this former utopia below the Mason and Dixon, dozens of decrepit old men and women usually tended by faithful nurses and servants are popping off like flies—abandoned by sons, daughters and grandchildren whose refusal to provide these doddering souls with bedpans and other soothing necessities results in their hasty, nasty, messy departures . . .

An equally wretched fate lurks in wait for juveniles of the town as hundreds of new born infants HUNGER for the comforting embraces of devoted nannies while being forced to endure the presence of strange parents . . .

But most critically affected of all by this complete drought of Afro-American resources are policemen and other public safety guardians denied their daily quota of Negro arrests. One officer known affectionately as "Two-a-Day-Pete" because of his unblemished record of TWO Negro headwhippings per day has already been carted off to the County Insane Asylum—strait jacketed, screaming and biting, unable to withstand the shock of having his spotless slate sullied by interruption . . . It is feared that similar attacks are soon expected among municipal judges prevented for the first time in years of distinguished bench-sitting from sentencing one single Negro to corrective institutions . . .

Ladies and gentlemen, as you trudge in from the joys and headaches of workday chores and dusk begins to descend on this sleepy Southern hamlet, we *repeat*—today—before early morning dew had dried upon magnolia blossoms, your comrade citizens of this lovely Dixie village awoke to the realization that some—pardon me! not some but *all*—of their Negroes were missing . . . Absent, vamoosed, departed, at bay, fugitive, away, gone and so far unretrieved . . .

In order to dispel your incredulity, gauge the temper of your suffering compatriots and just possibly prepare you for the likelihood of an equally nightmarish eventuality, we have gathered a cross section of this city's most distinguished leaders for exclusive interviews . . . First, Mr. Council Clan, grand dragoon of this area's most active civic organizations and staunch bellwether of the political opposition . . . Mr. Clan, how do you *account* for this incredible disappearance?

CLAN. A *plot*, plain and simple, that's what it is, as plain as the corns on your feet!

ANNOUNCER. Whom would you consider responsible?

CLAN. I could go on all night.

ANNOUNCER. Cite a few.

CLAN. Too numerous.

ANNOUNCER. Just one?

CLAN. Name names when time comes.

ANNOUNCER. Could you be referring to native Negroes?

CLAN. Ever try quaranteening lepers from their spots?

ANNOUNCER. Their organizations?

CLAN. Could you slice a nose off a mouth and still keep a face?

ANNOUNCER. Commies?

CLAN. Would you lop off a titty from a chest and still have a breast?

ANNOUNCER. Your city government?

CLAN. Now you talkin'!

ANNOUNCER. State administration?

CLAN. Warming up!

ANNOUNCER. Federal?

CLAN. Kin a blind man see?

ANNOUNCER. The Court?

CLAN. Is a pig clean?

ANNOUNCER. Clergy?

CLAN. Do a polecat stink?!

ANNOUNCER. Well, Mr. Clan, with this massive complicity, how do you think the plot could've been prevented from succeeding?

CLAN. If I'da been in office, it never woulda happened.

ANNOUNCER. Then you're laying major blame at the doorstep of the present administration?

CLAN. Damn tooting!

ANNOUNCER. But from your oft-expressed views, Mr. Clan, shouldn't you and your followers be delighted at the turn of events? After all—isn't it one of the main policies of your society to *drive* the Negroes away? *Drive* 'em back where they came from?

CLAN. Drivvve, boy! Driiiivvve! That's right! . . . When we say so and not befo'. Ain't supposed to do nothing 'til we tell 'em. Got to stay put until we exercise our God-given right to tell 'em when to git!

ANNOUNCER. But why argue if they've merely jumped the gun? Why not rejoice at this premature purging of undesirables?

CLAN. The time ain't ripe yet, boy . . . The time ain't ripe yet.

ANNOUNCER. Thank you for being so informative, Mr. Clan— Mrs. Aide? Mrs. Aide? Over here, Mrs. Aide . . . Ladies and gentlemen, this city's Social Welfare Commissioner, Mrs. Handy Anna Aide . . . Mrs. Aide, with all your freeloading Negroes seemingly AWOL, haven't developments alleviated the staggering demands made upon your Welfare Department? Reduction of relief requests, elimination of case loads, removal of chronic welfare dependents, et cetera?

AIDE. Quite the contrary. Disruption of our pilot projects among Nigras saddles our white community with extreme hardship . . . You see, historically, our agencies have always been foremost contributors to the Nigra Git-A-Job movement. We pioneered in enforcing social welfare theories which oppose coddling the fakers. We strenuously believe in helping Nigras help themselves by participating in meaningful labor. "Relief is Out, Work is In," is our motto. We place them as maids, cooks, butlers, and breast-feeders, cesspool-diggers, wash-basin maintainers, shoeshine boys, and so on—mostly on a volunteer self-work basis.

ANNOUNCER. Hired at prevailing salaried rates, of course?

AIDE. God forbid! Money is unimportant. Would only make 'em worse. Our main goal is to improve their ethical behavior. "Rehabilitation Through Positive Participation" is another motto of ours. All unwed mothers, loose-living malingering fathers, bastard children and shiftless grandparents are kept occupied through constructive muscle therapy. This provides 'em with less opportunity to indulge their pleasure-loving amoral inclinations.

ANNOUNCER. They volunteer to participate in these pilot projects?

AIDE. Heavens no! They're notorious shirkers. When I said the program is voluntary, I meant white citizens in overwhelming majorities do the volunteering. Placing their homes, offices, appliances and persons at our disposal for use in "Operation Uplift" . . . We would never dare place such a decision in the hands of the Nigra. It would never get off the ground! No, they have no choice in the matter. "Work or Starve" is the slogan we use to stimulate their awareness of what's good for survival.

ANNOUNCER. And a good one it is. Thank you, Mrs. Aide, and good luck . . . Rev? . . . Rev? . . . Ladies and gentlemen, this city's foremost spiritual guidance counselor, Reverend Reb Pious . . . How does it look to you, Reb Pious?

PIOUS (*continuing to gaze skyward*). It's in *His* hands, son, it's in *His* hands.

ANNOUNCER. How would you assess the disappearance, from a moral standpoint?

PIOUS. An immoral act, son, morally wrong and ethically indefensible. A perversion of Christian principles to be condemned from every pulpit of this nation.

ANNOUNCER. Can you account for its occurrence after the many decades of the Church's missionary activity among them?

PIOUS. It's basically a reversion of the Nigra to his deep-rooted primitivism . . . Now, at last, you can understand the difficulties of the Church in attempting to anchor God's kingdom among ungratefuls. It's a constant, unrelenting, no-holds-barred struggle against Satan to wrestle away souls locked in his possession for countless centuries! Despite all our aid, guidance, solace and protection, Old Beezlebub still retains tenacious grips upon the Nigras' childish loyalty—comparable to the lure of bright flames to an infant.

ANNOUNCER. But actual physical departure, Reb Pious? How do you explain that?

PIOUS. Voodoo, my son, voodoo . . . With Satan's assist, they have probably employed some heathen magic which we cultivated, sophisticated Christians know absolutely nothing about. However, before long we are confident about counteracting this evil witch-doctory and triumphing in our Holy Savior's name. At this perilous juncture, true believers of all denominations are participating in joint, 'round-the-clock observances, offering prayers for our Master's swiftiest intercession. I'm optimistic about the outcome of His intervention . . . Which prompts me—if I may, sir—to offer these words of counsel to our delinquent Nigras . . . I say to you without rancor or vengeance, quoting a phrase of one of your greatest prophets, Booker T. Washington: "Return your buckets to where they lay and all will be forgiven."

ANNOUNCER. A very inspirational appeal, Reb Pious. I'm certain they will find the tug of its magnet sincerity irresistible. Thank you, Reb Pious . . . All in all—as you have witnessed, ladies and gentlemen—this town symbolizes the face of disaster, suffering as severe a prostration as any city wrecked, ravaged and devastated by the holocaust of war. A vital, lively, throbbing organism brought to a screeching halt by the strange enigma of the missing Negroes . . .

We take you now to offices of the one man into whose hands has been thrust the final responsibility of rescuing this shuddering metropolis from the precipice of destruction . . . We give you the honorable Mayor, Henry R. E. Lee . . . Hello, Mayor Lee.

MAYOR (*jovially*). Hello, Jack.

ANNOUNCER. Mayor Lee, we have just concluded interviews with some of your city's leading spokesmen. If I may say so, sir, they don't sound too encouraging about the situation.

MAYOR. Nonsense, Jack! The situation's as well in hand as it could be under the circumstances. Couldn't be better in hand. Underneath every dark cloud, Jack, there's always a ray of sunlight, ha, ha, ha.

ANNOUNCER. Have you discovered one, sir?

MAYOR. Well, Jack, I'll tell you . . . Of course we've been faced wit a little crisis, but look at it like this—we've faced 'em befo': Sherman marched through Georgia—*once!* Lincoln freed the slaves—*momentarily!* Carpetbaggers even put Nigras in the Governor's mansion, state legislature, Congress and the Senate of the United States. But what happened? Ole Dixie bounced right on back up . . . At this moment the Supreme Court's trying to put Nigras in our schools and the Nigra has got it in his haid to put hisself everywhere . . . But what you spect gon happen? Ole Dixie will kangaroo back even higher. Southern courage, fortitude, chivalry and superiority always wins out. . . . SHUCKS! We'll have us some Nigras befo' daylight is gone!

ANNOUNCER. Mr. Mayor, I hate to introduce this note, but in an earlier interview one of your chief opponents, Mr. Clan, hinted at your own complicity in the affair—

MAYOR. *A lot of poppycock!* Clan is politicking! I've beaten him four times outta four and I'll beat him four more times outta four! This is no time for partisan politics! What we need now is level-headedness and across-the-board unity. This typical, rash, mealy-mouth, shooting-off-at-the-lip of Clan and his ilk proves their insincerity, and voters will remember that in the next election! Won't you, voters? (*Has risen to the height of campaign oratory.*)

ANNOUNCER. Mr. Mayor! . . . Mr. Mayor! . . . Please—

MAYOR. I tell you, I promise you—

ANNOUNCER. *Please, Mr. Mayor!*

MAYOR. Huh? . . . Oh—yes, carry on.

ANNOUNCER. Mr. Mayor, your cheerfulness and infectious good spirits lead me to conclude that startling new developments warrant fresh-found optimism. What concrete, declassified information do you have to support your claim that Negroes will reappear before nightfall?

MAYOR. Because we are presently awaiting the payoff of a masterful five-point supra-recovery program which can't help but reap us a bonanza of Nigras 'fore sundown! . . . First: Exhaustive efforts to pinpoint the where'bouts of our own missing darkies continue to zero in on the bull's-eye . . . Second: The President of the United States, following an emergency cabinet meeting, has designated us the prime disaster area of the century—National Guard is already on the way . . . Third: In an unusual, but bold, maneuver we have appealed to the NAACP 'n all other Nigra conspirators to help us git to the bottom of the vanishing act . . . Fourth: We have exercised our non-reciprocal option and requested that all fraternal Southern states express their solidarity by lending us some of their Nigras temporarily on credit . . . Fifth and foremost: We have already gotten consent of the·Governor to round up all stray, excess and incorrigible Nigras to be shipped to us under escort of the state militia . . . That's why we've stifled pessimism and are brimming wit confidence that this full-scale concerted mobilization will ring down a jackpot of jigaboos 'fore light vanishes from sky!

ANNOUNCER. Congratulations! What happens if it fails?

MAYOR. Don't even think *that*! Absolutely no reason to suspect it will . . . (*Peers over shoulder, then whispers confidentially while placing hand over mouth by* ANNOUNCER's *imaginary mike*) But speculating on the dark side of your question—if we don't turn up some by nightfall, it may be all over. The harm has already been done. You see the South has always been glued together by the uninterrupted presence of its darkies. No telling how unstuck we might git if things keep on like they have —Wait a minute, it musta paid off already! Mission accomplished 'cause here's Jackson 'head a time wit the word . . . Well, Jackson, what's new?

JACKSON. Situation on the home front remains static, sir—can't uncover scent or shadow. The NAACP and all other Nigra front groups 'n plotters deny any knowledge or connection wit the missing Nigras. Maintained this even after appearing befo' a Senate Emergency Investigating Committee which subpoenaed 'em to Washington posthaste and threw 'em in jail for contempt. A handful of Nigras who agreed to make spectacular appeals for ours to come back to us have themselves mysteriously disappeared. But, worst news of all, sir, is our sister cities and counties, inside and outside the state, have changed their minds, fallen back on their promises and refused to lend us any Nigras, claiming they don't have 'nuff for themselves.

MAYOR. What 'bout Nigras promised by the Governor?

JACKSON. Jailbirds and vagrants escorted here from chain gangs and other reservations either revolted and escaped en route or else vanished mysteriously on approaching our city limits . . . Deterioration rapidly escalates, sir. Estimates predict we kin hold out only one more hour before overtaken by anarchistic turmoil . . . Some citizens seeking haven elsewheres have already fled, but on last report were being forcibly turned back by armed sentinels in other cities who wanted no parts of 'em—claiming they carried a jinx.

MAYOR. That bad, huh?

JACKSON. Worse, sir . . . we've received at least five reports of plots on your life.

MAYOR. What?—We've gotta act quickly then!

JACKSON. Run out of ideas, sir.

MAYOR. Think harder, boy!

JACKSON. Don't have much time, sir. One measly hour, then all hell gon break loose.

MAYOR. Gotta think of something drastic, Jackson!

JACKSON. I'm dry, sir.

MAYOR. Jackson! Is there any planes outta here in the next hour?

JACKSON. All transportation's been knocked out, sir.

MAYOR. I thought so!

JACKSON. What were you contemplating, sir?

MAYOR. Don't ask me what I was contemplating! I'm still boss 'round here! Don't forgit it!

JACKSON. Sorry, sir.

MAYOR. Hold the wire! . . . Wait a minute . . . ! Waaaaait a minute—*goddammit*! All this time crapping 'round, diddling and fotsing wit puny lil solutions—all the while neglecting our ace in the hole, our trump card! Most potent weapon for digging Nigras outta the woodpile? All the while right befo' our eyes! . . . Ass! Why didn't you remind me?

JACKSON. What is it, sir?

MAYOR. *Me—That's what! Me!* a personal appeal from ME! *Directly to them!* . . . Although we wouldn't let 'em march to the polls and express their affection for me through the ballot box, we've always known I'm held highest in their esteem. A direct address from their beloved Mayor! . . . If they's anywheres close within the sound of my voice, they'll shape up! Or let us know by a sign they's ready to.

JACKSON. You sure *that'll* turn the trick, sir?

MAYOR. As sure as my ancestors befo' me who knew that when they puckered their lips to whistle, ole Sambo was gonna come a-lickey-splitting to answer the call! . . . That same chips-down blood courses through these Confederate gray veins of Henry R. E. Lee ! ! !

ANNOUNCER. I'm delighted to offer our network's facilities for such a crucial public interest address, sir. We'll arrange immediately for your appearance on an international hookup, placing you in widest proximity to contact them wherever they may be.

MAYOR. Thank you, I'm very grateful . . . Jackson, regrease the machinery and set wheels in motion. Inform townspeople what's being done. Tell 'em we're all in this together. The next hour is countdown. I demand absolute cooperation, citywide silence and inactivity. I don't want the Nigras frightened if they's nearby. This is the most important hour in the town's history. Tell 'em if one single Nigra shows up during the hour of decision, victory is within sight. I'm gonna git 'em that one— maybe all! Hurry and crack to it!

(ANNOUNCER *rushes out, followed by* JACKSON.

Blackout. Scene reopens, with MAYOR *seated, eyes front, spotlight illuminating him in semidarkness. Shadowy figures stand in the background, prepared to answer phones or aid in any other manner.* MAYOR *waits patiently until "Go" signal is given.*)

MAYOR (*voice combining elements of confidence, tremolo and gravity*). Good evening . . . Despite the fact that millions of you wonderful people throughout the nation are viewing and listening to this momentous broadcast—and I thank you for your concern and sympathy in this hour of our peril—I primarily want to concentrate my attention and address these remarks solely for the benefit of our departed Nigra friends who may be listening somewheres in our far-flung land to the sound of my voice . . . If you are—it is with heartfelt emotion and fond memories of our happy association that I ask—"Where are you . . . ?"

Your absence has left a void in the bosom of every single man, woman and child of our great city. I tell you—you don't know what it means for us to wake up in the morning and discover that your cheerful, grinning, happy-go-lucky faces are missing! . . . From the depths of my heart, I can meekly, humbly suggest what it means to me personally . . . You see—the one face I will never be able to erase from my memory is the face—not of my Ma, not of Pa, neither wife or child—but the image of the first woman I came to love so well when just a wee lad—the vision of the first human I laid clear sight on at childbirth—the profile—better yet the full face of my dear old . . . Jemimah—God rest her soul . . . Yes! My dear ole mammy, wit her round black moonbeam gleaming down upon me in the crib, teeth shining, blood-red bandana standing starched, peaked and proud, gazing down on me affectionately as she crooned me a Southern lullaby . . . Oh! It's a memorable picture I will eternally cherish in permanent treasure chambers of my heart, now and forever always . . .

Well, if this radiant image can remain so infinitely vivid to me all these many years after her unfortunate demise in the po' folks' home—*think* of the misery the rest of us must be suffering after being *freshly* denied your soothing presence!

We need ya. If you kin hear me, just contact this station 'n I will welcome you back personally. Let me just tell you that since you eloped, nothing has been the same. How could it? You're part of us, you belong to us. Just give us a sign and we'll be contented that all is well . . .

Now if you've skipped away on a little fun fest, we understand, ha, ha. We know you like a good time and we don't begrudge it to ya. Hell—er, er, we like a good time ourselves—who doesn't . . . In fact, think of all the good times we've had together, huh? We've had some real fun, you and us, yesiree! . . . Nobody knows better than you and I what fun we've had together. You singing us those old Southern coon songs and dancing those Nigra jigs and us clapping, prodding 'n spurring you on! Lots of fun, huh? . . . *Oh boy!* The times we've had together . . . If you've snucked away for a bit of fun by yourself, we'll go 'long wit ya—long as you let us know where you at so we won't be worried about you . . .

We'll go 'long wit you long as you don't take the joke too far. I'll admit a joke is a joke and you've played a *lulu!* . . . I'm warning you, we can't stand much more horsing 'round from you! Business is business 'n fun is fun! You've had your fun so now let's get down to business! Come on back, *you hear me!*

If you been hoodwinked by agents of some foreign government, I've been authorized by the President of these United States to inform you that this liberty-loving Republic is prepared to rescue you from their clutches. Don't pay no 'tention to their sireen songs and atheistic promises! You better off under our control and you know it! . . . If you been bamboozled by rabble-rousing nonsense of your own so-called leaders, we prepared to offer some protection. Just call us up! Just give us a sign! . . . Come on, give us a sign . . . give us a sign—even a teeny weeny one . . . ? (*Glances around checking on possible communications. A bevy of headshakes indicate no success.* MAYOR *returns to address with desperate fervor.*)

Now look—you don't know what you doing! If you persist in this disobedience, you know all too well the consequences! We'll track you to the end of the earth, beyond the galaxy, across the stars! We'll capture you and chastise you with all the vengeance we command! 'N you know only too well how stern we kin be when double-crossed! The city, the state and the entire nation will crucify you for this unpardonable defiance! (*Checks again*) No call . . . ? No sign . . . ? Time is running out! Deadline slipping past! They gotta respond! They gotta! (*resuming*) Listen to me! I'm begging y'all, you've gotta come back . . . ! *Look, George!* (*Waves dirty rag aloft*) I brought the rag you wax the car wit . . . Remember, George . . . ? Don't this bring back memories, George, of all the days you spent shining that automobile to shimmering perfection . . .? And you, Rufus! . . . Here's the polish and the brush! . . . 'Member, Rufus? . . . Remember the happy mornings you spent popping this rag and whisking this brush so furiously 'till it created music that was sympho-nee to the ear . . . ? And you— *Mandy?* . . . Here's the wastebasket you didn't dump this morning. I saved it just for you! . . . *Look*, all y'all out there . . . (*Signals and a three-person procession parades one after the other before the imaginary camera.*)

DOLL WOMAN (*brandishing a crying baby [doll] as she strolls past and exits*). She's been crying ever since you left, Caldonia . . .

MOP MAN (*flashing mop*). It's been waiting in the same corner, Buster . . .

BRUSH MAN (*flagging toilet brush*). It's been dry ever since you left, Washington . . .

MAYOR (*jumping in on the heels of the last exit*). Don't these things mean anything to y'all? By God! Are your memories so short? Is there nothing sacred to ya . . . Please come back, for my sake, please! All of you—even you questionable ones! I promise no harm will be done to you! Revenge is disallowed! We'll forgive everything! Just come on back and I'll git down on my knees— (*Immediately drops to knees*) I'll be kneeling in the middle of Dixie Avenue to kiss the first shoe of the first one to show up . . . I'll smooch any other spot you request . . . Erase this nightmare 'n we'll concede any demand you make, just come on back—please? . . . *Pleeeeeeeze!*

VOICE (*shouting*). Time!

MAYOR (*remaining on knees, frozen in a pose of supplication. After a brief, deadly silence, he whispers almost inaudibly.*) They wouldn't answer . . . they wouldn't answer . . .

(*Blackout as bedlam erupts offstage. Total blackness holds during a sufficient interval where offstage sound effects create the illusion of complete pandemonium, followed by a diminution which trails off into an expressionistic simulation of a city coming to a stricken standstill: industrial machinery clanks to halt, traffic blares to silence, etc. . . . The stage remains dark and silent for a long moment, then lights rise again on the* ANNOUNCER.)

ANNOUNCER. A pitiful sight, ladies and gentlemen. Soon after his unsuccessful appeal, Mayor Lee suffered a vicious pummeling from the mob and barely escaped with his life. National guardsmen and state militia were impotent in quelling the fury of a town venting its frustration in an orgy of destruction—a frenzy of rioting, looting and all other aberrations of a town gone berserk . . . Then—suddenly—as if a magic wand had been waved, madness evaporated and something more frightening replaced it: submission . . .

Even whimpering ceased. The city: exhausted, benumbed— Slowly its occupants slinked off into shadows, and by midnight the town was occupied exclusively by zombies. The fight and life had been drained out . . . Pooped . . . Hope ebbed away as completely as the beloved, absent Negroes . . . As our crew packed gear and crept away silently, we treaded softly—as if we were stealing away from a mausoleum . . . The face of a defeated city.

Blackout.

Lights rise slowly at the sound of rooster crowing, signaling the approach of a new day, the next morning. Scene is same as opening of play. CLEM *and* LUKE *are huddled over dazedly, trancelike. They remain so for a long count. Finally, a figure drifts on stage, shuffling slowly.*)

LUKE (*gazing in silent fascination at the approaching figure*). Clem . . . ? Do you see what I see or am I dreaming . . . ?

CLEM. It's a . . . a Nigra, ain't it, Luke . . . ?

LUKE. Sure looks like one, Clem—but we better make sure— eyes could be playing tricks on us . . . Does he still look like one to you, Clem?

CLEM. He still does, Luke—but I'm scared to believe—

LUKE. Why . . . ? It looks like Rastus, Clem!

CLEM. Sure does, Luke . . . but we better not jump to no hasty conclusion . . .

LUKE (*in timid softness*). That you, Rastus . . . ?

RASTUS (*Stepin Fetchit, Willie Best, Nicodemus, Butterfly Mc-Queen and all the rest rolled into one*). Why . . . howdy . . . Mr. Luke . . . Mr. Clem . . .

CLEM. It is him, Luke! It is him!

LUKE. Rastus?

RASTUS. Yas . . .sah?

LUKE. Where was you yesterday?

RASTUS (*very, very puzzled*). Yes . . . ter . . .day? . . . Yester . . . day . . . ? Why . . . right . . . here . . . Mr. Luke . . .

LUKE. No you warn't, Rastus, don't lie to me! Where was you yestiddy?

RASTUS. Why . . . I'm sure I was . . . Mr. Luke . . . Remember . . . I made . . . that . . . delivery for you . . .

LUKE. That was *Monday*, Rastus, yestiddy was *Tuesday*.

RASTUS. Tues . . . day . . . ? You don't say . . . Well . . . well . . . well . . .

LUKE. Where was you 'n all the other Nigras yesterday, Rastus?

RASTUS. I . . . thought . . . yestiddy . . . was . . . Monday, Mr.

Luke—I coulda swore it . . . ! . . . See how . . . things . . . kin git all mixed up? . . . I coulda swore it . . .

LUKE. *Today* is *Wednesday*, Rastus. Where was you *Tuesday?*

RASTUS. Tuesday . . . huh? That's somp'um . . . I . . . don't remember . . . missing . . . a day . . . Mr. Luke . . . but I guess you right . . .

LUKE. Then where was you?

RASTUS. Don't rightly know, Mr. Luke. I didn't know I had skipped a day—But that jist goes to show you how time kin fly, don't it, Mr. Luke . . . Uuh, uuh, uuh . . . (*He starts shuffling off, scratching head, a flicker of a smile playing across his lips.* CLEM *and* LUKE *gaze dumbfoundedly as he disappears.*)

LUKE (*eyes sweeping around in all directions*). Well . . . There's the others, Clem . . . Back jist like they useta be . . . Everything's same as always . . .

CLEM. Is it . . . Luke . . . ?

(*Slow fade.*)

CURTAIN

A Rat's Mass

ADRIENNE KENNEDY

Cast of characters:

ROSEMARY
BROTHER RAT
SISTER RAT
JESUS, JOSEPH, MARY, TWO WISE MEN, SHEPHERD

BROTHER RAT *has a rat's head, a human body, a tail.* SISTER RAT *has a rat's belly, a human head, a tail.* ROSEMARY *wears a Holy Communion dress and has worms in her hair. Mass said in prayer voices that later turn to gnawing voices. They were two pale Negro children.*

Scene is the rat's house. The house consists of a red carpet runner and candles. The light is the light of the end of a summer day.
BROTHER RAT *is kneeling facing the audience.*
At the far left of the house stands a procession of JESUS,

JOSEPH, MARY, TWO WISE MEN *and a* SHEPHERD.
SISTER RAT *stands at the end of the red aisle.*

BROTHER RAT. Kay within our room I see our dying baby, Nazis, screaming girls and cursing boys, empty swings, a dark sun. There are worms in the attic beams. (*Stands*) They scream and say we are damned. I see dying and grey cats walking. Rosemary is atop the slide. Exalted! (*Kneels again*) Kay within our room I see a dying baby, Nazis, again they scream (*Stands again*) and say we are damned. Within our once Capitol I see us dying. Rosemary is atop the slide exalted.

SISTER RAT. We swore on Rosemary's Holy Communion book.

BROTHER RAT. Did you tell? Does anyone know?

(*The procession watches.*)

SISTER RAT. Blake, we swore on our father's Bible the next day in the attic.

BROTHER RAT. Did you tell Sister Rat, does anyone know? (*Kneels*) It was Easter and my fear of holy days, it was because it was Easter I made us swear.

SISTER RAT. Brother Rat, it was not Easter. It was night after Memorial Day.

BROTHER RAT. No, it was not after Memorial Day. It was the beginning of winter. Bombs fell. It was the War.

SISTER RAT. It was the War.

BROTHER RAT. Our fathers said everyone was getting hung and shot in Europe. America wouldn't be safe long. (*Remains kneeling; procession marches across the house to center.*)

SISTER RAT. Remember . . . we lived in a Holy Chapel with parents and Jesus, Joseph, Mary, our wise men and our Shepherd. People said we were the holiest children.

(BROTHER RAT *turns face front.* SISTER RAT *comes down the aisle. Procession is still.* SISTER RAT *walking*). Blake, our parents send me to Georgia. It is a house with people who say they are relatives and a garden of great sunflowers. Be my brother's keeper, Blake. I hide under the house, my rat's belly growing all day long I eat sunflower petals, I sit in the garden Blake and hang three grey cats. (*Stands before* BROTHER RAT) Blake, I'm going to have a baby. I got our baby on the slide. (*Falls*) Gray cats walk this house all summer I bury my face in the sand so I cannot bear the rats that hide in our attic beams. Blake, why did the War start? I want to hang myself.

BROTHER RAT. Kay, stop sending me the petals from Georgia. Stop saying our mother says you have to go to the State Hospital because of your breakdown. Stop saying you have a rat's belly.

(*Procession marches across sound of rats.*)

BROTHER AND SISTER RAT. The Nazis! (*Marching*) The Nazis have invaded our house. (*Softer*) Why did the War start? We want to hang ourselves. The rats. (*Sound*) The rats have invaded our Cathedral. (*They rapidly light more candles. Procession returns, marches to the center.*) Our old Rosemary songs. Weren't they beautiful! Our Rosemary Mass. (*Procession watches; silence.*) Yet we weren't safe long. (*They look at Procession.*) Soon we will be getting shot and hung. Within our house is a giant slide. Brother and Sister Rat we are.

SISTER RAT. Blake, remember when we lived in our house with Jesus and Joseph and Mary?

BROTHER RAT. Now there are rats in the church books behind every face in the congregation. They all have been on the slide. Every sister bleeds and every brother has made her bleed. The Communion wine.

BROTHER AND SISTER RAT. The Communion wine. Our father gives out the Communion wine and it turns to blood, a red aisle of blood. Too something is inside the alter listening. (SISTER RAT *kneels.*) When we were children we lived in our house, our mother blessed us greatly and God blessed us. Now they listen from the rat beams. (*Sound rats. They remain kneeling. Sound rats.*) It is our mother.

Rosemary, Rosemary was the first girl we ever fell in love

with. She lived next door behind a grape arbor her father had built. She often told us stories of Italy and read to us from her Holy Catechism book. She was the prettiest girl in our school. It is one of those midwestern neighborhoods, Italians, Negroes and Jews. Rosemary always went to Catechism and wore Holy Communion dresses.

BROTHER RAT. Where are you going Rosemary? we say. And she says, "I have to go to Catechism." Why do you always go to Catechism? "Because I am Catholic"; then thinking, she says, "Colored people are not Catholics, are they?"

SISTER RAT. I don't think many.

BROTHER RAT. "Well I am. I am a descendant of the Pope and Julius Caesar and the Virgin Mary." Julius Caesar? "Yes, Caesar was the Emperor of all Italia." And are you his descendant? "Yes," she said.

BROTHER AND SISTER RAT. We wish we were descendants of this Caesar, we said, how holy you are, how holy and beautiful. She smiled.

BROTHER RAT. Our school had a picnic in the country and she took my hand. We walked to a place of white birch trees. It is our Palestine, she said. We are sailing to Italy, I said. She was the prettiest girl—the only thing, she has worms in her hair.

SISTER RAT. Great Caesars my brother and I were. Behold us singing greatly walking across our Palestine, my brother holding my hand and I holding his and we are young before the War O Italia. Rosemary was our best friend and taught us Latin and told us stories of Italy. O Rosemary songs.

BROTHER AND SISTER RAT. My sister and I when we were young before the War, and Rosemary our best friend, O Rosemary songs. Now we live in Rat's Chapel. My sister and I.

(BROTHER RAT *stares down the aisle.*)

BROTHER RAT. It is Rosemary. (*Stares*) Did you tell? Does anyone know? Did you tell? Does anyone know? You started to cry Kay and I struck you in the face with our father's rifle. It was the beginning of summer. Just getting dark, we were playing and Rosemary said let's go to the playground. After you lay down on the slide so innocently Rosemary said if I loved her I would do what she said. Oh Kay. After that our hiding in the attic rats in the beam. Now there is snow on the playground, ambulances are on every street and within every ambulance is you Kay going to the hospital with a breakdown.

SISTER RAT. Blake, perhaps God will marry us in the State Hospital. Our fellow rats will attend us. Every day I look under our house to see who is listening. (*Aisle bright. Procession marches out.*) I cry all the time now . . . not sobbing . . . Blake, did we really go on that slide together? What were those things made us do while she watched?

BROTHER RAT. We hide in the attic like rats.

SISTER RAT. I cry all the time now.

BROTHER RAT. Within every ambulance is you, Kay. Sister, all the time.

SISTER RAT. (*Sound rats.*) I am waiting for you Blake under the hospital so the Nazis won't see me.

(*Procession marches to center.*)

BROTHER RAT. The rat comes to the attic crying softly within her head down. She thinks she's going to have a baby. If I were a Nazi I'd shoot her. On the slide she said, Blake I am bleeding. Now there is blood on the aisle of our church. Before rat blood came onto the slide we sailed. We did not swing in chains before blood, we sang with Rosemary. Now I must go to battle. (*Heil. Salutes procession*) Will you wait for me again at last spring?

(*Procession does not answer.* BROTHER *and* SISTER RAT *fall down and light candles.* BROTHER RAT *stands. Stares down aisle*) Will they wait for me at last spring Rosemary?

(ROSEMARY *comes down red aisle in her Holy Communion dress.*)

ROSEMARY. Blake the Nazis will get you on the battlefield.

(ROSEMARY *and* BROTHER RAT *stand before each other.* SISTER *remains kneeling.*)

BROTHER RAT. Rosemary atone us, take us beyond the Nazis. We must sail to the Capitol. Atone us. Deliver us unto your descendants.

ROSEMARY. The Nazis are going to get you.

BROTHER RAT. If you do not atone us Kay and I will die. We shall have to die to forget how every day this winter gray cats swing with sunflowers in their mouths because my sister thinks I am the father of a baby. Rosemary will you not atone us?

ROSEMARY. I will never atone you. Perhaps you can put a bullet in your head with your father's shotgun, then your holy battle will be done.

(*The procession is at the edge of the house.*)

SISTER RAT (*kneeling*). O Holy Music return.

(*The procession marches to center.*)

ROSEMARY. Come with me, Blake.

BROTHER RAT. How can I ever reach last spring again if I come with you, Rosemary? I must forget how every day this winter gray cats swing with sunflowers in their mouths.

ROSEMARY. Perhaps you can put a bullet in your head.

SISTER RAT. I have a rat's belly.

BROTHER RAT. How can I ever again reach last spring if I come with you, Rosemary?

ROSEMARY. You must damn last spring in your heart. You will never see last spring again.

BROTHER AND SISTER RAT. Then we must put a bullet in our heads.

(*Procession marches out. Silence. They stare at* ROSEMARY. *Procession returns.*)

PROCESSION. Goodbye Kay and Blake. We are leaving you.

BROTHER AND SISTER RAT. Jesus, Joseph, Mary, Wise Men and Shepherd, do not leave. Great Caesars, we will be again, you will behold us as we were before Rosemary with the worms in her hair, a spring can come after the War.

PROCESSION. What Kay and Blake?

BROTHER AND SISTER RAT. A spring can come after the War

when we grow up we will hang you so that we can run again, walk in the white birch trees. Jesus, Joseph, Wise Men, Shepherd, do not leave us.

PROCESSION. We are leaving because it was Easter.

BROTHER RAT. No, no, it was not Easter, it was the beginning of June.

PROCESSION. In our minds it was Easter. Goodbye Kay and Blake. (*They walk out. A gnawing sound.* SISTER RAT *kneels,* BROTHER RAT *and* ROSEMARY *face each other. A gnawing sound.*)

ROSEMARY. In my mind was a vision of us rats all.

BROTHER RAT. If only we could go back to our childhood.

SISTER RAT. Now there will always be rat blood on the rat walls of our rat house just like the blood that came onto the slide.

BROTHER RAT. Beyond my rat head there must remain a new Capitol where Great Kay and I will sing. But no within my hot head I see the dying baby Nazis and Georgia relatives screaming girls cursing boys a dark sun and my grave. I am damned. No . . . when I grow up I will swing again in white trees because beyond this dark rat run and gnawed petals there will remain a Capitol.

SISTER RAT. A Cathedral.

BROTHER RAT. Now within my mind I forever see dying rats. And gray cats walking. Rosemary worms in her hair atop the slide. Our Holy songs in our parents' house weren't they beautiful.

BROTHER AND SISTER RAT. Now it is our rat's mass. (*From now on their voices sound more like gnaws*) She said if you love me you will. It seemed so innocent. She said it was like a wedding. Now my sister Kay sends me gnawed petals from sunflowers at the State Hospital. She puts them in gray envelopes. Alone I go out to school and the movies. No more do I call by for Rosemary. She made me promise never to tell if you love me she screamed you'll never tell. And I do love her. I found my father's rifle in the attic. Winter time . . . gray time dark boys come laughing starting a game of horseshoes gnawing in the beams. The winter is a place of great gnawed sunflowers. I see them in every street in every room of our house. I pick up gnawed great yellow petals and pray to be atoned.

BROTHER RAT. I am praying to be atoned. I am praying to be atoned dear God. I am begging dear God to be atoned for the Holy Communion that existed between my sister and me and the love that I have for Rosemary. I am praying to be atoned. (*He kisses* ROSEMARY. *He comes down aisle, movements more rat-like . . . voice more like gnawing.*) Bombs fall I am alone in our old house with an attic full of dead rat babies. I must hide.

BROTHER AND SISTER RAT. God we ask you to stop throwing dead rat babies.

(BROTHER RAT *kneels.*)

BROTHER RAT. When I asked you yesterday the day they brought my sister Kay home from the State Hospital, you said God, Blake perhaps you must put a bullet in your head then your battle will be done. God, I think of Rosemary all the time. I love her. I told myself afterward it was one of the boys playing horseshoes who had done those horrible things on the slide with my sister. Yet I told Kay I am her keeper yet I told Rosemary I love her. It is the secret of my battlefield.

SISTER RAT. Here we are again in our attic where we once played games, but neither of us liked it because from time to time you could hear the rats. But it was our place to be alone, Blake now that I am home from the hospital we must rid our minds of my rat's belly. Can you see it? You did not visit me in the hospital Brother Rat. Blake I thought you were my brother's keeper.

BROTHER RAT. Everywhere I go I step in your blood. Rosemary I wanted you to love me. (*He turns—aisles bright—gnawing sound—battlefield sounds.*)

BROTHER AND SISTER RAT. God is hanging and shooting us.

SISTER RAT. Remember Brother Rat before I bled, before descending bombs and death on our capitol we walked the Palestine . . . we went to the movies. Now the Germans and Caesar's army are after us, Blake.

(*He goes back to* ROSEMARY *whose back is to him and starts.*)

ROSEMARY. The Nazis are after you. My greatest grief was your life together. My greatest grief.

BROTHER AND SISTER RAT (*look up*). Now every time we will go outside we will walk over the grave of our dead baby Red aisle runners will be on the street when we come to the playground Rosemary will forever be atop the slide exalted with worms in her hair. (*They kneel then rise, kneel, then rise.*) We must very soon get rid of our rat heads so dying baby voices on the beams will no more say we are our lost Caesars.

ROSEMARY. It is our wedding now, Blake.

BROTHER AND SISTER RAT. Brother and Sister Rat we are very soon we must.

SISTER RAT. We are rats in the beam now.

ROSEMARY. My greatest grief was your life together. The Nazis will come soon now.

BROTHER AND SISTER RAT. Every time we go out red blood runners will be on the street. (*They kneel, then rise, kneel, then rise.*) At least soon very soon we will get rid of our rat heads and rat voices in beams will say no more we are your lost Caesars.

ROSEMARY. It is our wedding, Blake. The Nazis have come. (*Marching*) Brother and Sister Rat you are now soon you will become headless and all will cease the dark sun will be bright no more and no more sounds of shooting in the distance. (*Marching procession appears bearing shotguns.*)

BROTHER AND SISTER RAT. We will become headless and all will cease the dark sun will be bright no more and no more sounds of shooting in the distance. It will be the end. (*The procession shoots, they scamper, more shots, they fall,* ROSEMARY *remains.*)

CURTAIN

Tabernacle

A Black Experience in Total Theater

PAUL CARTER HARRISON

Cast of Characters

REV
ADAM
HAMM
BEGGAR-MUSICIAN
ATTORNEY JONES
ATTORNEY STUMBLE
DISTRICT ATTORNEY
JUDGE TAWKIN
CHORUS OF MOTHERS
FIVE BOYS (DANCERS)
BLACK POLICEMAN
FIRST POLICEMAN ⎫
SECOND POLICEMAN ⎬ All wear white masks
FIRST DETECTIVE ⎪
SECOND DETECTIVE ⎭
LOVEJOY (Homosexual prisoner)
PORTER

CLERK

MINISTER

EXECUTIONER

CHARACTER

TWO STAGE HANDS

FIVE PRISON GUARDS (Played by FIVE BOYS)

HOUSE USHERS

AUTHOR'S NOTE

The play is peripherally based on the events described in the documentary essay "The Torture of Mothers," written by Truman Nelson, who was no less inspired by the factum precipitating the Harlem (N.Y.) riots during the summer of 1964. Yet, though the play's foundation is rooted in fact, its reality is conceived in fantasy. No attempt has been made to establish a strict identification with the documented essay, though the events may allude to parallels of persons living or dead, which, in fact, was coincidentally intended.

As a source of reference, the Harlem episode is now used as a convenient vehicle to, firstly, articulate a Black experience, and, secondly, to achieve a totally theatrical experience which is cogent, expressive and edifying. The style of the work attempts to exploit all elements of the stage—plasticity of set design, role playing, dance movement, choral chants, animism of masks, pregnancy of light and silence—integrated in such a manner as to create concrete images of a unique quality of Black expression. It is a form which reaches out to bridge the moribund American theatrical traditions with the formlessness of contemporary revolutionary theater. It searches for a new unity of Black creative expression which is without peer in White American traditions.

Directorially—as directed by the author—the symbols, iconography, musical sound, and gesture reflect the attitudinal experience of Black Americans. Thus, the tonal quality of the play is dissonant, rather than harmonic: though structured as life, at times it appears to be played by ear. The approach is one of detachment, rather than the emotional self-indulgence found in psychological melodrama. Passion is derived from archetypical events which, however external, are recognizably human by definition of the characters' existence. The chorus of mothers is brought on stage with the robust voices of baritones: all male. Masks are designed for identification of certain characters, so as to suppress sentimentality and allow the emergence of acute reality. As a play within a play, the audience becomes a part of the total experience.

Tabernacle is set for a large cast; however, in most cases, it lends itself to double and triple role playing. For example—the BOYS *play the* POLICEMAN *and the* PRISON GUARDS *in the interrogation and flagellation scene;* ATTORNEY JONES *plays a* POLICEMAN *in the opening scene and street gathering scene;* LOVEJOY *plays a* POLICEMAN *in opening and the* EXECUTIONER *in closing scene;* CLERK *is played by one of the* BOYS; PORTER *is played by the* CHARACTER.

The production should preferably be played by an all black cast; otherwise, an all white cast in order to salvage the value of the masks. A mixed cast would be antithetical to the style.

Just as the musical sound tends to embrace both African and jazz traditions, the play can be observed as being classical or avant garde in form: it is neither a musical nor an opera, but a deliberate synthesis of theatrical techniques which best complement the Black experience.

ACT I

CURTAIN: *none! As the audience arrives in the theater, the play is already in progress. Situated within the frame structure of the metal scaffolding at stage right is the* MUSICAL ENSEMBLE; *they are visible to the audience and play freely while the audience locates its seats. At stage left—vacant—is a series of boxes, constructed upward toward a platform on which stands an enormous cross. Downstage, in front of the boxes, a panel of the ramps leading out into the audience is raised upright, exposing a smaller cross.*

Unceremoniously, HAMM *and* ADAM *climb the ladders leading up to the top of the scaffold—the roof— where they sit motionless around a large pigeon cage. As music builds emotionally, the* MOTHERS *file out intermittently, taking their positions in the cells of the lower level of the scaffold. The two cells just above are empty.*

As music reaches a heightened pitch, the lights begin to dim slowly and imperceptibly; REV *starts down the aisle, shaking hands and talking to the "congregation," moving down to the base of the extended ramps before beginning opening speech.*

REV. Brothers . . . and Sisters . . . all my Brothers and Sisters . . . just look at all of you out there. . . . Warms my heart to see you all turn out for this Tabernacle service. . . . The word must have gotten around, huh? . . . That this ain't no ordinary service, no, not on your garbage-pickin souls it ain't . . . (*Searching through the audience*) I bet some of yawl been here twice . . . hard to tell one face from the other in this light . . . but that don't matter . . . it don't change a thing in this meeting . . . cause you'll only shout twice as hard when it's over . . . (*Paces back and forth, speaks emphatically.*) . . . and after the shouting is over, you'll know once again why our flesh is seething to a hardened crust . . . you'll witness all the infernal ashes of Cain poured down on our souls . . . all of us . . . and you'll question your hearts how much more can we bear. . . . And your bodies will rumble with a fearful rock . . . not roll, but rock . . . and that won't be the fear of God . . . but the guilt-laden spirit coming out of reverie . . . and that means all of us. We been sitting like lambs out to pasture unimpressed with the shadow of the slaughter house . . . knowing all the time that the wrath and torment set against us was . . . and still is . . . enough to make cotton turn to stone and the desert spring a leak. Yes, Brothers and Sisters, after the shouting your eyes will be burned dry . . . burned out . . . there'll be no tears today . . . turn the other cheek died out with ole Saint Uncle Thomas . . . a quinine sipper . . . case-hardened . . . who believed white was Right . . . well, White ain't always Right . . . you'll see . . . you'll see . . . and stagger with disbelief as many of our Sisters have . . . watching their children yoked and tied to the rack . . . without cause . . . suspending their natural outrage with the hope that Justice might make possession . . . but it never do, Brothers and Sisters, and that's why we're here today . . . to bear witness to the sores infecting our souls . . . the passions our Sisters must cradle . . . and the dark hue of everlasting truth, yes, truth is Black . . . Black as Hamm and Adam up there . . . (*He gestures toward the two boys on roof.*) . . . . at least they're Hamm and Adam today . . . but their truth cannot be denied . . . certainly you wouldn't deny it? . . . or you, or you . . . maybe you? . . . (*Gestures toward* CHORUS.) . . . certainly not the Chorus of Mothers over there. Now I can see some of you making grim faces out there . . . mocking Rev. Rev ain't goin to do no preachin . . . Rev is just goin to bury his conscience and let things happen like it is . . . This ain't no ordinary meeting, remember? Even the music ain't ordinary . . . (To BEGGAR-MUSICIAN) . . . Give us some music, Brother. (MUSICIANS *begin to play tune similar to that at opening.*) Now when have you all heard music like that at All Souls? But this is what the Tabernacle needs to tell this story . . . a new tune . . . and this is just the beginning . . . our souls need refreshing . . . that's what the Tabernacle is for . . . to move our souls . . . to raise the scourge that has haunted us from the moment we crossed the dark threshold of the womb . . . (*Shouting*) . . . We want to make the guilty show his face . . . I'm sorry, Brothers and Sisters, I said I wouldn't do no preachin . . . that ain't what's needed cause we've heard it all before . . . but today, we're lucky to have some of the members of the congregation vent our wounds with a play of Passion . . . they've been waiting to come onto our humble stage . . . as you can see . . . by no means professional proscenium . . . (*Again shouting*) but we don't need no artifice, our stage is life . . . and we play right and wrong every day. Our souls are bare . . . so bear with us . . . bear with us . . . and bear witness.

(*Panel from ramp with cross falls, barely missing* REV, *whose back is to stage; lights come up on* HAMM *and* ADAM, *who become animated. Music stops.* REV *walks up ramp, as first* POLICEMAN *who had been behind ramp panel moves on;* REV *exits.*)

ADAM (*searching sky*). Gettin' late.

HAMM (*indifferently*). Um-hmm.

ADAM. Be getting dark soon.

HAMM. So what, stars ain't out yet.

ADAM. Just worried about the birds. They should have been home.

HAMM. Man, them birds are just like us. If they get a chance to hang out, they hang out. Can't blame them myself.

ADAM. But I got to be gettin home.

HAMM. Well, why didn't you say that instead of actin like you were worried about the birds? You are a very jive cat, Adam.

ADAM. I ain't jivin, I'm just hungry.

HAMM. You should've bought a hot-dog.

ADAM. Spent all my bread in pigeon feed.

HAMM. So that's why you're hungry and they are still flying. You done pepped them up with all that energy, man. They so high on your feed, they might never come down. That sure was a dumb sacrifice, Adam.

ADAM. Well, they had to eat, didn't they?

HAMM. Not if you don't eat.

ADAM. Aw man, you don't know nothing about duty.

HAMM. What kind of duty? In the jungle, your only duty is to survive, man. Ask your mama bout that.

ADAM. Don't be talkin bout my mama.

HAMM (*derisively*). I wouldn't talk bout your mama. Wouldn't let anybody else talk bout your mama. You mama is all right with me, Adam. In fact, she'll be my horse if she never wins a race.

ADAM. I don't play that shit, Hamm.

HAMM. Don't get uptight. All I'm trying to do is hip you, man.

ADAM. Save it for the birds. All I want to do now is get home.

HAMM. Go on, man, don't let me keep you.

ADAM. I'm waitin for the birds.

HAMM. And you're hungry.

ADAM. So what.

HAMM. So snot. Just stop cryin.

ADAM. Ain't nobody cryin.

HAMM. Don't tell me. You always cryin bout somethin. If it ain't bout the birds, it's the bees. If ain't bout the birds and bees, it's bout them little chicks on the block that keep a hurtin on you. You just ain't got no heart.

ADAM. You just jealous cause my heart's too big.

HAMM. Yeah. Covered with milk chocolate that melts in your mouth and not in your pants.

ADAM. Oh, I takes care of the business, all right.

HAMM. Sure, after playing "sugar daddy."

ADAM. They call me sugar, cause I sweet talks the be-jesus out a chick.

HAMM. Adam, you ought to be ashamed for God. You know damn well you ain't got no talk for nobody— You ain't nothin but a soft neck mother-hugger. Softer than a tit made of clouds.

ADAM. Aw man, you talk shit.

HAMM. If I'm lying, I'm flying.

ADAM. Hey Hamm. How high is up?

HAMM. You tell me, turkey. You the one up there, not me.

ADAM. You always got some jive, Hamm. Ain't a cat on the block that wears his pants any tighter in the crotch than me.

HAMM. Get that. Adam is a man. Your draws must be made of steel or something. Never wear thin in the ass, huh baby? Ain't you proud?

ADAM. You got a whole lot of lip, Hamm, but you really don't show me much.

HAMM. WHA! I've got more balls than Tracy's got dick!

ADAM. Must be pretty easy to get at, cause when the pigs are on the scene, all I ever hear you holler is LET EM GO!

HAMM. Hell, I ain't afraid of no pigs.

ADAM. Oh no?

HAMM. No, are you?

ADAM. Why should I be? Besides, I ain't into nothin but flying birds. Pigs don't bother you if your nose is clean.

HAMM. They don't scare me, if I never pick my nose! (*Hitting one hand against palm of other*) I've got something for em, if they start pushing me around. Let me see your hand, faggot.

ADAM. Pretty tough, huh?

HAMM. Like hell it is . . . soft as baby turd. This is a real hand . . . (*He raises hand, fingers drawn together karate style, threatens to smash the pigeon cage.*) . . . I could smash this thing with one blow.

ADAM. Raise up, baby. Don't take it out on the birds.

HAMM. There you go worrying about those birds again. Who's worrying about us? We'd be lucky if someone smashed up our homes . . . I'm just trying to prove a point . . . besides, I'd be doing the birds a favor . . .

ADAM. Hell-uv-a favor . . . tearing up their home.

HAMM. Hell-uv-a home, on top of a Harlem roof with the Hawk at the door.

(*He raises his hand again,* ADAM *breaks forward in gesture; the scene freezes. Simultaneously, the* CHORUS *becomes animated.*)

CHORUS.
For shame . . . for shame,
he knows not what he says
our homes are our homes,
we breathe there night and day.

For shame . . . for shame,
God knows our lives are urgent:
our children we shelter,
if only they'd be patient.

FIRST MOTHER.
How faint and feeble seems a mother's task,
When the stink of garbage is from weeks gone past.
And every seedy sanctuary 'way from home
attracts our lads too eagerly for right or wrong.
They the victims and we know it,
cause their young lives ain't too solid,

and no social team or Mister Clean can rid the anguish in our
   spleens.
We need courage more than prayers, dear mothers,
or we'll lose our lads to the mucky gutters.
   (CHORUS *freezes,* HAMM *and* ADAM *become animated again.*)
   ADAM (*preventing* HAMM *from smashing cage*). Lay off. Slaugh-
ter pigs not birds.
   HAMM. You and your dumb birds.
   ADAM. They're your birds too.
   HAMM. You know what you can do with those birds, don't you?
   ADAM. Maybe you'll feel differently when they come around.
   HAMM. The pigs ain't never changed nothing yet.
   ADAM. The birds . . . I mean the birds.
   HAMM. Pigeons . . . man, stop worrying . . . they're trained to
come home . . . just like us, huh, Adam? But we ain't got wings
like they have . . . so we could stay up there without comin down
. . . out of sight . . . no pigs to bug us . . . Man, wouldn't it be
great to drop a load on a pig's head? One of these days, Adam,
I'm going to take one of them.
   ADAM. I hope you're ready to give up as much as you're takin.
   HAMM. I know you ain't got much heart for that kind of action.
   ADAM. You'd better leave your heart at home and bring a whole
lot of ass . . . cause this new hog squad out here will try to tear
you another.
   HAMM (*sarcastically*). Oh, oh the HOG-SQUAD! Man, I ain't
afraid to do battle with no pig . . . they jes better keep out of my
way . . . cause I'm bad.
   ADAM. If you lookin for trouble, you sure don't have to go far to
find it . . . cause they all over the place . . . you jes walk right
on top of them and see what you get.
   HAMM. Then I'll have to walk right over them . . . That's all.
After all, they're in my back yard, and Harlem is like one great
big living room with wall-to-wall cops.
   ADAM. Yeah, and you'd damned well better keep your feet in
the air . . . with the birds.
   HAMM. You're really afraid of them, ain't you?

ADAM. I'm jes sensitive . . . sensitive to being whupped . . . and just for breathing too hard.

HAMM. Remember the last riot they had out here?

ADAM. I remember the whupping.

HAMM. Yeah, man, you sure did get your ass kicked!

ADAM. Out of sight don't make you out of mind!

HAMM. Ah, man . . . I got whupped too . . . you don't see me cryin.

ADAM. You jes ain't sensitive.

HAMM. I guess you spell that . . . A-F-R-A-I-D.

ADAM. Call it what you want, but I can't forget what happened to that Rico cat . . . They sure put something on him . . . and he wasn't even doin nothin but watchin.

HAMM. None of us was doin nuttin . . . but watchin . . . that's why we got in it . . . so those pigs couldn't whup-up those little kids.

ADAM. So they whupped us instead.

HAMM. For doin nuttin!!!

CHORUS (*rapidly*).
That's the truth . . . that's the truth.
Our boys they say they're doin nuttin
yet still they're always into somethin.
That's the truth . . . that's the truth.

HAMM (*gesturing with edge of palm*). Did you see how I bust that pig across his nose?

ADAM. No, but I saw his stick up-side your head.

HAMM. I got him first.

ADAM. How could you tell with your eye all messed up? . . . he put a hurtin on you . . .

HAMM. I felt his face sag . . . (*Rubbing edge of palm*) . . . right here.

ADAM (*animated recall*). I felt my ass drag . . . (*Rubbing his bottom*) . . . right here. Down at the precinct . . . you can believe me, baby, it was dragging. The pigs came in one at a time . . . even stood in line like it was Klein's bargain basement or somethin . . . took sticks in their hands . . . and they wailed

. . . yes, they wailed . . . (*Gestures*)

CHORUS (*groans with each gesture*). Ughumm, Ughumm, Ughumm.

ADAM. . . . pounding away . . . again . . . again . . . and again . . . they weren't lettin up for a minute . . . not missing a strike . . . my head started to roll . . . my knees took a dive . . . they propped me up and stroked some more . . . ugh . . . it was gettin good . . . ugh . . . like ass ain't comin cheaper at Sears . . . wham . . . the light ran out of my eyes . . . I started to heave . . . someone yelled . . . "my shoes goddammit."

CHORUS. UGH!

HAMM. Stop it, man, you're makin me sick. Remember, I was there too.

ADAM. Oh, I guess I was sort of gettin away, huh? Don't want you to think I was being too enthusiastic . . . I just don't want to get into nuttin . . . no more.

HAMM. Man, as long as you're Black and your tail points to the ground . . . you are in it. Whitey takes one look at your face and he starts swingin cause he's scared . . . he thinks you goin to kiss him or somethin . . . maybe if he'd stop hidin behind his mask, I would.

ADAM. Whitey wears a mask?

HAMM. The badge, baby, the badge.

(*Enter second* POLICEMAN. *He is wearing a white mask which partially covers his face. He joins another* POLICEMAN *who has been patrolling back and forth, downstage.*)

ADAM (*teasingly*). Good reason to stay off the streets . . . you'd look funny being kissed by a man you don't even know . . . Pow.

HAMM (*assumes karate pose*). Come on, I'll show you what I'd do . . . come on, take a swing at me . . . use the cage, if you dare . . .

ADAM. Ohhh . . . you got your karate trick together.

HAMM. My karate bag is so deep, you can't even see the bottom . . . come on . . . let's see what you know . . . swing at me.

(*The boys, including* HAMM *and* ADAM, *circle each other;* ADAM *swings at* HAMM; *they jockey back and forth as the* POLICEMEN *begin to sense the action and ascend the scaffolding to roof-top; the* CHORUS *becomes aroused and tries to warn the boys by cooing like pigeons.*)

CHORUS. Coo-ooo coo coo coo coo—coo coo

(*The boys become aware of the cooing and notice the birds.*)

ADAM. Look, they've come home! Let's take up the poles.

HAMM. Are they all back?

ADAM. I'm still counting . . . twelve . . . fifteen . . . sixteen . . .

HAMM. They sure ain't in much hurry to come down . . . angle them this way, Adam . . .

(*The* POLICEMEN *have reached the roof and confront the boys.*)

FIRST POLICEMAN. Unhand your poles.

(*The boys are startled; they face* POLICEMEN, *holding their poles.*)

SECOND POLICEMAN. And hold your ground.

ADAM. What's up, officers? Only pigeons flyin here.

FIRST POLICEMAN. You birds are coming down with us.

HAMM. Dig these pigs, Adam . . . they look a bit shaky . . . Better stop movin, officer, you might blow the whole roof down.

FIRST POLICEMAN. If you make the wrong move, you won't know the difference.

(ADAM *starts to raise the pole.*)

SECOND POLICEMAN. Freeze!

(*The figures on the roof freeze, the* MOTHERS *again become animated.*)

SECOND MOTHER (*rhythmically*).

Don't harm my boy.

CHORUS.

Don't harm my boy.

SECOND MOTHER.

He's done no wrong.

CHORUS.

He's done no wrong.

SECOND MOTHER.

He's made his flight to the tar beach,

to find some joy we all seek;
he bother no one,
only have some fun
away from the asphalt dung.
　CHORUS.
He bother no one
only having some fun,
away from the asphalt dung.
　SECOND MOTHER (*scale progression, with great indignation of character.*)
Don't harm him.
　CHORUS.
Don't harm him.
　SECOND MOTHER.
Don't harm him.
　CHORUS.
Don't harm him.
　SECOND MOTHER.
Don't harm him.
　CHORUS.
Don't harm him.
　SECOND MOTHER.
Don't harm him.
　CHORUS.
Don't harm him.
　SECOND MOTHER.
He's found relief on the tar beach.
　CHORUS.
He's found relief on the tar beach.
　SECOND MOTHER.
From the slag and the fetor paved below.
　CHORUS.
From the slag and fetor paved below.
　SECOND MOTHER.
He's only a boy,
with few pleasures to enjoy

provoke him not to temptation.
CHORUS.
Provoke him not to temptation.
SECOND MOTHER (*scale progression; highly indignant*).
He's not a criminal . . .
CHORUS.
. . . not yet.
SECOND MOTHER.
He's not a criminal . . .
CHORUS.
. . . not yet.
SECOND MOTHER.
He's not a criminal
CHORUS.
. . . not yet.
SECOND MOTHER.
He's not a criminal
CHORUS.
. . . not yet.
SECOND MOTHER.
Don't press his rancor to the wall,
only in the gutter can he fall,
don't goad him to his destruction.
CHORUS.
Don't goad him to his destruction.
SECOND MOTHER.
If he's done wrong,
relay a gong,
and I'll come,
pay any sum,
but please, don't goad him to destruction.
CHORUS.
Don't goad him to destruction.
(*Together*)
Don't harm my boy.

Don't harm my boy.
Don't harm my boy.
Don't harm my boy.

(*Figures on upper level become animated again.*)

FIRST POLICEMAN. For a half a second, I thought I saw your head rolling over the side.

HAMM. Bet you're sorry you missed your chance, huh, cop?

FIRST POLICEMAN (*jabs* HAMM *with gun*). A smart ape, huh? . . . (*Jab*) . . . how do you like them peanuts?

ADAM. We ain't doin' nuttin.

HAMM (*Gripping stomach, shouting*). Will you stop cryin?

SECOND POLICEMAN. You ain't crying, are you, sonny? . . . you just trying to tell us something.

FIRST POLICEMAN. We didn't mount these stairs for nothing . . . what are you hiding? . . . what have you got in that pail?

HAMM. Feed.

FIRST POLICEMAN. Feed . . . now who's feeding who . . . any special kind of feed?

HAMM. Pig feed.

(*He is beaten again.*)

FIRST POLICEMAN. This is for something, wise ass, this for nothing . . . this for something and again for nothing . . .

SECOND POLICEMAN (*searching pail*). Nothing.

FIRST POLICEMAN. All right, on your feet, we're going down.

(*The* POLICEMEN, HAMM, *and* ADAM *come down as a group of* BLACK BOYS *enter and converse with* MOTHERS *until they notice* HAMM *and* ADAM *and the* POLICEMEN. *The* BOYS *are carrying feed pails.*)

FIRST BOY. What's happening, Brothers?

HAMM (*breaks away from* POLICEMAN). Pigs want to corral us.

SECOND BOY (*coming in between* HAMM *and* ADAM *and* POLICE-MEN). Now what did yawl get into?

ADAM (*moves in close to* BOYS). Aw . . . jes shaking our poles in public, I guess.

FIRST BOY. Now that don't seem like a fair reason to take you in . . . Everybody got a right to air his pole now and then.

FIRST POLICEMAN. Step out of the way before we run the lot of you in.

THIRD BOY. We ain't doing nothing but standing around, officer.

FIRST BOY. Maybe we need a permit . . . or somethin?

FIRST POLICEMAN. Get out of the way.

FIRST BOY. Who's in the way? . . . We ain't in your way . . . pass on, officer.

SECOND BOY. But the brothers stay . . . a pig pen don't seem like home to me.

SECOND POLICEMAN (*reaches for gun*). Get out of sight . . . before one of you gets hurt.

FIRST BOY. Oh, we're leaving, officer . . . we're all gonna split . . . and the brothers too.

FIRST POLICEMAN (*draws revolver*). Over somebody's dead body.

FIFTH BOY. Oh-oh, he looks mean.

THIRD BOY. No . . . just ugly.

FIRST BOY. Blow us down . . . come on . . . officer, blow us down . . . we can't stop you . . . all we got is a little pigeon feed.

SECOND POLICEMAN. Shove off, you dumb son-of-a-bitches . . . (*Revolver drawn, hand shaking.*)

SECOND BOY. Uh, that officer has a nasty mouth.

FIRST POLICEMAN. You can't intimidate us . . . you're obstructing an arrest.

THIRD BOY. Arrest? . . . what arrest? . . . anybody see a cause for arrest? . . . who's getting arrested around here?

FIRST POLICEMAN. It's not up to you to decide, boy, so move out . . . we're leaving.

FIRST BOY. Let's all go down, unless you've decided none of us is particularly good company.

SECOND POLICEMAN. Clear out, before I throw a charge into one of you.

SECOND BOY. Solid.

(POLICEMEN *begin to realize hopelessness of situation and prepare to leave.*)

FIRST POLICEMAN (*to* HAMM *and* ADAM). We'll keep our date another time . . . there's always another time, isn't it? As for the rest of you monkeys, I'll have you all by the tail . . . sooner than later.

(POLICEMEN exit.)

HAMM (*shouting at exiting* POLICEMEN). Big faggots. You slip is showing, sweetie.

FOURTH BOY. Always said, a pig ain't shit . . . (*Ruminating*) . . . come to think about it, maybe he is.

HAMM. You brothers sure got an eye for trouble. What's doing tonight?

FIRST BOY. Just hangin-out, baby . . . that's all.

ADAM. I'm hungry . . . think I'll go home.

BOYS (*together*). Ahhh man-n-n-n—

FIRST BOY. Maybe that ain't too dumb . . . you'd better split too, Hamm, those pigs are gonna be after your ass tonight, man.

HAMM. Guess you're right . . . I can cool it for a couple of days . . . but I'm goin to keep my fingers greased.

FIFTH BOY. That's right, baby . . . keep those edges sharp.

HAMM. Did you thank the brothers, Adam?

ADAM. Yeah . . . sure . . . thanks.

HAMM. Let's go. See you guys on the block.

(*Exit.*)

SECOND BOY. Maybe we should all get back on the block . . . the Avenue's stinkin with pigs.

THIRD BOY. You can smell them before you see them.

FIRST BOY. Simple question of who's smellin who?

SECOND BOY. Their noses might be turned up on the Avenue . . . but on the block . . . we do the smellin . . . and they the stinkin.

FIFTH BOY. I hate pigs.

FIRST BOY. They hate you too.

THIRD BOY. Let's set 'em up again.

(*The pails are lined up side by side upstage, in front of the*

MOTHERS. *The* BOYS *line up, facing the pails, backs to the audience, and they progressively build up a growling sound at the height of which they charge on the pails, thrusting their fists into the pails.*)

BOYS. YAAAAWWWWWWWWWW!

(BOYS *become unanimated.*)

CHORUS.

Those boys are in an awful stink,
they'll surely end up in the clink;
they'd better bring their voices down,
or face a cuffing from a blue-suit clown.

They need some guidance soon, I think,
those social workers all are finks,
always harassed, they can't be mellow,
life has not been a bowl of Jello.

(*The* BOYS *now turn, and in turn they jump into position for their Karate Dance; before actual Karate Dance, they sing in position making a few preparatory moves.*)

BOYS.

On the block
On the block,
On the block we roll the piggies in our socks.

On the block,
On the block,
if they bug us they will surely get their knocks.

On the block,
On the block,
On the block we roll the piggies in our socks.

On the block,
On the block,
if they bug us they will surely get their knocks.

They may beat us off the Avenues,
and whip us till we bend,
but once we make the block,
every alley is our friend.

On the block
On the block,
On the block, we roll the piggies in our socks.

What more can the piggies expect?
they never treated us with no respect!

We are coming of age,
without rights, we can gauge;
so look out Whitey,
we're on the rage.

On the block,
On the block,
On the block, we roll the piggies in our socks.

On the block,
On the block,
If they bug us they will surely get their knocks.

(*The* BOYS *now go into actual Karate Dance. As the dance
ends, the* BOYS *exit as a blind* BEGGAR-MUSICIAN *enters.*

The BEGGAR-MUSICIAN *crosses stage left. As he passes* MOTHERS
*he makes a remark about being blind such as—"I see you moth-
ers are in the same place"—or—"can't seem to see around corners!" A* MOTHER *responds: "If you didn't drink so much you
wouldn't be so blind!"*

ADAM *enters. As he notices the* BEGGAR-MUSICIAN, *he makes
"violent" gestures to determine if* BEGGAR *is really blind.*

After he determines that BEGGAR *is blind,* ADAM *places a coin
attached to a string in the cup, jingles it and pulls it back out.
Begins to exit, smugly.*)

BEGGAR (*as he feels into cup*). Thank you . . . Brother!

ADAM (*curiously*). Hey man . . . why'd you call me brother?

BEGGAR. If you ain't black, I take it back.

ADAM. Oh yeah . . . but you can't know if I'm really black.

BEGGAR. I know what I'm dealing with on this corner.

ADAM. You sure you ain't jivin . . . I mean about being blind?

BEGGAR. I'm blind as a church-bat . . . you are black . . . ain't you?

ADAM. No . . . I'm brown . . . you know, somewhere between hazel-nut and burnt copper . . . but smooth as a cameo . . . get the picture?

BEGGAR. Oh . . . now I see . . .

ADAM (*astonished*). Can you?

BEGGAR. Yeah. You're a pretty feller, all right. Maybe I ought to kiss you on the back of your neck.

ADAM. Aw come off it, man . . . you know you ain't blind.

BEGGAR. Well, not exactly . . .

ADAM. See, I know what's happening.

BEGGAR. . . . I just can't see for looking!

ADAM. Ah man, I bet you can see a copper turn in your cup . . . faster than the flick of an eyelash.

BEGGAR. If a copper turns, I don't have to look . . . much less see.

ADAM. Did you see how much I put in your cup?

BEGGAR. That's easy . . . nothing from nothing ain't left something yet.

ADAM. How could you see that?

BEGGAR. Let's say, it's the glow of the roll that meets the eye. (ADAM *apologetically recovers the coin, removes the string and places the coin in the cup*.) Thank you, Brother . . . be you copper or bronze, your soul ain't rusty and you're still my pretty black nigger.

ADAM. For a blind man, you eyes are damn sharp at night, aren't they?

BEGGAR. Yeah, I guess I do all right in the dark!

ADAM. You probably don't miss a trick by daylight either.

BEGGAR. It's not the light, as much as the black hope which follows me everywhere I go.

ADAM. Sure ain't much to hope for out here. I mean just look around you.

BEGGAR. Keep your eyes open.

ADAM. Man, I've seen enough of this mess . . . uggh.

BEGGAR (*begins playing a chord*). Got any special tune you want to hear?

ADAM. No, you'd better not . . . you want the pigs on your heels?

BEGGAR. A little music never hurt anybody.

ADAM. If the pigs start swingin . . . you'll sing a different tune.

BEGGAR. As long as we're singin together . . . it's all right.

ADAM. Man, where you been? You must be blind or somethin. They'll come out here with those sticks and make you sing what they want you to sing . . . Whup. Hell, if my mama was home, I'd be home now . . . they could come anytime.

BEGGAR. Are you in trouble, boy?

ADAM. Yeah, as long as Black ain't white, and the blues is sung by Patti Page.

BEGGAR. No problem. Just pretend you're a cinnamon bun or a Rose tattoo.

ADAM. Man, the pigs might be dumb, but they got good eyes.

BEGGAR. 'Course, they're known to be a bit shortsighted.

ADAM. Seein is believin . . . ain't it? . . . They have got the bird's eye view, and here we sit grounded, without even wings.

BEGGAR. If I had wings, I wouldn't know what to do with them.

ADAM. Fly this coop. Get the Hell out quick. Get in the wind, Jack.

BEGGAR. But you've got to come down somewhere. So it just might as well be home.

ADAM. I'd come down in Africa. Why not? Home is where you find it, ain't it . . . ? At least there, a black man ain't some kind of monkey on a limb.

BEGGAR. Don't have to be here either . . . if you find the right tree to live in.

ADAM. Man, ain't nobody round here growing up to be no Tarzan. Ain't nobody dumb enough to sleep in a tree. And ain't none of us ever going to knock up no gorillas to bear one cheetah.

Man, Tarzan can't even talk straight. If he were black, walking around with that illegitimate monkey, and as a grown man, living with that Boy, rather than takin care of business with Jane, man, he'd get locked up . . . thrown under the jail. Now you know that ain't right.

BEGGAR. Times sure have changed in the old country. Even the honeywagon don't stop there anymore. You ain't got much of a bone to pick.

ADAM. I still got a bone to pick with Tarzan. So when I get on the other side, I'm gonna buy myself a Jane and let her pick it. (*Laughs.*) That ought give him something to do.

BEGGAR (*stops playing*). Shhh. (*Listens intently.*)

ADAM. What's happenin?

BEGGAR. Did you see something?

ADAM. No, did you?

BEGGAR. Remember, boy, darkness plays funny tricks on my eyes, but better senses tell me that the jungle is restless.

ADAM. Pigs. I'd better split.

BEGGAR. Good luck, little brother, but remember, Africa might not be sitting over the mountain top.

ADAM. You'll probably see Africa before me.

(BEGGAR *begins to play instrument;* TWO DETECTIVES *and* FIRST POLICEMAN *enter, searching the area.*)

FIRST DETECTIVE. Hey, you—

BEGGAR. Yeah?

FIRST DETECTIVE. Did you see some kids come by here?

BEGGAR. Get out the light, so I can see!

FIRST DETECTIVE. Then open your eyes.

BEGGAR (*walks past* POLICEMAN). Get out the light! Get out the light!

SECOND DETECTIVE. Come on, don't waste your time. He wouldn't tell you anyhow.

FIRST POLICEMAN. We'll find the little niggers . . . I know who they are.

FIRST DETECTIVE (*to* BEGGAR, *who has just about completed his exit*). Just keep your eyes on the sparrows, buster, they're killers.

(DETECTIVES *and the* POLICEMAN *exit, the* CHORUS *now crosses downstage left.*)

CHORUS.

The Law is now crawling in the neighborhood.

They break down our doors, they're no goddamned good;

they speak of a crime, a white lady killed this time,

THIRD AND FOURTH MOTHERS (*together*).

and they say our boys will pay.

Unhand our boys, don't blame them for some bloody deed;

they are tied to our apron strings, as you can see;

the seeds of suspicion are their famished history.

Cause they're Black, don't prove them guilty.

CHORUS.

Cause they're black, don't prove them guilty.

They speak of a crime,

a white lady killed this time,

and they say our boys will pay.

THIRD AND FOURTH MOTHERS.

At times our boys are rowdy, in the streets they play

when violence fans her skirts, they become easy prey.

The Law don't ask no questions, knocking boys down off their
    feet,

can't the Law see it's the company boys will keep.

CHORUS.

Can't the Law see it's the company boys will keep.

They speak of a crime,

a white lady killed this time,

and they say our boys will pay.

(*In the dimmed light, during the* CHORUS', *lines, the* POLICEMEN *and the* DETECTIVES *have entered with* HAMM *and* ADAM; *the boys are in prison dress, placed in a pool of light for interrogation scene.*)

POLICEMEN (*together*). We know you did it!

(FIRST POLICEMAN *and* FIRST DETECTIVE *carry lines; the* BLACK POLICEMAN *and* SECOND DETECTIVE *improvise as they beat boys.*)

FIRST POLICEMAN. Why did you kill that woman? (*The boys,*

who have been badly beaten, do not respond.) Speak up, you crummy apes.

FIRST DETECTIVE. Confess . . . and we'll make things light for you . . . I promise . . . don't be dummies . . . You can't hide the truth . . . whatever it may be.

FIRST POLICEMAN. I had you birds spotted all the time. Hiding on the roof, weren't you? You thought you could get out of sight . . . after playing with murder, didn't you? . . . you can't fly away now . . . speak up.

FIRST DETECTIVE. You can't hide from Justice, boys . . . ever hear that before?

FIRST POLICEMAN. We've got all the evidence.

FIRST DETECTIVE. We've got witnesses.

POLICE (*together*). We've got witnesses.

FIRST POLICEMAN. I told you we would have our date.

FIRST DETECTIVE. We've got all the goods, all the goodie goods.

FIRST POLICEMAN. You were seen at the scene of the crime.

FIRST DETECTIVE. Between the hours of four and nine.

FIRST POLICEMAN. You tried to stick up that shop.

FIRST DETECTIVE. The owner had no money so you stabbed her.

FIRST POLICEMAN. Stinkin lousy bums . . . why didn't you get a job?

FIRST DETECTIVE. Why didn't you stay in school?

POLICE (*together*). Why didn't you stay home?

FIRST DETECTIVE. Your homes were checked between four and nine . . . who was there . . . ?

FIRST POLICEMAN. Nobody! You've got no alibis . . . we've got all the evidence . . . we've got the witnesses . . . what have you got? . . . a rope around your neck.

FIRST DETECTIVE. Make it easy on yourselves . . . confess.

POLICE (*together*). Confess.

FIRST POLICEMAN. We'll get it out of you in the end.

FIRST DETECTIVE. You can't shake these charges easily.

CHORUS.

They speak of a crime,

a white lady killed this time,
and they say our boys will pay.

FIRST POLICEMAN. We're scraping you scum off the streets once and for all.

FIRST DETECTIVE. You won't win in a trial whether you speak or not.

FIRST POLICEMAN. Here is all the evidence we need . . . we can wait all night.

FIRST DETECTIVE. Your parents haven't all night.

FIRST POLICEMAN. They've been waiting for hours . . . but what do you birds care?

FIRST DETECTIVE. Confess . . . and they can go home. (*Boys are not responding.* FIRST DETECTIVE *loses patience.*) Well, I've had it . . . take them boys.

CHORUS. No.

(ADAM *is defenseless as* POLICE *close in;* HAMM *springs to his feet, assumes Karate stance, backing away from the* POLICE.)

FIRST POLICEMAN. Look what we've got here . . . a cop fighter.

SECOND DETECTIVE. A regular killer.

BLACK POLICEMAN. You stinkin garbage.

POLICE (*together*). Killers!

CHORUS. No.

(POLICE *now begin to beat boys with sticks, etc., then, as the* POLICEMEN *hit the boys, the* CHORUS *slams feet down to indicate thuds.*)

BLACK POLICEMAN. You bastards have enough yet?

HAMM. Not you too, Brother!?!

BLACK POLICEMAN. I'm not your brother . . . we don't even look alike . . . We ain't the same and I don't want no part of you.

(BLACK POLICEMAN *slams* HAMM *once again and turns to audience. Everything freezes except the* BLACK POLICEMAN *and the* CHORUS. *Atonal.*)

What part should I take.
beyond my own stakes,

these boys should know better.
  CHORUS.
These boys they know better.
  BLACK POLICEMAN.
A certain death has brought shame—
why should I share their blame?—
Black or White, it's the same.
  CHORUS.
Black and White's not the same.
  BLACK POLICEMAN.
When boys lack ambition,
parents bow with contrition,
I've got kids of my own.
  CHORUS.
These are kids of our own.
  BLACK POLICEMAN.
Harlem streets are one cesspool,
that's why I retreat restful
back to my Queens home.
  CHORUS.
A home is a home.
  BLACK POLICEMAN.
I am merely doing my job.
I cannot show sympathy for slobs.
I've got a life of my own in Queens.
  CHORUS.
We've got no life at all, it seems.
  BLACK POLICEMAN.
The City pays my wages to clean the streets of spew,
the bank it has my mortgage, so I function as I'm due.
My conscience knows no favorites, be it Black or White.
  CHORUS.
Your conscience should tell you these kids are Black not White
  BLACK POLICEMAN. What the hell is the difference?
  CHORUS.
There's a helluva difference.

BLACK POLICEMAN.
Why should I contrive to look them in the eye?
CHORUS.
There are mirrors in their eyes, look, you'll see a black magpie.
BLACK POLICEMAN. I'm not their brother, their sister, or their
mother.
CHORUS.
You're as black as their brother, you *could* even be their mother.
BLACK POLICEMAN.
I've got kids of my own.
CHORUS.
These are kids of our own.
BLACK POLICEMAN.
What does it matter the streets will lose some scum,
and the mothers can relax their all-day vigil for the bums.
It's no feather in my cap to deal the guilty punishment,
be he black, white, or green or sometimes unpigmented.
In the end it doesn't matter to me,
I will turn my back on the very next track, and head for Queens
    on the BMT,
'cause that's where I have my home . . .
CHORUS.
No home is a home 'way from home . . .
BLACK POLICEMAN.
. . . and I've got kids of my own . . .
    (*Turns to boys.*)
. . . I'd do the same if they were wrong.
CHORUS.
But who's to say that ours are wrong.
    (BLACK POLICEMAN *strikes* HAMM *again.*)
    FIRST POLICEMAN. Shall we go a little further?
    ADAM. No.
    FIRST DETECTIVE. Got any more lies to tell?
    HAMM and ADAM. No.
    FIRST DETECTIVE. Hold it boys, sit them up.
    FIRST POLICEMAN. No lying down on the job. Are you all right?

. . . can you hear me? . . . are you out? . . . speak up.

HAMM. No.

FIRST DETECTIVE. Now for some facts. You're not mean boys, are you?

HAMM. No.

FIRST DETECTIVE. You don't need to carry knives, do you?

HAMM. No.

FIRST DETECTIVE. You could hurt somebody, and you don't want to do that, do you?

HAMM. No.

FIRST DETECTIVE. You didn't plan to rob that shop, did you?

HAMM. No.

FIRST DETECTIVE. It just came over you suddenly, right? . . . when you walked into that woman's shop . . . that's how it happened, right?

ADAM. No.

FIRST POLICEMAN. Are we going back to the same old guff?

ADAM. No.

FIRST DETECTIVE. Were you with a gang this afternoon?

HAMM. No.

FIRST POLICEMAN. The ape is lying. I'll straighten him out . . .

FIRST DETECTIVE. Hold it. (*To boys*) We know you didn't do the job alone. Now, can you name other members of the gang?

HAMM. No.

FIRST POLICEMAN. So it was just the two of you?

ADAM. No.

FIRST DETECTIVE. O.K., then you can name the others.

ADAM. No.

FIRST DETECTIVE. You boys are hopeless. Aren't you part of a gang that's been romping around here . . . pestering people . . . agitating?

ADAM. No.

FIRST POLICEMAN. Who you kiddin . . . you're one of them . . . you're a Blood Brother.

ADAM. No.

FIRST DETECTIVE. Muslim?

HAMM. No.

FIRST POLICEMAN. What do you call yourselves? . . . open up. Aren't you part of a gang that's been going after white people?

FIRST DETECTIVE. You don't have to answer that . . . that can't be true, is it?

HAMM. No.

FIRST DETECTIVE. Ever mangle anybody before?

HAMM. No.

FIRST DETECTIVE. This is the first time you killed anybody?

HAMM. No . . . I . . .

FIRST POLICEMAN. There've been others, how many others?

HAMM. No . . . no . . .

FIRST DETECTIVE. You didn't mean to kill, did you?

HAMM. No . . . I . . .

FIRST DETECTIVE. We're on to a confession . . . get out a piece of paper.

(*One* DETECTIVE *takes out a pad.*)

FIRST POLICEMAN. Did you know the woman was dead?

ADAM. No.

FIRST POLICEMAN. You just left her there and ran.

ADAM. No . . . no . . . no . . . I . . .

FIRST DETECTIVE. Yes . . . what is it? You knew she was dead.

ADAM. No.

FIRST POLICEMAN. Don't you birds know anything else besides "no"?

CHORUS. No.

FIRST DETECTIVE (*Speaking to other* DETECTIVE). Get all this down. (*To* HAMM) You tried to intimidate the woman . . . there was a struggle . . .

HAMM. No.

FIRST POLICEMAN. . . . She recognized you . . . You got scared . . . So you stabbed her . . .

HAMM. No.

FIRST DETECTIVE. Then you killed her for nothing.

HAMM and ADAM. No.

FIRST DETECTIVE. Then the whole thing was a mistake, it's all a mistake, right?

HAMM. Yes.

FIRST DETECTIVE. That's it, boys, we got our confession.

HAMM. I . . . I . . . mean, no . . . no . . . we didn't mean it . . . we didn't do it . . .

FIRST DETECTIVE. Book them on homicide.

CHORUS. No.

FIRST DETECTIVE. Tell the mothers they can go home, now.

CHORUS. No . . . No . . . No . . . No . . .

(BOYS *are led into jail cells, chairs are removed,* BEGGAR *enters,* CHORUS *crosses further left to court scene ramps.*)

BEGGAR.
They've locked them up,
they've got their victim,
the white court screams . . .
out for conviction.

If a white man dies,
in a Harlem case
society brands it
a crime of race.

CHORUS.
But we,
we fail to see,
how the law can act so hastily
and bring down a curtain on these young lives.
They've accused them,
they've abused them,
they've confused them,
they've misused them,
who can show some evidence?
Who'll take charge of their defense?

BEGGAR.
They've locked 'em up,
they've got their victim,
the white court screams . . .
out for conviction.

CHORUS.
But who will come to our aid?
Our mendacity can't pay . . .
we need evidence
to prove innocence
and innocence needs a defense
and defense can't be paid in cents.
BEGGAR.
They've locked 'em up,
they claim a witness,
yet unrevealed,
silence is skeptic.
CHORUS.
Still we, we fail to see,
how the law can act so hastily;
and bring down the curtain on these young lives.

They've accused them,
they've abused them,
they've confused them,
they've misused them . . .
who can show some evidence?
Who'll take charge of their defense?
BEGGAR.
Now all the neighbors
are gripped in shame,
they turn in fear
of sharing blame.
CHORUS.
Where art thou, social sages,
who may free our boys from their cages . . . ?
we need evidence,
to prove innocence,
and innocence
needs a defense,
and defense,
and defense can't be paid in cents.

REV (*exhorting audience*). I want to know . . . yes, Brothers and Sisters, I want to know . . . where were you . . . you . . . and you . . . when these mothers needed you most. You . . . whose belly is huge and whose clothes burst with the new life . . . there you were, sucked in by the hungry eye of the boob tube . . . which shocked you into buying things you don't need with money you ain't got to impress people you don't even like, shocked you into buying horror . . . and shame . . . and timidity! . . . Cause that's easy to digest . . . guaranteed to flush the soul . . . and once sated with shame, you took your Alka Seltzer and went off to sleep. . . . The misery of the day was over . . . until the following morn . . . when you'd strain your eyes at a newspaper and eat up the next advertised plum . . . which wrenched your stomachs into indignation . . . this time requiring a laxative to vent your frustrations . . . and no longer having the energy to ask, "What is the truth about advertising?" . . . The anxiety of not knowing, thus not caring, threw your minds into a fit of panic . . . and you prayed . . . that your local pharmaceutical gods had at least one more librium to free your conscience from the body, yes, and relieve you of those critical decisions . . . What is right or wrong . . . But it just occurred to me, where was everybody when these mothers needed you most? . . . and I want to know.

CHORUS. Yes indeed.

REV. What were you thinkin about when the storms of Cain swept through this valley and flushed Hamm and Adam into the shadow of death?

CHORUS (*response can vary*). Yes indeed.

REV. Now, I'm supposed to get angry . . . our homes invaded . . . our mothers bullied . . . and where was God? . . . He who is cold in the slums of winter, whose playmates are rats . . . four-legged ones that live with you . . . two-legged ones who imprison you . . .

CHORUS. Yes, Lord.

REV. . . . Yes, pouring shame on the community . . . drowning our children in questionable testimony . . . Still God lives on though no one knows His name . . . Even He must know He is nobody . . . That Old Man in the sky with the long white beard, He's dead. He's not omnipotent, he's not omnipresent, he's not omniscient.

CHORUS. Fix it!

REV. . . . And nobody can know, what troubled souls we have . . . Sure, we're sorry about that old woman . . . but that don't make Harlem a hell.

CHORUS. Yes indeed.

REV. No, don't go drawing your hands up around your nose . . . every time you hear the name Harlem . . . All I want to know is where was everybody?

CHORUS. Yes indeed.

REV. . . . Where were you, you who are dressed up, lookin all homogenized, dressed up from the church clothing store in the suburbs.

CHORUS. Yes indeed.

REV. . . . What happened to all those professional samaritan gods?

CHORUS. Talk bout 'em, Rev!

REV. Not a single fanny was uncorked from the Y.M.C.A. . . . and we all know why the N.A.A.C.P. stayed away . . . cause niggers ain't all colored people.

CHORUS. Fix it up, Rev!

REV. But one black tom fool did come runnin from the press . . . and where's God's proof that our boys did the crime? Killing ain't something that comes easily for our souls. One white lady's death don't make it right to contemplate the death of two black boys.

CHARACTER(*male voice in audience*). Bullshit. (*Bolts up from seat, prepares to leave theater.*) You cats are jiving, man . . . and these people goin for it, but I ain't.

REV (*traces voices through audience*). Hold on, Brother.

CHARACTER. For what? To hear you cats run your program down?

REV. What's your beef, man?

CHARACTER. You ain't tellin it like it is, Rev.

REV. You know something we don't know?

CHARACTER. I know what everybody else knows. Somebody killed that old lady.

REV. Who?

CHARACTER. One of those niggers up there, that's who.

REV (*goaded by audience, going after* CHARACTER). Wait a minute, you seem pretty sure about that, Brother. I mean you talk like you really know what went down . . . Come here a minute. No, no don't run away, Brother. You got something to tell us, come on over and run it down. That's what the Tabernacle is for.

CHARACTER. Aw, man, I'm goin forget it.

REV. We ain't forgettin it. You come in here and break up our meetin with some accusations and you say forget it. Well, we ain't forgettin it. You got so much mouth, come on and tell us what's happenin.

CHARACTER. Okay, so you really want to know what happened . . . okay. There was this Jewish woman in Harlem who owned a second-hand clothing store, you dig it? We called her Anna the Panhandle, cause she sold boss rags, cheap! Now . . .

REV. Wait a minute, Brother . . . why don't you show us what happened.

CHARACTER. Aw man, I ain't gonna get up here and make a fool out myself in front of all these people. I ain't no actor.

CHORUS (*goading* CHARACTER; *improvises*). Show us something . . . He don't know nothing about shucking and jiving, go on and prove it.

REV. This ain't got nothing to do with acting. Just play the scene like you know it. Come on, we'll help you.

CHARACTER. Man, this place don't even look like the Panhandle.

REV. Give us a Panhandle.(*A rack of old clothes is rolled out by* STAGE HANDS *as* REV *gestures.*) Okay, Brother, here's your shop, what next?

CHARACTER. Well, a bunch of black brothers came into the

shop, I don't know how many, about five of them.

REV. Give us shadows.

(FIVE BOYS *enter, wearing black stockings on their heads; they roam around the clothes as if they were going to buy.*)

REV. They were in the shop to buy clothes, right, raggy old clothes to put on their backs.

CHARACTER (*as audience and* CHORUS *chide him*). But cheap . . . don't knock it, Brother, if you ever get uptight, you can appreciate Anna the Panhandle. It might look like rags on the rack, but on your back, you is sharp for days. Sharp as rat turd. Look at them cats sniffin . . . They know what's good. And all Anna was tryin to do was help them get their vine together.

REV. At what price?

CHARACTER. It varies with the goods, man. I don't know.

REV. Why don't we ask Anna?

CHARACTER. Aw man, you know Anna is dead.

REV. Then I guess you'll have to play Anna.

CHARACTER. Oh no. I told you I ain't no actor. Besides, how am I going to play a woman?

THIRD MOTHER. The same way you play a man!

REV. It's your idea, Brother. You claim to know the truth. Okay, then you play Anna's ordeal. That ain't like playing the woman. You simply play your own conscience. (*Shouts.*) Bring on Anna.

(STAGE HAND *brings on mask of Anna.* CHARACTER *hesitates at putting it on.*)

SECOND MOTHER (*raucously*). Put it on!

REV (*after* CHARACTER *puts on mask*). Do your thing, Anna. Show us where it's at.

(*The* BOYS, HAMM, *and* ADAM *become animated, stage left. The* JUDGE, STUMBLE, *and the* D.A. *enter and assume their places. They remain throughout the scene.*)

CHARACTER. Can I . . . can I help you, boys?

FIRST BOY. We just lookin.

CHARACTER. Anything in particular you want?

SECOND BOY. You got anything in particular?

CHARACTER. Here's a nice overcoat. Warm, very warm. You like an overcoat?

FIRST BOY. You call this an overcoat? What do it cover? The lining?

THIRD BOY. Man, the hawk would eat you up in that thing. Hell, you couldn't even give this thing away.

CHARACTER. It's a hundred percent wool. Try it on. We don't talk about the price now.

ADAM (*shouts from cell*). Try it on.

FOURTH BOY. Try it on.

FIRST BOY (*trying coat on*). You mean you wanna sell me this raggity damn thing? It couldn't keep a bedbug warm. (*Throws coat on floor.*)

CHARACTER. Try something else.

HAMM. Boss suit.

(*One of the* BOYS *is trying on the jacket of a suit.*)

FIRST BOY. That's a boss suit. Let me try it.

FIFTH BOY. Naw man, it might be something for me.

FIRST BOY. Aw man, you ain't gonna buy nothing. Come out the goddamn coat.

CHARACTER. Careful, boys . . . don't stretch the material. Please be gentle with the fabrics.

FIRST BOY. Back off me, woman. You don't tell me how to handle clothes.

CHARACTER. I just want you to be careful. If you wanna buy it, that's another thing . . . but if you don't, I've still got to sell it.

THIRD BOY. And if you don't sell it, it would sit here untouched, right? I mean, how you spect to sell somebody something if it ain't got the right touch, you dig it?

HAMM. Tear it up.

FIRST BOY. If it weren't so pretty, I'd tear it up.

CHARACTER. You like it, you pay me for it, then do what you want.

CHORUS. Attitude. Attitude. Always an attitude.

ADAM. The lady asked if you liked it.

FOURTH BOY. She wanna know if you like it?

FIRST BOY. It don't fit.

CHARACTER. It's a beautiful fit. All you got to do is let the sleeve out a tiny bit. And look at the trousers . . . Perfect. What do you want for the money?

SECOND BOY. What kind of money?

CHARACTER. You tell me if you wanna buy it, I'll tell you what kind of money.

FIRST BOY. You mean you wanna sell me something that don't fit?

CHARACTER. Don't buy it. (*Gestures to remove jacket.*)

FIRST BOY. Don't touch me.

CHARACTER. It's my fabric I'm touching, not you.

FIFTH BOY. Now you'd better think twice and be nice, Anna. We ain't goin for no oakie doak.

CHARACTER. Why don't you simply try another suit? There are plenty suits here. Anything that makes you happy.

FIRST BOY. I want this one.

CHARACTER. But it doesn't fit. You said it doesn't fit.

THIRD BOY. Then stop jivin and find the right size.

CHARACTER. What do you want from my life? There's only one suit in that size and one size in that suit. If you don't want it, don't buy it. Take it or leave it.

HAMM. Take it.

FIRST BOY. I might just take it.

CHARACTER. It's up to you. The price, I assure you, is right.

FIRST BOY. I ain't thinkin about the price.

ADAM. Maybe you've got another suit?

FOURTH BOY. Look here, Anna, maybe you've got another suit.

CHARACTER. You see what I've got. Look for yourself. Nothing like he's got on, but see, here are others, plaids, worsted, gabardines, that should look good on you . . . this one comes with two pair of trousers, the extra one I give for the same price. I think it's only fair. A bargain is a bargain. But only if you buy today. Tomorrow, that's something else. You want it?

FIRST BOY. I want this one.

CHARACTER. Then take it.

FIRST BOY (*cunningly*). I think I will.

FIFTH BOY. Boss suit, man. What you gettin for it, Anna?

CHARACTER. I don't know. What can I say? It's a very good suit. Hardly ever worn . . . go on, you can touch the material now. Very well made. It must have cost a hundred dollars. It's hard to say what I should ask for a suit of that quality.

CHORUS. Same old jive and shuck. That's all it is, jive and shuck.

THIRD BOY. Stop jivin and give the price.

CHARACTER. What do you want to pay?

FIRST BOY. Nothing.

CHARACTER. Nothing? You got to pay something.

FIRST BOY. It don't fit.

CHARACTER. Then you don't have to buy it.

HAMM. Ain't gonna buy it.

FIRST BOY. Ain't gonna buy it . . . but I'll take it just the same.

CHARACTER. You're not taking my suit without paying.

FIRST BOY. Ain't I?

CHARACTER. No you're not. Now stop playing around. You boys could get into trouble. Give me something and you can have the suit.

SECOND BOY. She thinks you're kiddin.

FIRST BOY. It ain't worth it at any price.

CHARACTER. Then take it off. (*She starts to remove jacket from* BOY*'s back.*)

FIRST BOY. Don't touch me, bitch. (*Pushes her away.*) Don't ever put your hands on me.

CHARACTER. You're not going to take my suit. You're not going to take it.

FIRST BOY. I just took it.

(*The* BOYS *begin to leave.*)

ADAM. Nothing you can do about it, Anna.

FOURTH BOY. There's nothing you can do about it.

CHARACTER. I'll call the police.

FIFTH BOY. Call the fuckin pigs.

CHARACTER. Stop . . . stop, police, police. I won't let you take it, I won't, I won't. (*She pulls on* FIRST BOY.)

FIRST BOY. I told you not to pull on me, didn't I, huh, didn't I, huh?

(*The* BOYS *surround her.*)

CHARACTER. You're no good. Why don't you get a job. I work hard for a living, and now you want to take from me. Is that what makes you feel better . . . ? you think it's smart you got nothing better to do than steal from an old lady? Would you do it if I were a man?

FIRST BOY. Shut up, bitch.

CHARACTER. I won't shut up. Not in my own shop. You've got what you wanted, now get out get out, all of you. You thieves, get out.

SECOND BOY. Put me out.

CHARACTER. Out . . . out . . . out.

FIRST BOY. Keep your hands off me.

(*The* BOYS *grapple with her, finally beat her; someone has a knife with which she is stabbed, but no one can see who did it. The scene ends with* CHARACTER *on the floor; mask is removed and* REV *approaches.* BOYS *have fled.*

For the most part, parts of this scene can be improvised, with CHARACTERS *still adhering to the main vein of the script;* HAMM *and* ADAM *represent a second layer of consciousness.*)

REV. Is that how it went down, Brother?

CHARACTER. That's right.

REV. Who did it? Which one of these niggers did it?

CHARACTER (*exits disgustedly*). I don't know!

REV (*As* STAGE HANDS *roll off clothing stand*). The white press did it.

CHORUS. Yes indeed.

REV. Exploited the horror of the day without proof . . .

CHORUS. Deedy!

REV. And sent one of those brand new Negroes down to fix the label of guilt . . .

CHORUS. Tell it, Rev!

REV. Made a stooge out of our own, now that ain't right.

CHORUS. No indeed.

(*The* D.A. *now steps into the area of clothing shop scene and is examining the area.* PORTER, *a young flashy black man, enters and also looks around, making notes in a note pad.*)

D.A. What's going on here? Who are you?

PORTER. Who me? . . . I'm Porter.

D.A. You really came dressed to kill, huh, Porter?

PORTER. Just part of my job. One meets all kinds of people, you know.

D.A. I don't remember seeing you around. You must be a new boy on the job. Man, how times are really changing.

PORTER. Actually, this is my first assignment.

D.A. Are you reliable?

PORTER. I got my job through the *New York Times.*

D.A. Good source all right . . . but hell, I bet you come expensive.

PORTER. Reasonably, buy fair, when the price is right.

D.A. I suppose it pays to read the ads sometimes . . . (*Hands* PORTER *a dollar.*) . . . Here, run down and get me a cheeseburger . . . lots of mustard, no onions . . . and keep the change.

PORTER. What?

D.A. I said keep the change . . . surprised you, huh? . . . you'll like it around here, Porter.

PORTER. Sir, I'm afraid you're making a mistake.

D.A. Maybe you're right . . . no point in inflating standards, and the union. I forgot the union . . . take the usual twenty-five-cent tip.

PORTER. Sir, you've got it all wrong . . . my name is Porter.

D.A. Good . . . that's good enough for me . . . you just call me D.A. . . . Now hurry along before the Judge reconvenes . . . (PORTER *still stands, looks at dollar.*) . . . Look, Porter, I don't think you've got the gist of the job, you're kind of slow, now you just tell me who hired you and . . .

PORTER (*emphatically*). The *New York Times*!

D.A. So, what do you want . . . your picture spread out on a Lenox Avenue bus . . . I got my job through the *New York Times* . . .

PORTER. I work for the *Times*.

D.A. Then what the hell are you doing here . . . who let you in?

PORTER. I'm a reporter.

D.A. Reporter . . . well, I'll be damned, I thought you said porter.

PORTER. I did say Porter . . . my name is Porter.

D.A. Oh-h-h, well why didn't you say so?

PORTER. I did . . . what else could I say?

D.A. Oh, O.K., it was just a case of mistaken identity.

PORTER. Yeah, but I should think any fool could see I'm no porter.

D.A. Look, if you've seen one porter, you've seen them all . . . Hell, anybody could make that mistake, mistaken identity being what it is these days.

PORTER. That, sir, is a conclusion . . . a-prior-i . . . which I doubt you can afford . . . correct me if I'm wrong.

D.A. Yeah . . . yeah, you might have something there . . . Porter . . . by the way, how about my dollar?

PORTER. What dollar?

D.A. The one you've got choked in your palm for dear life. (PORTER *returns dollar*.) A reporter, can you beat that. Well, what can I do for you . . . Reporter?

PORTER. I need information. I'm following the track of the murder case.

D.A. You've got a "gold brick" with the *Times* . . . you're on a very short track to the nearest gallow.

PORTER. Then it's safe to say that the boys in custody are the actual killers?

D.A. Open and shut case.

PORTER. And there's no reason to doubt that these boys killed the woman simply because she was white.

D.A. I don't doubt it, do you?

PORTER. From where we sit at the *Times,* the motive does have that tint.

D.A. Tint, hell . . . it's more like a smear . . . They would have raped her for sure, if she wasn't so old . . . her underwear were intact . . .

PORTER. That's admirable.

D.A. . . . but you know, damn well, there's an anti-white conspiracy active up in Harlem.

PORTER. I assume from your statement that these boys are part of a terrorist gang.

D.A. Did you just figure that out all by yourself?

PORTER. And they're after white blood?

D.A. Not bad, Porter, not bad for a beginner. Now, maybe you can tell me why there is so much hostility up there.

PORTER. Once, I heard rumors.

D.A. Rumors? Just for the record, Porter, would you object to being called brother?

PORTER. Brother what?

D.A. Brother rat . . . brother cat . . . what does it matter, that's what they're all shouting uptown.

PORTER. But you see, I don't live uptown. I would hardly be recognized as a brother.

D.A. You never can tell . . . what with mistaken identity today.

PORTER. You're trying to tell me something, aren't you?

D.A. You tell me.

PORTER. Well, I can't be certain . . .

D.A. Come on, you're on to it . . .

PORTER. Then . . . then . . . shall we conclude that the terrorists are called brothers?

D.A. That sounds like a tenable conclusion.

PORTER. And they're trained perhaps?

D.A. I'm told, well enough to maim.

PORTER. Would your confidential source link the terrorists . . . thus, consequently the killers in custody, with other white fatalities?

D.A. You know, Porter, I think you got a story.

PORTER. Have you any witnesses?

D.A. Come now, Porter, need you ask?

PORTER. Who are they?

D.A. I could name one, if it would be of any help to you.

PORTER. It's something my readers want to know.

D.A. Come here . . . (*Cupping hand to* PORTER*'s ear.*) . . . Jesus . . . (*He shouts.*)

PORTER (*angry*). Christ.

D.A. A Puerto Rican cop in disguise. All other witnesses are held in strictest confidence, you understand.

PORTER. Oh . . . I see . . . but do you have sufficient evidence?

D.A. Being reviewed this very moment by Judge Tawkin.

PORTER. And the defense?

(*The* JUDGE *now becomes more animated, slams his gavel down;* ATTORNEY STUMBLE *comes to attention;* PORTER *and* D.A. *move toward* JUDGE.)

JUDGE TAWKIN.

Order, order, Judge Tawkin, if you please.

I've reviewed this case for the State,

and find no reason to debate

the firmness of the arraignment plea.

Murder in the first degree.

PORTER (*writing*). Murder in the first degree.

JUDGE TAWKIN.

Since question of defense has risen,

appointed counsel is my decision,

the parents' fortunes being quite insolvent,

our Law by God defends the indigent.

CHORUS.

Hush up your mouth, Judge Tawkin,

we have let you have your say;

we'll seek our own counsels

if we slave both night and day.

We'll drag ourselves down to the bone,

and tarry not a whit,

our boys must have their lawyers
no legal counterfeit.

JUDGE TAWKIN (*slams gavel*).
Dear Mothers, the court recognizes your pleas
as being those unmistakably of mothers;
you obviously have not been advised of the magnitude your fees
    must cover,
since legal counsel is at three hundred a day,
enjoy your savings, don't throw them away.

D.A. (*to* PORTER). You heard the good Judge Tawkin, the case
is as good as closed.

JUDGE TAWKIN.
The court being endowed with judicial prudence
must necessarily appoint counsel of equal prudence
entrusted with the selection since no others have appeared,
meet Attorney Stumble, a Democrat and fair.

STUMBLE (*stands slovenly*). I . . . I . . . er . . . yes . . . er
. . . thank you . . . er obliged . . . er . . . Judge . . .

CHORUS.
Democrat or Plutocrat, he's a sod and that's a fact,
We don't want no stumble bum, who needs a handout for his
    crumbs.
Our boys, they're fighting for their lives, we'll work
ourselves until we're paralyzed, who needs a stumble bum,
who surely can't invent the slightest base, for a case, in our boys'
    defense.

JUDGE TAWKIN. This is a Court of order. If there is no further
testimony at this time, the session is closed.

STUMBLE. If it pleases the court . . . ?

JUDGE TAWKIN. Make it quick, Stumble.

STUMBLE. . . . er . . . the Democratic Club would like permission to bestow upon your honor a pair of tickets to the next
Giants football game . . . er . . . at home.

JUDGE TAWKIN. Permission granted.

(*As* JUDGE *prepares to exit, the* CHORUS *exits singing.*)

CHORUS.
The judge sure is funky . . . the judge sure is funky . . .

JUDGE TAWKIN (*pompously strides across stage, exiting*). Funky indeed.

D.A. Good luck, Stumble . . . only the best case wins, you know?

STUMBLE. Yes, I remotely recall that maxim having a touch of truth . . . yes, but anyway, you may have a pair of tickets for the Giants too.

D.A. Send them around, Stumble . . . we're still in the same place . . . see you in court . . . and remember, don't let the side down. (PORTER *is writing as* STUMBLE *exits.*) Well, Porter, you've got the facts, print them loud and clear.

PORTER. Nothing to it, looks like an open and shut case.

D.A. That ought to reassure your readers, Porter . . . oh, and don't forget how to spell my name . . . it's D.A. . . . and so long, Porter. (*Starts to exit, returns.*) Say, Porter, I just thought, in your line of work, you must get to meet many famous people?

PORTER (*grinning*). Oh yes . . . fringe benefits, you know.

D.A. Well, I can usually call a spade . . . a spade . . . but there's one face that always eludes me, what's the name of that gal, whose face appears on the box of pancake flour? (PORTER *looks bewildered.*) . . . Don't know her huh? I thought she might be a relative or something.

(*Exits.* PORTER *looks after him for a moment, then exits also.*

Lights dim, then strobe lights begin to flash: cataclysmic sounds from musicians. HAMM *and* ADAM *become animated, they look frightened. From the back of the audience,* FOUR PRISON GUARDS *come trotting in a quick-time cadence; they ascend to boys' cages and begin to remove their pants. From stage right, a* FIFTH PRISON GUARD *enters, carrying a broad paddle; he climbs into boys' cages and begins to beat them as the other* PRISON GUARDS *hold them. He strokes each boy five times. After the final stroke, the executing* PRISON GUARD *exits as he entered, and the other four climb down and exit up aisle in the same manner as before. Two of them return as before; this time, however, the one on* HAMM's *side of the stage is followed by* STUMBLE *and the other is followed by* HOMOSEXUAL PRISONER, *who is wearing a handker-chief. They ascend the ramps also as before; however* STUMBLE *stumbles, the* GUARD *aids him, and they climb to the boys' cells.)*

STUMBLE. Make yourself decent . . . you can't lie around like that.

LOVEJOY (*holding* ADAM'*s trousers*). There's a draft in here . . . wouldn't you rather put these on?

STUMBLE. Listen, whenever you come out of it, we can get down to the bottom of things. I haven't much time.

LOVEJOY. . . . or would you rather not? Frankly, I always sleep that way myself . . . but then you're so young.

STUMBLE. I know you weren't expecting to see me, were you?

LOVEJOY. I bet you're surprised to see me, aren't you?

STUMBLE. Come along now, the sooner you pull yourself together . . . the sooner I can help you.

LOVEJOY. You look like you've seen a ghost . . . is there something I can do for you?

HAMM. Who are you?

STUMBLE (*tries to get card from briefcase, entire contents fall, he retrieves one, offers it to* HAMM). My card . . . J. D. Stumble, your attorney.

ADAM. Who are you?

LOVEJOY. Lovejoy . . . Evelyn Lovejoy . . . my intimate friends call me Eve. But then sharing the same cell as we do couldn't make things more intimate . . . so you can call me Eve . . . though I loathe easy familiarity . . . but somehow, I have the feeling that we've met before.

ADAM. Are you kidding?

LOVEJOY. But of course, I know all about you. You're Adam . . . you're a lady-killer, ain't you?

ADAM. I'm innocent.

LOVEJOY. Seems I've heard that line before.

STUMBLE. Want a cigarette?

LOVEJOY. You want a fag?

ADAM. No.

LOVEJOY. No harm asking . . . (*Searches for match.*) . . . as usual, one is always without a proper match around here.

STUMBLE. Well, have you nothing to say?

HAMM. Did my mother send you?

STUMBLE. I've never had the pleasure of her acquaintance.

HAMM. Then why are you here?

STUMBLE. You're in trouble, boy.

HAMM. Like I really need you to tell me that.

STUMBLE. I've been appointed by the State to defend you.

HAMM. The State, you?

STUMBLE. God willing.

HAMM. Does my mother know about this?

STUMBLE. She's hardly in a position to equivocate.

HAMM. Quiv-a-cate . . . my ass . . . I don't know nothin about that . . . all I want to know is when are you gettin me outa here?

STUMBLE. You're asking a little too much, don't you think . . . you're not in here on some misdemeanor.

HAMM. Then you might as well split, man . . . until I see my mother.

STUMBLE. In the straits you're in, boy, you can't afford such a lofty tone . . . can't you see I'm trying to help you?

HAMM. Who asked you?

LOVEJOY. I must say you're not the chattiest of roommates . . . I mean, some of the mates just go on forever . . . chat . . . chat . . . chat.

ADAM. Why did they put you in here?

LOVEJOY. Hmm, for a while there I thought you'd never ask.

ADAM. O.K., what are they up to now?

LOVEJOY. It seems obvious, they wanted us to share . . . this solitary confinement. Why, I always said, one week alone is more than anybody should have to bear, don't you agree?

ADAM. No I don't. And you ain't saying nuttin.

LOVEJOY. Now don't get cheeky with me . . . It wasn't my idea . . . around this place, one never knows with whom one might have to bed down with next . . . Now you should know that.

ADAM. Why don't they leave me alone?

LOVEJOY. Oh come now, don't be disagreeable.

ADAM. This dump is loaded with garbage . . . up to the ceiling, it stinks.

LOVEJOY. It gets better by starlight.

ADAM. I want out.

LOVEJOY. Dear, dear, the violent type.

STUMBLE. Now you're not acting reasonably.

HAMM. Who's not . . . how do you expect me to act . . . gettin my ass kicked in every day . . . they ain't supposed to do that . . . tell me how do you expect me to act, I'm not acting reasonably. Take a look, go on . . .

STUMBLE. No, no, let's not be ugly.

ADAM. If they beat me again . . . if they beat me again . . .

LOVEJOY. Have you been beaten?

ADAM. What does that look like to you?

LOVEJOY. How lucky, I haven't been beaten in years.

ADAM. Are you sure you're all together?

LOVEJOY. Heavens no, but I sure hope they keep you in one piece.

ADAM. You know they're trying to break me, don't you?

LOVEJOY. Did you bleed?

ADAM. Nothin to do but . . .

LOVEJOY. Splendid.

ADAM. What was that?

LOVEJOY. Mend it . . . your wounds, would like for me to mend it?

ADAM. Nothing doin, you don't look like no Red Cross nurse to me.

LOVEJOY. Of course you know the secret to a successful beating is not to resist.

STUMBLE. You probably tried to resist.

HAMM. Man, how you goin to resist when the sides ain't even . . . but if I could only have one of them alone . . . just one . . .

STUMBLE. Listen, boy, you provoked the Law . . . and you know . . .

HAMM. I ain't doin nothing . . . I wish I could do something.

STUMBLE. You inflicted the first blow by killing that woman.

HAMM. I didn't kill no woman.

STUMBLE. Wise up, boy, you can come clean with me . . . I'm your lawyer.

HAMM. You cats are all in the same dirty bag . . . I'm telling you like I told the others . . . I didn't do it.

STUMBLE. If you hold on to that story, I don't see how I can help you, you're just wasting time.

HAMM. I read you right the first time. You ain't my lawyer, you're the D.A.'s flunky. Who sent you anyway? . . . you're just like the rest of them . . . trying to make me say something what ain't true, well I ain't comin . . .

STUMBLE. You are resisting the Law.

HAMM. Call it what you want . . . but I ain't confessin . . .

STUMBLE. Why not, there's still a chance . . . we'd all be better off . . .

HAMM. Why don't you kiss my a— . . .

STUMBLE. Don't say it . . . contempt won't help you! . . . the cards are stacked against you.

HAMM. They're stacked against me because I'm black.

STUMBLE. They're stacked because Adam said you did it.

LOVEJOY. You know, Adam, you don't look like any tough type to me, no indeed, and I've seen some types . . .

ADAM. I bet you have . . . but you haven't seen them all . . . I'm real tough.

LOVEJOY. Oh no . . . I can tell by your hands . . . you couldn't raise a crab off your balls, much less harm a hair on a delicate head.

ADAM. All right, smarty . . . go tell it to the warden, he ain't so sure.

LOVEJOY. Oh, forget about him, I'm convinced.

ADAM. That ain't goin to keep him off my ass.

LOVEJOY. Do you mean that? . . . How'd you get in so thick with the police?

ADAM. All you got to do is wear the right shade of make-up and you get kissed with a stick every night, Black.

LOVEJOY. Now, now, Adam . . . you're beginning to sound bitter, not much fun.

ADAM. What load of shit are you packin?. . . they ain't beatin on you.

LOVEJOY. Maybe I'm just not as deserving as you.

ADAM. That's what all you white people think . . . We deserve the beatin and y'all don't . . . y'all hate us, that's all.

LOVEJOY. Now, that is going too far . . . that's absolutely untrue, Adam, why I just love colored boys! Why I'm here now because of a sun-baked boy, that's the story of my life . . . It all started with my selling him an American Legion ribbon . . .

ADAM. I don't want to know . . . I couldn't care a fart about your sickness.

LOVEJOY. Call it love, Adam . . . Now that's something some of you boys know nothing about . . . Love . . . you're all so busy, busy, busy trying to be hostile, you can't recognize love.

ADAM. Don't tell me nuttin bout love, cause it damn sure ain't comin from you.

LOVEJOY. But you're wrong, Adam, I'd gladly give you love . . . if you wouldn't turn it away, think of it, Adam, think of it.

ADAM. Who do you think you are, the "white hope"? You phony.

LOVEJOY. Surely, Adam, you can't hate me . . . not Eve?

ADAM. You make me vomit.

LOVEJOY. That's the most unkind hurt of all . . . I must confess, I'm injured.

ADAM. You're injured . . . I'm bleeding to death. Don't talk that shit to me, you've got everything working for you baby, all you have to do is lick your fuckin wounds.

LOVEJOY. Oh dear . . . I'm afraid we're on the brink of a disastrous misunderstanding. It's at times like these, dear Adam . . .

ADAM. Shove it up your ass.

LOVEJOY. Is that the voice of Love or Hate talking? (LOVEJOY *approaches* ADAM.) . . . Now I can appreciate your desperation,

Adam. But as long as we must share the same cell, we've got to learn to love each other. I just loathe hostility . . . people are always hating each other and always for the wrong reasons . . . and that always leads to something unpleasant. Love is more desirable . . . Oh, I can see you're really a good boy. . . . Adam . . . It's hard to believe you could even maim a bedbug.

ADAM. I didn't do it.

LOVEJOY. I know, Adam, it's just the company you keep . . . I wish we could have gotten together sooner to avoid these strains in our relationship, cause I've always said, hate is infectious, deceitful, even your best friends let you down in the end, and you, Adam, you're so young.

ADAM. You know nuttin about it . . . so back up from me.

LOVEJOY. I'm just trying to be your friend in spite of it, Adam . . . I love you.

ADAM. Just stay away from me, you don't love me, man.

LOVEJOY. You need a friend, Adam, you've lost Hamm . . . you can forget about him.

ADAM. Hamm is black, it's me and Hamm, not me and you.

LOVEJOY. Well a fine friend you've got, baby, he's gone screaming mad, told the cops everything.

ADAM. I'm tired of your jive.

LOVEJOY. That ain't no jive, baby, he told them how you did it . . . how you stabbed that old lady . . . it's all over the jail . . Adam the Lady-Killer . . . Now I ask you, does that sound like love, that's hate, baby, but I know love, I want you to love me, Adam, Eve needs love . . .

ADAM. You lying bitch.

HAMM. I don't believe you.

STUMBLE. Go on, take that attitude . . . then there's nothing that I can do for you.

LOVEJOY. You're hostile, that's all, just hostile.

STUMBLE. Why don't you confess?

HAMM. I'm not guilty.

LOVEJOY. Even a killer needs love.

ADAM. I'm not guilty.

STUMBLE. Then there's one chance, tell the court Adam did it.

HAMM. You can't put me in your trick-bag, you goddamned hack.

LOVEJOY. I believe you, Adam . . . I believe you because I love you . . . I'm sure Hamm did it . . . tell me it's true, Adam, Hamm did it . . .

ADAM. You don't have to believe me . . . I don't want you to believe me. (*Throws* LOVEJOY *to the floor.*) Stay away from me, you queer.

HAMM and ADAM. Get out of sight.

STUMBLE. That's no way to cooperate . . . you're just hurting your own defense.

(HAMM *throws* STUMBLE *to the floor.*)

LOVEJOY. Go on and hate me . . . see where it gets you . . . you'll die for it, you'll see you've just lost Eve.

HAMM and ADAM. Get out of sight.

(LOVEJOY *and* STUMBLE *get themselves together and call for the guards. The same* TWO GUARDS *who led them on come onstage from right and stand jumping in the same cadence.*)

STUMBLE and LOVEJOY. Guard, guard, guard.

STUMBLE (*to* GUARD). Tell the warden that my visits will be much fewer.

(*They exit.*)

LOVEJOY (*to* GUARD). Take me to the warden. I know my rights, I don't have to sleep with no goddamned killer.

(*They exit.*)

As in the scene with the BOYS *and the* CHARACTER, *this scene in* HAMM*'s cell may also be improvised, in keeping with the general theme of the scene.*

REV *blandly anounces to audience that they should take ten minutes to think about what they witnessed.*)

END OF ACT I

ACT II

Just before the Second Act begins, the FIVE BOYS *mingle with the audience and discuss the situation that* HAMM *and* ADAM *are in; they spot* PORTER *in the crowd; they pursue him down the aisle as he looks for a seat: mostly improvisation.*

SECOND BOY. Man, if you ask me, it's all one big smelly drag.

FOURTH BOY. Hamm and Adam are really uptight.

THIRD BOY. Yeah, I bet they get all knotted up in a rope.

FIRST BOY. That's Whitey's favorite trick, man.

FIFTH BOY. JAMF.

FOURTH BOY. Those damn newspapers talk like they goin to tie up the whole block.

FIRST BOY. Well, that's one knot we don't have to worry about . . . cause we all know you can't read.

(BOYS *laugh, notice* PORTER.)

PORTER. What do you say there, fellers?

THIRD BOY. Wow . . . dig what's floatin on the block . . .

SECOND BOY. You sure is clean, Brother . . . sportin a groovy vine . . .

FIRST BOY. Yeah, you is really hooked up . . .

FIFTH BOY. Brother, you so sharp, you look like a Mississippi sheriff on election day.

(BOYS *laugh,* PORTER *does not, they are aware of his nonparticipation.*)

FIRST BOY. What's your trouble, Brother, ain't you in on the joke?

PORTER. Somehow, I missed the point . . . you know, I couldn't get with it.

THIRD BOY. Man, this cat sure is funny.

PORTER. Frankly, I didn't come up here for laughs.

FIRST BOY. Oh I see, you ain't from up here.

PORTER. Well not exactly in body, but very well in spirit.

THIRD BOY. Oh . . . and just where did you leave your body . . . downtown somewhere?

PORTER. Oh, it's just hanging out, you know . . . it's just out there.

FIFTH BOY. Well if you not here in body, I guess that makes you a spook. You sound like you lost your soul, baby, ain't nothing up here for you.

PORTER. Maybe you boys can help me find what I'm looking for, a story.

BOYS (*except* FIRST BOY). Man a wha a a a? . . .

FIRST BOY. Hold on a minute, what kind of story you lookin for, Brother?

PORTER. Well you see, I'm doing a story for the *New York Times* . . . maybe you know it, the big paper?

SECOND BOY. You mean the big-big paper . . . bout so wide . . . ?

PORTER. Yeah.

SECOND BOY. And about so long, . . . with all that small print . . . ?

PORTER. Yes . . . yes, that's it.

SECOND BOY. Never heard of it.

FIRST BOY. Let's drop the jive, Brother, you're sniffin' under a white woman's dead ass.

FIFTH BOY. JAMF!

PORTER. You've got me all wrong, I'm really not the type . . . What I'd really like to know is why do you call me Brother?

FOURTH BOY. Man, if you were blood, you wouldn't have to ask us that.

PORTER. Then . . . all bloods are brothers.

FIRST BOY. Haven't you heard, man . . . "blood is thicker than water" . . . and all Whitey's got in his veins is piss.

PORTER. Oh, the message is coming through, boys . . . sounds like, Blood Brothers . . . that's it, isn't it?

FIRST BOY. Somebody school this dude!

FIFTH BOY. JAMF.

PORTER. Tell me one thing . . . how much blood do the brothers figure on getting?

THIRD BOY. Wait a minute, who said the brothers are after blood?

PORTER. Certainly, it's a fact that Whitey, as you say, has sound reason to believe that . . . shall we say the Blood Brothers are out to get him?

FOURTH BOY. Yeah, and his Mama too.

SECOND BOY. He ain't wrong . . . want to know what we're goin to do when we get him . . . we're goin to rip off his head . . . then we're goin to shrink his skull in piss and lye . . . and put a key chain through his nose, then twirl him around our fingers as a good luck charm and walk up Lenox Avenue singing "I've got the world on a string."

PORTER. You don't really mean that, do you?

FIRST BOY. That's what's happening uptown, Brother.

FIFTH BOY. Cause Whitey is a JAMF.

PORTER. Would you mind elaborating for the records?

BOYS. Cause Whitey is a Jive Ass Mother Fucker.

(BOYS *begin dance movement.*)

FIRST BOY.

You're a JAMF
if you sit light in your pants
and you dare not let an eye stare you deadpan in your pie.

BOYS.

A JAMF . . .

SECOND BOY.

Stand tall,
don't grin and let your carriage fall
when you pass by Whitey's door,
that ghost can't bluff you no more.

BOYS.

A JAMF.

THIRD BOY.

Out of sight . . .

BOYS.

They yell

THIRD BOY.

. . . the World Fair's coming and you're blight . . .

BOYS.

They tell

THIRD BOY.

. . . though our friends you'd like to meet . . .

BOYS.

Like hell

THIRD BOY.

. . . man, you stink and that ain't discreet.

BOYS.

A JAMF . . .

FOURTH BOY.

I'm a junky

cause my life is drab and funky,

can't get no job with pay that's chunky,

on my back, rides a honky monkey.

BOYS.

A JAMF . . .

FIFTH BOY.

Who needs school?

Teachers only think we're fool,

instituting blackball rules—

progressive education, drop out tools

BOYS.

A JAMF . . .

Exemplary . . .

Whitey no longer smokes tea,

Sailing high on LSD,

dreaming of the Great Society.

A JAMF . . .

J-A-M-F . . . JAMF!!!

(*End of song, music fades.*)

FIRST BOY. Let's go, Brother, we're goin to make a little tour of the block.

PORTER. No . . I . . . really, I have a deadline to meet.

(*The* BOYS *hustle him offstage. As they exit,* STAGE HAND *brings on clerk's stenograph;* JUDGE *enters and sits on chair which is on lowest level;* MOTHERS *are in the same position as for earlier court scene, on platforms, stage left.* CLERK *enters, sits,* ATTORNEY JONES *enters; he is a black man.*)

JONES. Clerk, I demand to see the Judge on the basis that the boys in custody are without proper counsel.

CLERK. And who are you, may I ask?

JONES. I am Attorney Jones, the chosen counsel for the defendants, by the mothers of the defendants . . . and I demand to see both defendants promptly.

CLERK. Impossible, the Judge has already appointed counsel.

JONES. The appointee is a hoax . . . further, incompetent.

CLERK. This blessing from the Court is more than suitable as spokesman for the defense.

JONES. You call that anal prolapsus a mouthpiece? The moment he opens his jowls, he stinks out loud.

CLERK. May I remind you, Attorney, that gratis bears only the sweetest of aromas. The Court's choice is final.

JONES. This decision is a blatant mockery to the Court.

CLERK. Tell me, Attorney, are the mothers paying your fees?

JONES. The mothers are without resources and the Court knows it.

CLERK. Then, how, pray tell, did you expect to compete with the Court's choice?

JONES. There is such a thing as moral assignation . . . particularly on the mothers' request.

CLERK. That Attorney is a mockery to this Court.

JONES. I demand to see the Judge.

JUDGE TAWKIN. This is Judge Tawkin . . . the chambers are open for petition . . . thereafter, all must hold their peace.

JONES. Your Honor.

JUDGE TAWKIN. Yes . . . this is the honorable Judge Tawkin . . . and I must advise you before you speak further that the Court is not obliged by moral predilection or legal prerogative to tolerate scoffing of its rightful decisions and judgments, and further, will not be coerced by social intimidation to follow any procedure other than that found propitious in the past . . . and . . . er had you something to say?

JONES. I wish to represent the . . .

JUDGE TAWKIN. Permission denied. The session is closed.

JONES. I will appeal to a higher court.

JUDGE TAWKIN. Clerk, direct the Attorney to the higher court.

(*The* CLERK *stands, claps his hands,* TWO STAGE HANDS *come out and move the* JUDGE*'s chair and stand to a higher level.*)

CLERK. The Court of Appeals is now in session . . . Judge Tawkin.

JONES. Begging your pardon, Your Honor, but I could have sworn on a stack of Bibles that I'd seen your face before.

JUDGE TAWKIN. Like a vestal virgin, Counselor, Justice always wears the same face. State your case.

JONES. Your Honor, I am petitioning for a writ of habeas corpus for the accused on the grounds that they are being denied the right to counsel of their choice . . . and secondly, because they are being physically agitated to extract incriminating testimony.

JUDGE TAWKIN. Er . . . which of the accused did you say you represented, Counselor?

JONES. As yet, neither. I was denied by the lower court.

JUDGE TAWKIN. Oh . . . do I detect a smug tone of prejudice, Counselor? Justice makes no distinctions between levels.

JONES. Quite true, Your Honor, but as long as polluted water doesn't seek its level . . . we can easily detect the dreg from the fresh springs.

JUDGE TAWKIN. Counselor, your facility for eloquence is indeed admirable, yet what is relevant in fact is that you represent no one.

JONES. I represent the mothers of the accused, who wish me to represent their sons.

JUDGE TAWKIN. The mothers are not on trial.

JONES. Your Honor, we are all on trial.

JUDGE TAWKIN. Fortunately, Counselor, the Court has relieved you and the mothers of any responsibility for this ordeal . . . by delegating counsel of the Court's choice. This thereby nullifies your petition and as for the second item on your petition which implies brutality at the hands of a correction officer, I must ask you to submit before the Bench any such evidence to support your claim.

JONES. Your Honor, if you would only listen to the mothers . . . I doubt that you could challenge the truth . . . that from their own sons . . .

JUDGE TAWKIN. You must admit, Counselor, that's rather limited evidence.

JONES. The State's evidence against the accused is equally limited.

JUDGE TAWKIN. You're out of order, Counselor . . . that will be determined under due process of other proceedings not answerable at this session.

JONES. Then I challenge the Court to disprove my complaint . . . and penalize me if you like with contempt of court.

JUDGE TAWKIN. That would only dignify the charges . . . hardly worth damaging your mantle, is it Counselor?

JONES. Let my mantle rot in a dung heap . . . I'd even gladly stand at the gallows, Your Honor, if you would stick your neck out . . . to be used for the dry hemp that it is.

JUDGE TAWKIN. I will not enter into a personal discussion, Counselor. You have abused your privilege to show cause to petition which, in case you haven't noticed, had been declined . . . The session is closed.

JONES. I'll summon the Supreme Court.

JUDGE TAWKIN. Clerk, direct the Attorney to the Court Supreme.

(*Again the* CLERK *stands and claps his hands; the* STAGE HANDS *reenter, this time wheeling in a stage tower-lift.* JUDGE TAWKIN *is then raised to the ultimate height.*)

CHORUS.
They've locked them up,

they've got their victim,
the white court screams out
for conviction.

If a white man dies
in a Harlem case,
Society brands it a
crime of race.

To face a trial poor
is no disgrace,
though absolution
needs a money base.

A rich man's crime
is defrayed by cost,
his life refunded,
without a lost.

They've locked them up,
they've got their victim,
the white court screams
out for conviction.

Equality is not the
case, when one must judge a crime of race.

JUDGE TAWKIN (*getting order with gavel*). Order in the Court Supreme . . . what this Court needs is order.

JONES (*Bending backward to see the* JUDGE). I humbly note, Your Honor, that your face is embarrassingly familiar.

JUDGE TAWKIN. What you recognize, Counselor, is the smile of charity . . . a common feature of the Court.

JONES. Then I trust, Your Honor, that your smile shall not elude the pleas of the mothers in question, who are without adequate means to carry out a life and death struggle.

JUDGE TAWKIN. Suffer the little mothers that come unto me for mine is the Kingdom of Justice . . . state your case.

JONES. If I may be permitted, Your Honor, here at the Bench of Supreme judgment . . . where the rights . . .

JUDGE TAWKIN. Drop the prologue . . . a more appropriate description is in order, but impermissible in Court . . . Just get to the point.

JONES. Very well, Your Honor, it would please the Court . . .

JUDGE TAWKIN. Brevity, Counselor, brevity . . .

JONES. I shall present my first citation.

JUDGE TAWKIN. Is there more than one?

JONES. Only the necessary documentation for my brief, Your Honor.

JUDGE TAWKIN. Make it very brief.

JONES. I bring to the Court's attention the Supreme Court's decision in the Scottsboro case, which upheld the ruling that the right of counsel meant the right of counsel of one's own choice . . . thereby, any . . .

JUDGE TAWKIN. The Court is aware of all that. We have no time for recapitulations.

JONES. I'm presenting facts.

JUDGE TAWKIN. Do you claim exclusive ownership of facts?

JONES. If you'll pardon my impertinence, Your Honor, even crusty old facts at times can use some airing from under the Court's Supreme skirts.

JUDGE TAWKIN. As supreme Judge, one does not lay oneself open to dirty laundry. Proceed, Counselor, with haste.

JONES. I'd like to advise the Court . . .

JUDGE TAWKIN. Scratch advise from the records. The Court is infallible.

JONES. Then I shall indulge the Court's good graces to deliberate on the apparent denial of equal protection of the law for the accused, based on a class distinction.

JUDGE TAWKIN. The Court will not indulge the kindling of such odious fiction . . . the mere assertion of which places a blinding smoke screen over the due process of law.

JONES. If the Court would unharness her political girdle, her eyes would open on the light.

JUDGE TAWKIN. I don't see where this helps your case, Counselor; in fact the Court is growing impatient.

JONES. There's reason to believe that the Court's patience is water soluble, if the sweat on your temples is any indication.

JUDGE TAWKIN. From where I stand, Counselor, you seem to have exhausted your plea for the indigent, so perhaps we should conclude.

JONES. Why don't you listen, before you dismiss the mothers' pleas?

JUDGE TAWKIN. You'll have to speak louder . . .

JONES. What about the mothers' pleas?

JUDGE TAWKIN. What is all the shouting about . . . ? I can't hear you.

JONES and CHORUS. The mothers' pleas.

JUDGE TAWKIN (*searches through book, finds page*). Oh yes, the mothers, we're coming to that . . . We have a citation which covers the case summarily and uncontestably . . . ah yes . . . here we are . . . Clerk . . .

CLERK (*gestures toward audience*). Order in the Court, Judge Tawkin . . . the final decision is Supreme. All rise. (*The* CLERK *picks up an incense burner and proceeds to swing it in front of the* MOTHERS, JONES, *the audience, etc.*)

JUDGE TAWKIN. . . . the decision of Pauper Criminal, the Assignment of Attorney . . . ah . . . can best be defined by the case of the People vs. Fuller, Court of General Sessions, May 1901, and best reflects the decision of this hearing . . .

(*Monotone voice.*)

. . . A destitute defendant,
charged with murder in the first degree,
can have no part in selecting the counsel
authorized to be assigned to him by the Court
and paid for by the county.

CHORUS (*litany response*).
O Mother of God,

pray for our sins
now and every hour of their lives . . .
  JUDGE TAWKIN.
It seldom happens
that a defendant is arraigned
charged with murder in the first degree,
without many applications for such assignments being made
to the judge
before whom the arraignment is held by counsel
claiming previous retainer,
or special familiarity with the case,
or claiming to represent the wishes of the accused,
or his family
or some other equally cogent reason.
  CHORUS.
O Mother of God,
who is without power,
voiceless in our sons' destiny,
we pray with you . . .
  JUDGE TAWKIN.
It has, indeed, been a matter of common rumor that
zealous counsel have sometimes offered
to divide their prospective fees
with the family and friends of the accused
in consideration of their inducing the accused
to ask the Court for their assignment as counsel.
  CHORUS.
O Mother of God,
whose hem line is frayed,
whose breasts hang like sacks,
help us to know you in this hour of our lives . . .
  JUDGE TAWKIN.
The accused
in prison,
and with a relatively limited acquaintance
as to the capability and suitability of counsel

and oppressed with the gravity of his situation,
is often but poorly able to choose or recommend.
   (*At this point, the* STAGE HANDS *reenter and wheel the* JUDGE
offstage.)
It is the plain duty of the Court
to protect the defendent from such improper influences;
and to permit him under the circumstances,
to suggest counsel to be assigned by the Court,
and paid for by the county,
is to open the door to such grave abuses
that I am unwilling to encourage it.
   CHORUS.
O Mother of God,
the tides have moved against us
have mercy on us . . .

You've abandoned us, Lord,
You've lost faith in us, Lord.
   (*The* MOTHERS *move on—stage right* [*center*]*; the* FIVE BOYS
enter, and climb among the scaffolding. REV *enters, speaks to*
MUSICIANS.)
   REV. Play on, Brothers . . . loud and strong. We don't want
the congregation to fall asleep around here . . . they been sleep
too long already. Bout time they all woke up before we get shook
up . . . yes, wipe that moonshine from your eyes . . . those
promises that today's bed of thorns will be tomorrow's cushion of
roses . . . Wake up, cause this meetin ain't over yet . . . not less
the Man, whom we all know is waiting outside the door this very
moment . . . crashes down our walls, and stamps out our burning spirits . . . you know, he don't knock . . . then slip under
the door . . . no more . . . the only knockin he does is up-side
your head . . . cause he don't want our heads together . . . not
when we talkin bout him . . . not when he can't understand the
message, and only knows the fear of darkness . . . Now we've
witnessed that, Brothers and Sisters . . . he's afraid of our message . . . just afraid that we might fall under some improper

influences . . . start rakin hell till it boils over . . . and sure as
hell it will. How much sleep do you need before you realize
you're dead? . . . If you're goin to raise yourself and act among
the livin, then you've got to summon your bodies to act right now
. . . and you know that's the truth, Brothers and Sisters . . .
right or wrong . . . right or wrong? . . . What's the matter, has
the drug of contentment numbed your tongues? Well, there's no
need to answer, that's why we're holding this meeting now here
at the Tabernacle, the Mothers will speak for us all . . . When
the great father put you out his house, come home . . . that's
what the Tabernacle is for . . . like the Chinese Book say, put
your house in order . . . just like the Mothers have done . . .
here with the other orphans . . . all survivors of Cain . . . all
turned out into the streets . . . all sharing that common lend
lease on life.

(FIRST MOTHER *has ascended the ramps somewhat.*)

FIRST MOTHER.
We have lost our pleas
down on bended knees
where they belong;
we seek supplication,
neighbors,
though talk
may not be
free.

(FIRST MOTHER *crosses back upstage, another* MOTHER *comes down.*)

CHORUS and BOYS.
We are here for your cares to share,
we are all locked in one Black fraternity.
Why try to believe
in Ideology?
Democracy has been long dead,
we've been asked to honor its tranquility,
still every day our lives reap its futility,
there's no chance of it, no more.

FOURTH MOTHER (*a bit shy*).
Our common burdens
bring us to these grounds,
love is lost
until it can be found.
We implore you without
pity,
at least here,
Equality's
Free.
    CHORUS and BOYS.
You are right in what you say
cause we pay in a way
that our blood
starts to flood
with frustration;
mutual respect is our indemnity
since Black is forced to be our sole identity.
What you say is true, yes true.
    FIFTH MOTHER.
Our forlorn hopes are
riding on a ghost;
we're the seeds of
a battled legacy.
Now the gray winds hold
us captive,
while the hangman's
rope hangs
free.
    CHORUS and BOYS.
There's one reason
for this tragedy
that should not escape our view;
we cannot even own our own debauchees,
paternity is simply chattel slavery,
yes, the ghost still haunts us too.

SECOND MOTHER.
Let me warn you
Brothers,
bait your children from the gutters,
there is thunder brooding in the air
so we know your woes too well.

(POLICEMAN *enters through audience.*)

POLICEMAN (*wearing white mask*). That's it . . . that's it . . .
break it up, break it up.

REV. What do you want broken, Officer . . . an arm . . . a leg
. . . or will a few hearts do?

POLICEMAN. It's all over, Reverend, we've had enough loitering
out here.

REV. Don't you stand there and tell me . . . we're loitering
. . . This is a meeting.

POLICEMAN. In my book, it's loitering.

REV. I say it's a meeting . . . and further, you weren't invited.

POLICEMAN. Are you kiddin me, what are you doing . . . selling tickets?

REV. Just take a look around you . . . there ain't even standing
room left.

POLICEMAN. Look here, Rev, the Law is used to being the uninvited guest . . . now I'm telling you, pack it in.

REV. If you ask me, the uninvited guest had better think twice
and be nice and that's advice, Mr. Law.

POLICEMAN. I didn't ask for your guff . . . I want this corner.

REV. Then take it.

POLICEMAN (*sensing hostility in crowd*). All right, go on with
your namby-pamby, but you'd better keep the noise down. I've
got an eye on all of you. (*To audience.*)

REV. You heard him say it's all right, they don't bite when you
pet them, but we ain't goin for that, right?

CHORUS and BOYS. Right.

REV. Now it's time to take our usual collection for the mothers
. . . don't forget our guest, Brother . . . maybe you can spare a
dime. Yet a thousand dimes can't repay the sorrow these mothers

have suffered . . . One good little mother just showed you the strain that she was under, right or wrong?

(USHERS *come down aisle and pass baskets for collection.*)

CHORUS and BOYS. Right.

REV. . . . but she's strong . . . she's got to be strong . . . we all got to be strong to survive the Hell-raisin Cain . . . yes brought down upon our rooftops, shakin all the roaches out the walls, if that ain't right, what is it?

CHORUS and BOYS. Wrong.

REV. . . . we can't have nothing. The scriptures say that . . . From Him That Hath Not, Shall Be Taken Away Even That Which He Hath . . . even if we don't want roaches and vermin, it ain't left up to us to decide if we want them.

CHORUS and BOYS. Right.

REV. . . . I'd rather wade through rat stools . . . bare feet and bare handed, than to be exposed to the virus of oppression that has strangled Hamm and disillusioned Adam . . . right or wrong?

CHORUS and BOYS. Right.

REV. Yes, that Cain is a terror . . . that Cain who smells and has no place to bathe . . . Cain who is fifteen and in the sixth grade . . . Cain whose name is spick, black nigger, bastard, guinea, and kike . . . Cain, who hangs out on the street corners with a pocket full of needles, looking for a taste of honey . . . Cain, whose toys are broken bottles and tin cans . . Now you know we got to get rid of this Cain . . .

BOYS and CHORUS. Right.

REV. . . . and we're goin to do so, if there's not another *Mayflower* . . . And Hamm will be a man . . . and Adam will be redeemed . . .

BOYS and CHORUS. Right.

REV. . . . And the Great White Father will have no alibis on Judgment Day.

BOYS and CHORUS. Right.

REV. Cause we're tired of corruption . . . tired of being stuffed in the Great White Father's hip pocket . . . we got to have our chance to wear the pants . . . oh yeah, we'll show him . . . ain't no reason we can't corrupt as good as him.

BOYS and CHORUS. Right.

POLICEMAN. Why don't you knock it off, Reverend, and stop being a hard-on.

REV. How can you recognize a hard-on unless you're capable of the feat, and you don't look capable to me.

POLICEMAN. I'm warning you, Reverend, you can't raise Cain on this corner.

REV. Well, shut my mouth and call me dopey . . . maybe we ought to just raise cotton.

BOYS and CHORUS. Wrong.

REV. So as we shall not be guilty of disturbing the peace . . . shall we all have a moment of silence? . . .

(REV, MOTHERS, *and* BOYS *stand silently.* POLICEMAN *stalks the group; the silence is heightened by sharp ejaculations of* MOTHERS *or the pounding of a fist.*)

REV. I feel like shouting!

CHORUS and BOYS (*eruption*). Right.

REV. We hollered in Sharpsville . . .

BOYS and CHORUS. Right.

REV. . . . and we hollered in the Congo . . .

BOYS and CHORUS. Right.

REV. . . . the mercenaries hollered too . . . and they'll holler right here in Harlem.

CHORUS and BOYS. Right.

REV. . . . till they move out of our paths . . . and take their mousetrap laws with them . . . What's that Law?

CHORUS and BOYS. Stop and Frisk.

REV. Let me hear you talking.

CHORUS and BOYS. Stop and Frisk.

REV. Like we need that shuffle like a blind man needs glasses, right?

CHORUS and BOYS. Wrong.

REV. I'm so moved by your spirit today, Brothers and Sisters, I could forget about the second collection for myself.

CHORUS and BOYS. Right.

REV. But on the other hand . . .

CHORUS and BOYS. Wrong.

REV. Of course, I know you're right . . . for these are not times for selfish gains . . . when the only harvest to be reaped from the poor is famine . . .

CHORUS and BOYS. Right.

REV. And even when the harvest is ripe . . . you still go hungry . . . but there are always some of us with selfish desires . . . and you all know that's not me . . . who will stuff his pockets with bread and try to ride the gravy train into manhood . . . and when he arrives at the door of the Great White Father, he finds out that he's as hungry as when he started . . . you know why?

CHORUS and BOYS. He's Black.

REV. He might be poor, but he's got a lonely ride back.

POLICEMAN. What in God's name are you trying to do, Reverend, start a riot?

REV. I'm not sure that your God bears any resemblance to my God.

POLICEMAN. Now you're really asking for it, Reverend.

REV. . . . God who is black and who wishes he were white . . . No. Not that he were white, but that white would not wish he were black . . . so in what God's name do you speak?

POLICEMAN. In the name of the Law, I want this corner cleared in another second . . . get moving.

REV (*as the* BOYS *begin to act hostile*). Hold it . . . contain yourselves, Brothers . . . keep yourselves cool for just a second to review . . . Be polite to the invader . . . cause God is everywhere . . . he may be among us this very moment . . . You can never know who is standing in a crowd . . . We've been infiltrated before . . . so think twice and be polite . . . look around you . . . The eyes of God are everywhere, and his hand delivereth the law . . .

(MUSICIANS *begin to play minuet and the* BOYS *and* MOTHERS *go into minuet formation, and begin to sing and dance*.)

THE GROUP.

O you never know just who is who

˙counting heads over you
so it's best to keep your voice low keyed
and pretend
polite society.

    (*The* BOYS *break away and do a wild dance.*)

REV. Be polite.

(BOYS *re-form with* GROUP.)

THE GROUP.

Is there not a face that one can trust,
when you're in for a bust
must not play the numbers lottery,
less you are polite society.

    (*The* BOYS *repeat previous pattern.*)

REV. Be polite.

THE GROUP.

Every downtown avenue we turn,
scolding eyes brand and burn;
they can't see if we are you or me;
what a dumb
polite society.

    (*The* BOYS *repeat previous pattern.*)

REV. Be polite.

THE GROUP.

If a wino ever breaks his flask,
smell the badge, in the splash
precinct cars jam traffic in the streets,
cept when in
polite society.

    (*The* BOYS *break away as before, only the hostility is increased
and this time they provoke the* POLICEMAN *to shoot one of them.
Music stops, the* BOYS *and* MOTHERS *crowd around him.* MUSI-
CIANS *go into* HAMM *and* ADAM*'s song as the* BOYS *exit with dead
member. The* MOTHERS *follow them off, and* REV *exits last.*)

    HAMM and ADAM.

O moon dust over Harlem,

tonight we say good-bye;
you'll have to harbor others,
cause we have no alibis.

Embrace our dear old mothers, tell them good-bye;
there's no hope for our pardons,
and you know why.

Fixed in the stars,
we could be
anywhere, anywhere, anywhere,
far from this despair.

O moon dust over Harlem
   O take us on a star and sail us very, very far.
     (HAMM) tonight we say good-bye
   at night we could be there, suspended without care
     (HAMM) you'll have to harbor others
   we know the poolroom halls, the sleepless nights and brawls.
     (HAMM)
Embrace our dear ole mothers,
   We'd brighten up their souls, no burdens to unfold.
     (HAMM)
Tell them good-bye,
   we could be anywhere, a star is anywhere.
There's no hope for our pardons,
   how far the distant stars, much freer than we are,
     (HAMM)
and you know why.
O moon dust over Harlem,
Tonight we say good-bye;
You'll have to harbor others,
and you know why.
   (*While the boys are singing, the* D.A. *has come onstage. He beckons for* STAGE HANDS, *who bring on table and two chairs.*)
    VOICE (*offstage*). Attorney Jones to see the District Attorney.

D.A. Sit down, Attorney . . . State your business.

JONES. I represent the people of Harlem.

D.A. In response to what declaration?

JONES. The immediate prosecution of one Officer Whitey, for the heedless slaying of a teen-age boy . . . that is to say . . .

D.A. Take it easy, Attorney, you're sniffing up the wrong tree.

JONES. As long as I can support one leg on the ground . . . this tree will suit me fine.

D.A. I'd like to share your optimism, but I think you're wasting your time.

JONES. Time is only wasted by lack of measures to proceed . . . Now in the case of Officer Whitey . . .

D.A. I'm afraid that's not within your jurisdiction, Attorney.

JONES. I am executor of the People's legitimate Rights of Inquiry.

D.A. The People are the State . . . and I am the administrator of Justice for the State. Your claim is null and void.

JONES. By my interpretation, you mean the people of Harlem are nullified of the equities of State jurisprudence.

D.A. Don't be an ass . . . that's not even worthy of debate.

JONES. Oh no, we won't do that . . . much too infectious . . . spreads germs . . .

D.A. Listen, Attorney, what do you want of my life?

JONES. You might start by recognizing our statutory rights as residents of this state . . . and avail yourself to the issues.

D.A. Issues . . . issues, did you say . . . what damn issues? You have no grounds for any issues.

JONES. Would that be a denial of a confirmation?

D.A. Let's not niggle, Attorney, this is a closed session . . . we can speak frankly.

JONES. Good. Then it comes as no great blow on the head to learn that the People intend to force their claim.

D.A. Nonsense. That would be an open challenge to State prerogative.

JONES. So you call it a challenge when a mouth once sealed . . . opens wide.

D.A. Open mouths only draw flies. Now, let's get to the heart of the matter.

JONES. The People of Harlem demand the immediate confinement and subsequent trial of Officer Whitey.

D.A. There has already been an inquisition.

JONES. By the people?

D.A. The State . . . you know, the civilized thing.

JONES. Oh yes, very civilized indeed. Just a question of who's holding the cock by the tail . . . or is it the tail before the cock?

D.A. Choose whatever end you like . . . the officer was doing his duty.

JONES. Was it the officer's duty to shoot a defenseless boy?

D.A. The boy threatened him with a knife.

JONES. The boy was unarmed.

D.A. Not according to testimony.

JONES. Testimony . . . what testimony? . . . I read the State's extracted penny dreadful, the pertinent facts were never published.

D.A. Much too lengthy for public interest . . . the idea is to give the public information, and you know as well as I do most people can't even handle the classified ads, much less a massive judicial document. One must break down the facts . . . our task is prudent dissemination.

JONES. Well, it's comforting to know that the State assumes responsibility for the People's reading habits . . . including the editing of shall we say burdensome materials?

D.A. I shouldn't press my cunning if I were you, Attorney, this audience is not obligatory.

JONES. Mr. District Attorney, your humility embarrasses me to blushing red, correction, color that blue.

D.A. Don't be pompous.

JONES. I think you mean uppity.

D.A. Nigger.

JONES. Bigot.

D.A. Varlet.

JONES. Honky.

D.A. Journeyman.

JONES. Hypocrite.

D.A. Now that we've gotten that pleasant exchange of niceties out of the way, I suppose that we can consider the issue closed.

JONES. Closed, it was never opened.

D.A. Thus, shall we say, let us conclude this entertainment . . . I think the State has been more than indulgent with its arena.

JONES. Particularly when it presents such a crummy farce.

D.A. Traditional stage, you know.

JONES. Hackneyed stock lines.

D.A. But then it could be the lighting.

JONES. Yes, the darkness is blinding.

D.A. Then you couldn't have possibly seen the joke . . .

JONES. Your trouble is that you laugh at your own jokes.

D.A. Attorney, the joke is over.

JONES. When I tell the People, they're goin to have a fit . . . and it won't be all giggles.

D.A. In due time, Attorney, you and your people will come to know the subtle compensations of the Law . . . then shall you receive your long awaited deserts.

JONES. You sound as flat as the rest of this Pepsi Generation . . . save your bubbles.

D.A. The issue is closed.

JONES. The issue is now in the hands of the People.

D.A. I've heard enough.

JONES. I place the State responsible for all pending demonstrations.

D.A. There will be no demonstrations.

JONES. May all the maimed and dead rest on your conscience.

D.A. For your further amusement, Attorney, there has been a restraining injunction placed in Harlem against any demonstrations or mass assembly. Any infraction of this order will be observed as civil disobedience. The State's conscience is clear.

JONES (*exiting up aisle*). Bull shit.

(*Previous scene has been played on apron. After* ATTORNEY *leaves, the lights come up onstage and* D.A. *speaks to audience.*)

D.A. The State vs. Hamm and Adam.

(MUSICIANS *begin to play violently, loud noises emanate from rear of house, as in a riot. Platform that was raised for* D.A.'s *scene is lowered and* JUDGE's *chair is brought from stage left to stage right. The* JUDGE *enters and sits. The* FIVE BOYS *and* JONES *enter from rear of the house after the* JUDGE *sits. They are dragging with them a large dummy to represent Officer Whitey.*)

JUDGE TAWKIN. Does the counsel for the defense wish to submit a plea? (*No response.*) Is there a plea for the defense? (*No response.*) Where is the appointed counsel for the defense?

(STUMBLE *enters.*)

STUMBLE. Here . . . here . . . right here . . . Your Honor.

JUDGE TAWKIN. The defense plea, if you please.

STUMBLE. Yes . . . yes . . . I have it right here . . . um . . . er . . . not guilty.

JONES. Guilty, Officer Whitey is guilty.

D.A. The State charges the defendants with first degree murder.

JONES. As offender of the People, he must be tried by the People for murder without decree.

JUDGE TAWKIN. The Court is open to testimony.

JONES. Lay the streets bare for open testimony.

D.A. We see before us the offenders of that onerous Black deed, Murder.

JONES. Root out the evil . . . Death's face has that known white pallor.

STUMBLE. Objection.

JUDGE TAWKIN. Objection overruled. Black is merely descriptive of the event . . . not the principals of the event.

BOYS. JAMF.

JONES. Acting on his natural instinct to inflict pain, this devil's apprentice stalked a life and claimed it.

JUDGE TAWKIN. Is there one among us who can swear . . . that testimony entered against the accused . . . is without reasonable doubt . . . more or less true?

(CHARACTER, *dressed as Anna, enters and sits on platform between* JUDGE *and* JONES.)

CHORUS.
On our oaths as Mothers, grieved to the womb,
we swear by the countenance of the Heavenly Mother
the torment we have witnessed at the hands of the accused
is now and ever shall be true.

JONES. Officer Whitey stands accused.

JUDGE TAWKIN. Is there proof?

BOYS.
Puddin ain't pie, the eye don't lie,
Puddin ain't pie, the eye don't lie.

D.A. The State's witness was interviewed in closed sessions, Your Honor, and advised not to appear in Court, because of her minor age.

JUDGE TAWKIN. Objection sustained.

STUMBLE. This appears to the defense as an improper denial of minor's rights.

JONES. Death has robbed us of one more minor . . . cut down by Officer Whitey, denied the right to dissent and raise himself from the ashes of depression . . .

JUDGE TAWKIN. Evidence . . . The Court petitions the testimony of the officer responsible for collecting the evidence.

CHORUS.
Gathered there, as we were,
on our common ground, as we do,
straining our breaths in a way,
venting wounds of the day,
there blazed a sudden heated wind;
the earth shook loose a mighty roar;
one boy fell, he breathed no more.

D.A. Unfortunately, Your Honor, the officer in question is now detained in custody of the law to answer charges of illegal complicity in a case outside this one currently being judged. However, due to the officer's previous fine record, bravery and uncountable citations, the State takes full responsibility for his submitted testimony, having formerly displayed veracity and conscientious service to his department.

STUMBLE. Objection.

JUDGE TAWKIN. Objection overruled. Committed performance in past service is a vital index to character.

HAMM and ADAM. We have no alibis, so surely we must die.

JONES. Here there should be a face . . . but there is no face . . .

BOYS. JAMF.

JONES. . . . no soul to feel the guilt . . . just a hollow shadow . . . a shadow created by a ruling psychopath still to haunt our streets . . .

BOYS. We ain't sad . . . we just men . . . Drive us mad . . . Drive us mad.

JONES. . . . then disappearing into the darkness from whence it came . . . leaving behind a bath of blood.

CHORUS. Don't harm our boys . . . Please save our boys.

(STUMBLE *breaks into laughter.*)

JUDGE TAWKIN. Order . . . Order, Counselor.

(STUMBLE *reduces laughter.*)

The Court fails to appreciate the nature of your amusement.

STUMBLE. Well . . . well . . . it's just that . . . suddenly . . . it occurred to me that this trial is earmarked for disaster.

JUDGE TAWKIN. Your contention is well taken, Counselor, but your procedure . . . the Court finds quite unusual.

D.A. But of course, it's a closed case.

(STUMBLE *breaks into laughter again;* D.A. *and* JUDGE *also laugh a little.*)

CHORUS.

Hah-hah-haa-hah
Hah-hah-hah-hah
Hah-hah-ahah-ahah
Hah-hah-hah-hah

JUDGE TAWKIN (*slams gavel to get order*). Order. Judge Tawkin, here, wants order.

HAMM and ADAM. We're on trial for our lives, we have no alibis, so surely we must die.

JONES. There he sits . . . white with fright . . . pale as Ballantine ale . . . flat as unleavened bread . . . the drought that brought famine to our security . . . strangling our roots . . . and causing chaos everywhere.

D.A. The ruthless assault committed by the accused was contrived and premeditated by an insidious design of hate . . . the locus of which being racism.

JONES. We will be redeemed.

BOYS. O say can you see . . . any bedbugs on me? Look and see, look and see.

JUDGE TAWKIN. The facts of the case seem to point rather strongly to the willful abuse and contempt of Democracy's great plan . . . that under God, all men are created equal.

JONES. We've faced the scourge of Boss-lords, Task-lords, and Land-lords, but Officer Whitey is the most infamous of War-lords to invade us.

STUMBLE. Objection.

JUDGE TAWKIN. Objection sustained.

STUMBLE. In review of the charges, it comes to mind . . . are the accused being tried for their crime . . . or their color?

D.A. The crime of the accused was an act of racial bias.

JONES. It is said that the War-lord cast the fatal blow out of duty . . . Adorned in a white cloak, his duty is merciless . . . but he shan't reign forever.

CHORUS.
For he shan't reign
forever
and ever.

D.A. Racial hostility is at the marrow of this crime.

JONES. And he expects us to love him.

BOYS. Cast a stone, break his bones. Cast a stone, break his bones.

JUDGE TAWKIN. Have the accused anything to say on this matter?

HAMM and ADAM. We have no evidence to call to our defense, so surely we must die.

FIRST MOTHER. My baby!

D.A. The State demands the firmest possible penalty as the only retribution for the crime.

BOYS. Crucify him.

JUDGE TAWKIN. It appears to the Court, by the testimony presented, that the accused acted without moral restraint.

STUMBLE. Objection.

JUDGE TAWKIN. Objection sustained.

STUMBLE. For the record, Your Honor, would that be a case of loose morals?

JONES. I excuse the mothers, to condemn the accused for the violence he has brought on you, in violation of all sense of moral prudence.

BOYS. Brand him.

D.A. The State rests . . . and awaits verdict.

JUDGE TAWKIN. Has all testimony been heard?

(*Anna crosses to* JUDGE *as if to whisper something in ear, hesitates, then exits.*)

D.A. There's nothing left to be said.

BOYS. Ain't no use in talkin deep . . . we all know that talk is cheap . . . talk is cheap . . . talk is cheap.

JUDGE TAWKIN. The Court, having heard all testimony, will sit in final judgment.

JONES. The judgment of the mothers is final.

HAMM and ADAM. We have no alibis . . . so surely we must die.

CHORUS. O Mother of God, pray for their sins . . . now and every hour of their lives.

JUDGE TAWKIN. A verdict has been entered to the Court . . .

CHORUS. Don't harm our boys . . . Please save our boys.

JUDGE TAWKIN. Guilty.

JONES. Show your wrath, Mothers.

CHORUS. Guilty.

JONES. Officer Whitey is condemned.

JUDGE TAWKIN. By the jurisdiction accrued me as arbiter of Justice, it is the Court's judgment that the accused be sentenced to death.

BOYS(*begin a steady pounding on limbs of Dummy: crucifixion*) Kill him . . . Kill him . . .

REV (*enters briskly*). Scatter the Devil's ashes.

D.A. The State welcomes your decision, Your Honor. (*Exits.*)

CHORUS.
Have mercy on us, Lord.
Sanctus. Good God Almighty.
   REV. Spiritus Sancti.
   CHORUS. Sanctus. My Jesus.
   REV. Spirit Sancti.
   CHORUS. Sanctus, Lawd have mercy.
   REV. In nova fert animus mutatas dicere formas coepore.
(STAGE HANDS *have entered and led* HAMM *and* ADAM *up to the gallows where the* EXECUTIONER *awaits them.*)
   CHORUS. Sanctus, save me, Jesus.
   REV. . . . di coeptis nam vowmutatas et illas . . .
   CHORUS. Sanctus, thank you, Jesus.
   REV. Adspirato meis prima qua aborgina mundi . . .
   CHORUS. Sanctus, fix it, Lawd.
   REV. . . . ad mea perpetuum de dicere tempora carmes.
(*One of the* BOYS *is doing a wild dance with a spear. As the time of execution draws near he slows up; then charges on the Dummy at the height of sonorous shouts of* BOYS.)
   BOYS. Ywaaaawwwaaaw!
(*At height of scream, the lights black out, the* BOYS, HAMM, *and* ADAM *are hung, and the Dummy of Officer Whitey is killed with the spear. Two areas relight simultaneously as everybody freezes.*

As the lights come up, the cast removes their masks and come forward with REV, *who addresses audience.*)
   REV (*as* REV *begins to address audience, the cast becomes animated, and moves forward downstage onto the ramps*). The dialogue is over, Brothers and Sisters, you have witnessed it all . . now come and take your places with us . . .
   Rev ain't preachin to you . . . Rev just tellin it like it is . . . now he's goin to shut up so you can shout . . . well, go on . . . go on . . . I can't believe this silence . . . I can't hear you . . . am I shoutin alone?
   Brothers and Sisters . . . I can't believe this silence on my ears . . . I mean ain't you with us . . . ain't you goin to do something . . . ain't you even mad or something?
   Yawl ain't goin to just sit there, are you? . . . No, I can't

believe that . . . I ain't goin to believe that . . . I'm just goin to pretend you been knocked dumb . . . ain't yawl feelin the spirit yet? . . . let me know we ain't here in vain . . . let us feel the spirit . . . let us feel the spirit . . . in your silence, Brothers and Sisters, ask yourselves . . . Have you brought your cross today?

(The play ending is determined by the audience: if the audience responds with shouts, then the cast enters the audience, shaking hands and joining in with jubilation; if the audience answers with silence, the cast, with the exception of REV, *who finishes his speech as designed, laughs at the audience and exits offstage left and right.*

There is no curtain call once actors have left the stage.)

END

Goin'a Buffalo

A Tragifantasy

ED BULLINS

Sometimes . . .
I'd like to be
a Stranger in town . . .
Sort'a mysterious.
Strange tales would be
told about me . . .
And they would be
FANTASTIC!

MARTIN P. ABRAMSON

Cast of Characters

CURT: *29 years old.*
RICH: *28 years old.*
PANDORA: *22 years old. Curt's wife.*
ART: *23 years old.*
MAMMA TOO TIGHT: *20 years old.*

SHAKY: *36 years old. Mamma Too Tight's man.*
PIANO PLAYER.
BASS PLAYER.
DRUMMER.
BARTENDER.
DEENY.
BOUNCER.
CUSTOMERS.
SHOWGIRL.
VOICE.

Synopsis of Scenes
   ACT ONE: *Evening.*
   ACT TWO: *Later that evening.*
   ACT THREE: *Three days later.*
   The action of the play takes place in Curt's apartment and at the Strip Club.

ACT I

Scene I

This play is about some black people: CURT, PANDORA, ART, RICH, *and* SHAKY, *though* MAMMA TOO TIGHT *is white. The remainder of the cast is interracial, but two of the musicians are black and if* DENNY, *the* BOUNCER *and one of the* CUSTOMERS *are white, there might be added tensions. But it is left to the director's imagination to match the colors to the portrayals.*
   Time: Early 1960's, late evening in January.
   Scene: A court apartment in Los Angeles in the West Adams district. The room is done in white—white ceiling, white walls, white overly elaborate furniture—but a red wall-to-wall carpet covers the floor. A wall bed is raised. Upstairs, two doorless entrances stand on each side of the head of the bed. The right entrance is to the kitchen; the backstage area that represents the kitchen is shielded by a filmy curtain, and the actors' dim silhou-

ettes are seen when the area is lighted. The left entrance will be raised and off stage right at the head of a short flight of stairs and a platform which leads into the combination bathroom–dressing-room–closet. When the actors are within this area, their shadows will be cast upon the wall fronting the stairs. And when the bed is lowered a scarlet spread is shown.

Within the interior of the front room the light is a mixture of red, blues, and violet, with crimson shadows bordering the edges of the stage to create the illusion of a world afire, with this pocket of atmosphere an oasis.

A telefunken, turned very low, plays the local jazz station, and CURT *and* RICH *lean over a chess board.* CURT *squats upon a stool, and, facing him across the coffee table and chess board,* RICH, *a stocky, brooding man, studies his next move, seated on the edge of the couch. Each has an empty beer bottle and a glass close at hand.*

CURT. I just about have you up tight, Rich.

RICH (*annoyed*). Awww . . . Curt, man . . . don't try and hustle me!

CURT (*looks at him*). Did I say somethin' to upset you, man? (RICH *shakes his head and curses to himself.*

A shadow appears at head of stairs and pauses as if the figure is listening for conversation. Then PANDORA *enters—a beautiful black girl wearing tight white pants, a crimson blouse, and black boots—and slowly descends the stairs while looking at the men. She crosses behind them and walks toward the kitchen.* RICH *looks a second at her behind, but drops his gaze when* CURT *begins tapping the chess board with a finger nail.* CURT *gives no discernible attention to* PANDORA. *She enters the kitchen; a light goes on.*)

CURT (*staring at Rich*). This game's somethin' else . . . man.

RICH (*studies board, looks up at* CURT, *and concentrates upon the board again. Mutters to himself*). Ain't this somethin' else though . . . (*Looking up*) You almost got my ass, man.

CURT (*mocking*). I have got your ass, Rich.

RICH (*half-hearted*). Awww . . . man . . . why don't you go fuck yourself? (*He places hand upon a piece.*)

CURT (*warning and placing hand upon one of his pieces*). Wouldn't do that if I were you, good buddy.

RICH (*frowns and takes hand from board. He shakes head and mumbles, then curses his own caution*). Sheeet! (*He makes move.*) Let's see what you're goin' ta do with that, man!

CURT (*deliberately*). Checkmate!

RICH (*half rising*). What you say, Curt?

CURT (*toneless*). Checkmate, man.

(CURT *looks toward the rear of the apartment; the faucet has been turned on, and in the kitchen* PANDORA *leisurely crosses the entrance doorway*).

CURT. WE'RE READY FOR ANOTHER ONE, PAN-DORA!

PANDORA (*off*). Already?

CURT. That's what I said, baby!

PANDORA (*crosses doorway again*). Okay.

RICH (*mumbles and studies chessboard*). Well . . . I'll be god-damned.

(*Faucet sound goes off.*)

PANDORA (*off*). You don't need fresh glasses, da ya?

(*Sound of refrigerator opening.*)

CURT (*surely*). NO, PANDORA, JUST THE BEER!

PANDORA (*raising voice*). Okay . . . Okay . . . wait a fuckin' minute, will ya? Be right there!

(*Rattles of bottles.*)

CURT (*glowering toward the kitchen, then staring at* RICH *who sits stoop-shouldered*). How 'bout another one, Rich?

(RICH *reaches into pocket and brings out a small roll and pulls off two bills and places them beside* CURT's *glass. He mutters to himself*).

RICH. I wonder why in the fuck I didn't see that?

PANDORA (*with a cross expression, enters carrying two bottles of Miller's Highlife).* Just because you're pissed off at the world don't take it out on me! What'ta hell ya think ya got 'round here, maid service? (CURT *stands to meet her; she slows. Whining).* Awww . . . Curt . . . *(A knock comes from backstage; relieved, she looks at* CURT.) I wonder who would be knocking at the kitchen door, honey?

CURT *(reaches down, palms and pockets the money).* There's only one way to be sure, sugar. *(Sits down, looks at* RICH) You clean, man?

RICH *(nods).* Yeah . . . Curt.

CURT *(nods to* PANDORA *as the knock sounds again).* Just watch your mouth, pretty baby . . . it's goin' ta get you in trouble one of these days, ya know. (PANDORA *places bottles on the edge of the table and briskly goes to open back door.)*

PANDORA. Maybe it's little Mamma already.

CURT *(mostly to himself).* She wouldn't come around to the back door for nobody. *(Disregards the noise of the kitchen door's lock snapping back and the rattle of the night chain being fixed in its hasp)* I have the black men this time, right, Rich?

RICH *(reaching for the beer).* Yeah.

ART *(off).* Hello, is Curt home? My name's Art. I ran into Curt this afternoon and he told me to drop by.

PANDORA *(off).* Just a minute . . . I'll see. *(The sound of the door closing is heard, and* PANDORA *returns to the main room.)* Curt . . . Curt?

CURT *(setting up his chess pieces; in a bored voice).* Yeah, baby?

PANDORA. There's a guy named Art out here who says you told him to drop around.

CURT *(not looking at her but down at the board).* Invite him in, baby.

(PANDORA *exits.)*

RICH. Is this the guy?

CURT (*nods, in low voice*). Never a dull moment . . . right, Rich?

RICH (*sarcastic*). Yeah. We're really in ta somethin', man.

(*The music changes during the remainder of this scene. "Delilah" and "Parisian Thoroughfare" as recorded by Max Roach and Clifford Brown play. These will be the themes for the scenes between* ART *and* PANDORA, *except when other music is necessary to stress altering moods. If Act I extends long enough, "Sketches in Spain" by Miles Davis is to be played also, but "Delilah" should be replayed during* PANDORA'S *box scene.*)

PANDORA (*off*). Just a minute.

(*noise of the lock and chain.*)

ART. Good evening.

(*She leads him into the living room.* RICH *has poured beer for* CURT *and himself; he stands and saunters to the radio as if to change stations, but turns after* ART *has passed behind him and sizes up the stranger from the rear.*)

CURT (*stands*). Hey, good buddy! You found the place okay, huh?

ART (*pleased by greeting*). Yeah, it wasn't so hard to find but I guess I came around to the wrong door.

CURT (*with a wave*). Awww . . . that's okay. One's good as the other. It's better to come in that way if you're walkin' from Washington Boulevard. You live somewhere 'round there, don't ya?

ART (*hesitant*). Well . . . I did.

CURT (*gesturing*). Here, I want you to meet my wife and a buddy of mine. (*Introducing* PANDORA) This is my wife, Pandora . . . and . . .

PANDORA (*smiles brightly*). We already met, kinda. He told me his name at the door.

CURT (*ignoring* PANDORA). . . . and this is Rich.

RICH (*remains in same spot.* ART *turns and* RICH *gives him a casual salute*). What's happen'n, brother?

CURT (*to* PANDORA *and* RICH). This is a guy I met in jail. (*Introduces* ART) Art Garrison. (*Shows* ART *a seat on the couch, downstage from Rich.*) Yeah, Art was one of the best young cons on Tier Three . . . (*To Pandora*) Get my boy here a drink, baby.

PANDORA (*starts for kitchen*). You drink beer, Art?

ART. Sure . . . that sounds great.

PANDORA (*over her shoulder*). We got some scotch, if you want it.

ART. No, thanks.

(RICH *sits, makes opening move, not looking at* ART.)

CURT (*to* RICH). Yeah, if it wasn't for Art here I wouldn't be sittin' here.

RICH (*bored*). Yeah?

CURT. This is the kid who banged Scooter aside the jaw during the riot last summer in the joint.

RICH (*sounding more enthused*). Yeah . . . you were doin' a stretch down at county jail when that happened, weren't you?

CURT. Yeah, man. I was there bigger den shit. (*Takes seat*) Yeah, that paddy mathafukker, Scooter, was comin' down on me with an ice pick, man . . . we had all been rumblin' up and down the cell block and I slipped on somethin' wet . . . I think it was Cory's blood 'cause Miles and his boys had stomped the mathafukker so good . . .

(*During the telling of the incident,* PANDORA *stands framed in the kitchen doorway, watching the men.*)

CURT. And I went to look up and all I could see was that gray-eyed mathafukkin' Scooter comin' at me with that ice pick of his . . . He reached down and grabbed my shirt front and drew back his arm and WHAMMO . . . (*Indicating* ART) just like a bat out'ta hell my boy here had scored on the sucker's jaw.

ART (*pleased*). Well . . . I couldn't let that white sonna bitch do you in, man.

RICH (*dryly*). What was the beef about, man?

CURT. Well you know Miles goes for the Muslims though he

ain't one hisself. Now the Muslims were in a hassle at the joint with the guards and the big people on top because of their religious beliefs, dig?

RICH (*interested*). What do you mean?

CURT. Well the guards didn't want them havin' their meetin's 'cause they said they were organizing' and plottin'. And the Muslims wanted some of the chow changed 'cause they don't eat the same kind'a food we do.

RICH. Yeah!

CURT. So while this was all goin' on, Cory . . . a young, wise nigger who thinks he's in ta somethin' . . . well he started agitatin' and signifyin' bout who the Muslims think they was. And what made it so rank was a lot of the ofays, ya know, Charles, the white man, start in sayin' things they had held back before, so Miles and some of the boys got together one day and caught that little jive-sucker Cory outside his cell block and stomped him so bad the deck was greasy wit' his blood, man. That's when the shit started really goin' down, right there, man. Bumpy, Cory's cousin come runnin' up, man, and that big nigger kicked Miles square in the nuts and laid out two of his boys before the rest of them got themselves together. By that time some of the whiteys come runnin' up and a few more of Miles's boys. Yeah, the whole shit started right there where Cory lay almost done in . . .

RICH. Yeah . . . I heard a couple of cats got stabbed, man.

CURT. Yeah, man, it was pretty scary for a while, mostly black cons against white ones except for the studs who just tried to stay out of the shit and the Uncle Toms . . . those Toms we were really out to cool.

RICH (*heated*). Yeah, you should have done those mathafukkers in!

CURT. Even the guards wouldn't come into the cell block and break it up at first . . . a whole lot of shit went down that day. (*Looking at* ART) I owe my boy here a lot for that day.

ART (*embarrassed*). Yeah, man, I would have liked to have stayed out of it but I couldn't.

CURT. Yeah, Art, I us'ta wonder about that . . . (*A two-beat pause*) How could you just go about your business and stay in the middle all the time in that place when so much crap was goin' down?

ART. I just stayed out of everything, that's all.

CURT. But didn't you care about anything, man? Didn't you feel anything when that shit was happen'n to you?

ART. Yeah, I cared but I just didn't let it bother me too much. I just froze up on everything that tried to get in and not too much touched me.

PANDORA (*from doorway*). Talk about somebody bein' cold!

CURT (*having noticed her in doorway for first time, stares at ART*). But you don't know how I appreciate what you did, man. It wasn't your fight, man. You weren't takin' sides. You were one of the quiet guys waitin' for trial who just kept his mouth shut and minded his own business.

ART. I never do try and take sides in stir, just serve my time and forget about it, that's all.

(PANDORA *has moved out of the doorway.*)

CURT. Well, I'm glad you did that time, man, and if there's anything I can ever . . .

RICH (*interrupting*). What were you in for, Art?

(CURT *takes a drink of his beer, lights a cigarette and blows smoke across the table above the two men's heads.* PANDORA *drops something made of glass in the kitchen and curses.*)

ART. Well . . . I was waiting for trial . . . attempted murder.

RICH. That's a tough one to have on your rap sheet.

ART. Yeah, it doesn't do your record or you any good, especially when it ain't for money.

CURT (*finally makes answering chess move*). It was over a broad, wasn't it?

ART (*lights a cigarette, offers* RICH *a light but is refused*). Yeah. I guess girls are my main weakness.

RICH (*with unlit cigarette dangling from his lips, makes move*). How much time did you do?

ART. Waited on my trial for nine months at county when the husband of the girl dropped the charges and left town.

CURT (*replies to move*). That's who you shot, the girl's husband?

ART (*his eyes following game*). Yeah.

RICH (*moves quickly*). You pretty good with a gun?

ART (*caught up in game*). I can usually hold one without it blowing my foot off.

RICH (*sharply*). Any simple ass can do that! I asked you are you any good with one!

(*The three men are fixed in tableau for a three-beat interval:* ART *strains forward from his seat and is about to speak.*)

CURT (*to* RICH *as he makes his move*). This move's goin' ta show ya to stop fuckin' with Curt the Kid, good buddy.

(*Noise of refrigerator opening and slamming, and* PANDORA *enters with a bottle and a glass. She pours beer for* ART *and sets the glass down beside him as the men all look at the chessboard.*)

PANDORA (*in a light mood*). Sorry I took so long, Art. I just dropped the supper. (*To Curt*) Honey, the beans are all messed up. Little Mamma won't have anything to eat 'cept eggs.

CURT (*not looking at her*). Didn't want no fuckin' beans anyhow! And I know Mamma Too Tight don't want any either . . . what kind'a shit is that . . . givin' that broad beans on her first night on the streets?

PANDORA (*defensively*). That's all we got, honey . . . You know we won't have any spendin' money until Deeny pays me.

RICH. Why don't you have a seat, Pan?

PANDORA. I gotta finish cleanin' the kitchen . . . I don't want no roaches 'round here. Last place we had we had to split 'cause the roaches took it over. The little mathafukkers got mo' of the food than Curt or me. Soon as I bring in a little money to get some food with . . . (CURT *looks at her sharply but she is turned toward* RICH *and* ART.) there's mo' of them little mathafukkers there than your eyes could see. And I put too much time in fixin' this pad up nice the way it is to have them little mathafukkers move in on me and try to take it over.

CURT. You better finish up, sweetcake, so I can take you to work. (*The term sweetcake is used with derision and seldom with affection.* PANDORA *picks up* CURT's *empty bottles and exits.*)

CURT. Your move, Richie.

RICH. Are you sure, man?

CURT. Just ask Art, he's been watchin' the game.

ART. Well, I ain't in it, man.

RICH. That's right, you ain't in it.

CURT (*watching* ART's *face*). Yeah, it's your move, Richie, babe.

RICH (*to* ART). That was pretty nice of that girl's ole man to let you off, Art.

ART. Nawh . . . he wanted his ole lady to leave the state with him so he had to drop the charges against me to let her off the hook too.

RICH. She was in it too, huh?

ART. She shot him with me.

CURT. You play this game, Art?

ART. Yeah, some. But I haven't had much practice lately.

CURT. Well, this one's about over.

RICH (*snorts*). Sheeet!

CURT. Maybe you'd like ta play the winner.

RICH (*grimacing before making hesitant move*). Where ya livin' now, Art?

ART. I just got locked out of my room.

RICH. Yeah, Curt said you wanted to make some money.

ART (*intensely*). I have to, man. I'm really on my ass.

CURT. Check!

RICH (*makes move*). Not yet, sucker.

ART. I gotta get out of this town.

RICH. You got a car, ain't ya?

CURT (*moves*). Not long now, Rich.

ART. Yeah, that's about all I got. A car and a suitcase. I've also gotten more jail time in this town than in my whole life, and I've been halfway round the world and all over this country.

RICH (*moves and acts angry*). Yeah, L.A.'s no fuckin' good, man. If I was off parole now I would get the first thing on wheels out of here. How bout you, Curt? If you weren't out on bail wouldn't you make it?

(CURT *doesn't answer. Stage left, a knock sounds and* PANDORA *comes out of the kitchen striding toward the entrance which serves as the front door to the apartment.*)

PANDORA. That must be little Mamma.

CURT. Sure hope it is . . . I would really like to see that little broad.

PANDORA (*peers through window*). Yeah, there's that chick. (*Calling outside in jocular way*) Hey, broad, what they doin' lettin' you out'ta jail? (*An indistinct shout and a laugh comes from outside.*)

CURT (*to Rich*). Checkmate, man!

(*Lights lower to blacken the stage.*)

ACT I

Scene II

When the lights go up MAMMA TOO TIGHT *and* SHAKY *sit upon the lowered bed. Faintly reflecting a glow, the bedspread gives them the appearance of sitting upon smoldering coals.* MAMMA TOO TIGHT, *a small, voluptuous girl, is dressed well. Her shift complements her creamy complexion and full-blown build.* SHAKY *is nondescript but dresses in expensive casual clothes.*

CURT, RICH, *and* ART *sit in the same area, stage right, facing*

the bed, forming the lower lip of a half-moon, and PANDORA
*has changed to a black cocktail dress and sits upon the stairs to
the bathroom. She faces front with a bit of red ruffled slip peek-
ing beneath and around her black stockinged legs.*

*They all eat chicken from cardboard containers and reach
for beers and cigarettes. The light in the kitchen is off, and the
radio plays.*

ART. Thanks again, Curt . . . if you hadn't invited me to eat
I don't know what I'd do . . . probably had to drive downtown
on what little gas I got and eat at one of those Rescue Missions.

MAMMA TOO TIGHT (*nudging* SHAKY *in the ribs*). Well, I'll be
damned . . . Ole Curt done saved himself a soul . . .

SHAKY (*slow and languid*). Easy, baby, you gonna make me
spill my beer.

MAMMA TOO TIGHT. What you know 'bout eatin' at Rescue
Missions, boy?

PANDORA (*interjecting*). You better stop callin' that guy ah
boy, Mamma . . . ha ha . . . girl . . . you got mo' gall.

RICH (*drinking beer*). Yeah, Mamma, how fuckin' big do boys
grow where you come from?

CURT (*with food in mouth*). Forget about it, Art, glad to have
ya. One more don't mean a thing.

PANDORA. Listen to that, Mamma Too Tight . . . (*Mocking*)
"One mo' mouf don't mean a thing." . . . We eat beans all week
and when you and Curt's friends come in we play big shit! . . .
And call out for food and beer.

(CURT, SHAKY, *and* ART *stop eating.* CURT *stares at* PANDORA
and ART *holds his plate like it is hot and he is trying not to
drop it on the floor.* SHAKY *eyes* MAMMA TOO TIGHT *and gives a
mean scowl.* MAMMA *has seen the look on* CURT'S *face before.*
RICH *goes on enjoying his meal.*)

MAMMA (*in a jolly tone, to* PANDORA). Girl, you don't have ta
tell me a thing . . . these here men think that money can be
just picked up off'a them pavements out there like chewin'

gum paper . . . until they got ta get out there for themselves. (*She swings off the bed and shows flashes of lingerie.*) Like this pretty boy here with the fuzz on his face. (*She approaches* ART *and stands so her hips form a prominent profile to* CURT's *line of vision.*) He ain't even eatin' no mo' . . . and Curt's not either, honey. What I tell ya? These men are somethin' else. So weak from plottin' what we should be doin' to bring some money in that they can't eat themselves. (*Puts her plate on coffee table*) I knows that Curt is a big strong man . . . he's always lettin' Pan know. (*Strong dialect*) So he don't need no help from us frail ass women but maybe ole fuzzy wuzzy face here needs some help. (*Her audience is in better humor once more. To Art*) You wants Mamma Too Tight to feeds him some food, baby boy?

SHAKY. Cut out the Magnolia act. Everything wears thin, *Queenie!*

MAMMA (*sudden anger*). Don't you call me no fuckin' Queenie!

SHAKY (*sarcastic*). Anything you say, baby.

(PANDORA *guffaws at* SHAKY's *tone.*)

PANDORA (*mimicking Mamma's drawl*). But ain't dat yo name, hooneee?

(MAMMA *ignores* SHAKY *and* PANDORA, *picks drumstick from plate and offers it to* ART *who frowns, and pulls it away and puts it to her mouth imitating a mother feeding a reluctant child. Finally,* ART *smiles at her as* SHAKY *speaks.*)

SHAKY. Why don' chou lighten up, woman!

MAMMA. Lighten up? . . . Damn . . . man . . . I ain't here ten minutes before I see your face and you tell *me* to lighten up! I been with you since I hit the streets at noon and you still checkin' up on me . . . don't worry, man . . . I'm goin' ta get right ta work.

SHAKY (*slow and languid*). I know that, baby.

MAMMA (*to* PANDORA). Girl you should of seen Shaky . . . ha ha ha . . . almost swept me off my feet, girl. Said he loved me and really missed me so much the last ninety days that he almost went out of his mind . . . ha ha . . . (*Coyly*) I was so embarrassed and impressed, girl, I liked to have blushed and nearly peed on myself like a sixteen-year-old girl. (*Change of voice*) But the ole sonna bitch didn't fool me none with that shit . . . The only thing he missed was that good steady money!

CURT (*picqued*). Why don't you check yourself, Mamma!

MAMMA (*waving* CURT's *threat off and returning to the edge of the bed*). But, girl, he sho threw some lovin' on me . . . hee heee . . . sheeet, I should go away again after this afternoon. (PANDORA *laughs throughout*.) Ummm . . . chile . . . I nearly thought I was on that honeymoon I never had.

PANDORA. You should after that routine, baby.

MAMMA. And then when the sun start goin' down and things got really gettin' romantic, girl . . . this mathafukker says . . .

(*Lights lower; spot on bed.* SHAKY *speaks the line.*)

SHAKY. I want you to bring in a yard tonight, baby.

(MAMMA *resumes speech. Bed spot off; colored spot on* MAMMA.)

MAMMA. You what, man?

(*Colored spot off; bed spot on.*)

SHAKY. A hundred stone cold dollars, baby. Tonight, baby!

(*Spot off; lights go up.*)

MAMMA (*to* PANDORA). And girl, do you know what I said?

PANDORA. Yeah, I know what you said.

MAMMA. That's right, baby, I said to Shaky, "How do you want them daddy . . . in fives or tens?"

(*Laughter halts the speeches; the glasses are filled and fingers cleaned of chicken grease and cigarettes lit.*)

CURT (*to* SHAKY). Don't let Mamma try and fool you . . . she wanted to see you so bad . . . everytime Pan us'ta go visit her she would say to Pan, "How's that ole dirty Shaky doin?"

MAMMA. Yeah, I'd ask . . . cause I'd be wonderin' why ain't the mathafukker down here.

SHAKY. Now, let's not go into that again, baby.

CURT. Yeah, Mamma . . . you know what's happen'n behind that. You know why Shaky didn't come down . . . you never can tell when they might have a warrant out on him or some-thin' and keep him too. You remember what happened at court, don't cha?

MAMMA. Yeah, I remember. How can I forget? The judge said for Shaky to leave the court cause every time I'm on trial he's in the back row hangin' round and that last ole woman judge said she knew who Shaky was an' she'd like to put him behind bars instead of me . . . but comin' down to visit me in jail is different, Curt!

SHAKY (*pleading*). Now, baby . . .

CURT. Listen, Mamma . . . how old are you?

MAMMA. Twenty.

CURT. That means you're a big girl now, a woman who should be able to understand things, right?

MAMMA. Yeah, but . . .

CURT (*cutting*). Right! Now listen, baby . . . and listen hard . . . now how many times you been busted?

MAMMA. Thirty-three times . . . but I only fell this once for more than ten days and that was because I got that new fuckin' woman judge. I got the best record in town of any broad on the block I know. Pandora's rap sheet is worse than mine and I was on the block two years before she was.

CURT. Exactly, baby. Now if you didn't have an old man like Shaky out there workin' for you, you'd be out of business and servin' some big time . . . right? Wouldn't that be a drag to be servin' some grand theft time behind givin' up a little body! Pan ain't been snatched since before we were married . . . ain't that right, Pandora? See there? Now let me tell you, baby, and listen hard. (*Intensely*) A self-respectin' man won't let his ole lady stay in jail. If he can't get the bail for her or the juice to pay off somebody downtown like Shaky done you to have your time cut to one third . . . (*Disgust*) he's a punk! And any broad that even looks at the jive-sucker should get her funky ass run into the ground like a piece of scum!

MAMMA (*on defensive*). I know all that, Curt, but I got so lonely down there. Nothin' down there but broads and most of them are butches.

PANDORA. Mamma . . . don't even talk about it. Makes cold chills run up my back just thinkin' 'bout it.

CURT. Yeah, we know it was hard, baby, but you can't afford to lose your old man by his gettin' busted behind a jail visit. That would be a stone trick, Mamma. Nothin' but a hummer . . . Right?

MAMMA. Awww . . . Curt, you try and make it sound so smooth.

PANDORA. He can really make it do that, girl.

RICH (*finishes drinking the last of his beer*). Hey, Shaky, I want you to take a walk with me, okay?

SHAKY (*standing slowly and visibly rocking*). Yeah, man. (*To Mamma*) I'll see you back at the house, baby. Watch yourself.

MAMMA. I'll probably be in early, Shaky. Unless I catch somethin' good.

(RICH *and* SHAKY *exit by the front door.* PANDORA *accompanies them and checks the outside before they step out.*)

MAMMA. Sheeet, Pandora, I thought Shaky was the Chicken Delight man when he knocked. I wasn't here ten minutes before he was knockin' on the door to see if I had my ride to the club. Didn't even think about feedin' me. (*Soulful*) Just give me some good lovin' ta show me where it's at.

PANDORA. These men are somethin' else, girl . . . 'spect a girl to go out'ta here on an empty stomach and turn all kinds of tricks . . . but Curt and me did have some beans for you, girl, but I dropped them.

MAMMA. Well, I'm glad you did.

CURT (*packing away chessboard*). I told her you didn't want no beans, Mamma.

MAMMA. I got too many beans in the joint.

PANDORA (*peeved*). Well that's what I had for you, chick.

MAMMA (*to* ART). Hey, pretty baby, why you so quiet?

ART. Oh, I ain't got much to say, I guess.

CURT. This is my boy Art, Mamma. I introduced you when you came in.

MAMMA (*sultry*). I know his name . . . ha ha . . . I just want to know his game, dat's all. Hey, fuzz face, what's yo game? Is you kinda fuzzy wuzzy 'round the edges?

ART. I'm sorry . . . I don't know . . .

CURT. Awww . . . he's okay, Mamma . . . he was in the joint with me. He's just quiet, that's all. Reads too much . . . somethin' you should do more of.

PANDORA. Why should she? Ain't heard of nobody gettin' no money readin'.

MAMMA (*to* ART). Now I know your name, fuzzy boy, now you say my name.

ART (*surprise*). Your name?

MAMMA. Yeah. Say MAMA TOO TIGHT!

ART. I know your name.

MAMMA. But I want you to say it.

ART. I don't have to with you broadcasting it all over the place ever since you been here.

MAMMA (*cross*). You must think you're wise, man.

ART (*in low, even voice*). I am, you big-mouthed bitch and I want you to stop jivin' with me.

(PANDORA *giggles*. CURT *looks on enjoying the surprise showing on* MAMMA's *face.*)

MAMMA. Well . . . 'scuse me, tiger. (*Walks over to* ART *and sits beside him.*) Aww . . . forget it. I always act this way, ask Pan and Curt. 'Specially when I'm ah little bit loaded . . . Hey, Pandora, your friend here ain't got no sense of humor.

PANDORA. Nawh . . . he's too much like Curt. Serious. That's why they probably get along so good, girl . . . they probably made for each other.

(*The girls laugh.*)

CURT. C'mon, Pan . . . it's almost time for you to go to work. Deeny will be callin' nex' thing and that's one mathafukker I don't even want to see much less talk to. Go on and get the stuff.

(PANDORA *exits through the bathroom door.*)

MAMMA (*to* ART). You want to know why they call me Mamma Too Tight, pretty baby?

CURT. If Shaky ever heard you callin' my boy that he'd break your arm, Mamma.

MAMMA. Yeah, he might. But Shaky ain't where nothin's shakin' at the moment. . . . Just out givin' Rich a fix . . .

CURT. Both of you bitches talk too much!

MAMMA (*to* ART). You know what, fuzz wuzz? I sho wish I had a lil fuzzy wuzzy like you up there some of those cold nights in the joint. (*She gets up and walks to stand before the men. She plays it strictly for laughs, swinging her hips to the radio music, and singsongs in a hearty, brazen voice like one of the old-time red hot mamma's. Singing*) Why do they call me what they call me, baby. When what they call me is my name.

ART (*dryly*). I have suspicions but I'm not positive.

MAMMA (*ridiculing, but friendly*). You have suspicions as every little fuzzy wuzzy does but let me tell you . . . because my real name is Queenie Mack! Queenie Bell Mack! Ain't that some shit? No self-respectin' whore in the world can go 'round with a name like that unless she's in Mississippi . . . sheeet . . . Queenie!

ART. So you named yourself Mamma Too . . .

MAMMA (*cutting*). No! It just happened. I don't know how. I just woke up one day with my name that way . . . And I like it that way . . . it's me! (*Turning toward* ART) Don't you think it fits, honey?

ART. I think it really does.

MAMMA. Damn right it does. It makes me feel so alive. That's why I'm glad to be out . . .

CURT (*yelling*). Hey, Pandora!

MAMMA. Man, but it's so good to be high again. It's so good to be free.

(PANDORA *enters from the bathroom and descends the stairs and places a cardboard box on the table as the lights blacken briefly and the music rises.*)

ACT I

Scene III

As the lights go up and the music lowers, the scene has shifted. CURT *and* PANDORA *sit upon the couch, across from* ART, *and* MAMMA TOO TIGHT *has taken the stool* CURT *was seated on. Uncovered, the box waits in the center of the table.* CURT *is licking a brown cigarette as the theme plays.*

CURT. Yeah. We want to make some money, Art, so we can get out of this hole. (*Lights the cigarette and inhales fiercely. Drops head. Two-beat pause. In strained voice, holding smoke back*) We're makin' it to Buffalo, man. You hip to Buffalo?

ART. No, I don't think so . . .

CURT (*takes another drag*). It's a good little hustlin' town, I hear. I got a case comin' up here for passin' some bad paper, ya know, forgin' payroll checks . . . and when I get the money to make restitution and give the people downtown some juice, ya know, man, pay them off, I'm makin' it East. But I need some grand theft dough.

ART. But won't you get some time with your record?

CURT. Nawh. Probably not. You see, I'm a good thief. I take money by my wits . . . ya know, with a pen or by talkin' some sucker out of it. It's only seldom that I'm forced to really take any money by force. If I make full restitution for these checks and fix my lawyer up and the other people downtown, I'll get probation. They'll reduce it to a misdemeanor and breakin' probation for somethin' like that ain't nothin' . . . besides, Buffalo's a long way away, man.

PANDORA (*receiving cigarette from* CURT). It's supposed to be a good little town. A different scene entirely. I'm due for a good scene for a change.

CURT. Yeah, but we have to get that juice money first, baby. We gotta get us some long money.

MAMMA. Any place is better than L.A. but I heard that Buffalo is really boss.

PANDORA (*languid*). It sho is, baby.

MAMMA. I wonder if I could get Shaky to go?

CURT. Sure you could, Mamma. He can get connections to deal his stuff there just like here. That's the idea. When we make our hit and split out of here we're gon'a take as many as we can with us. You know, set up a kinda organization.

PANDORA (*passing cigarette to* MAMMA). They really got respect for cats from the coast back there.

ART (*getting caught up in the mood*). Yeah, they really do . . . when I . . .

PANDORA (*cutting speech*). With me workin' on the side and with Curt dealin' we'd be on our feet in no time.

CURT. We want to be on our feet when we get there, baby.

ART. And that's where I come in, right?

CURT. Right, good buddy.

MAMMA (*handing cigarette to* ART). Here, baby.

ART (*waving it away*). So what's on your mind, Curt?

MAMMA (*extending cigarette*). I said here, baby, I just don't like to hold this thing and see all this bread go up in ashes.

ART. I don't want any.

(*A three-beat stop, all caught in tableau staring at* ART, *then* PANDORA *snickers and breaks into a tittering laugh, looking at* CURT.)

PANDORA (*ridicule*). You and your friends, Curt . . . I thought . . .

CURT (*heated*). Shut up, bitch . . . you talk too much!

PANDORA (*rising anger*). Why shouldn't I when you bring some square-all little . . . (CURT *slaps her; she jumps to her feet and spins to claw him but* CURT *lunges forward and slaps her again, causing her to trip backwards across the edge of the coffee table. From the floor, removing one of her shoes)* God- damn you Curt . . . (*She begins to crawl to her knees and* CURT *moves around the table after her. Then* ART *steps between them and pushes* CURT *backward on the couch. Surprise is upon* CURT's *face and* MAMMA TOO TIGHT *seems frozen in place.*)

CURT. *What the fuck's goin' on, man?*

ART (*low*). Don't hit her any more, Curt.

CURT (*incredulous*). What? . . . Man, are you payin' this woman's bills . . . have you got any papers on her?

PANDORA (*to* CURT). *Are you payin' my bills, mathafukker?*

CURT (*rising to attack* PANDORA; ART *blocks his way*). I've told you to keep your mouth . . . (*To Art when he won't let him pass*) Now listen, Art, you're like a brother to me but you don't know what's goin' down, man.

ART. Why don't we all sit down and try and relax, Curt? Why don't you do it for me, huh? As a favor. I'm sorry for buttin' into your business between you and your ole lady but somethin' just happens to me, man, when I see a guy hit a girl.

(*After a minute,* CURT *is soothed and sits upon the couch again, glaring at* PANDORA *who holds her shoe like a weapon.*)

MAMMA (*partially recovered*). Oh, man, I just hit the streets and this is what I run into . . .

CURT (*intense, to* ART). What are you doin', man? Squarin' out on me? Man, I've went a long way . . .

ART (*leaning forward*). Well, look, Curt . . . I can split . . .

(CURT *stands and looks down on* ART. *Changing expression,* PANDORA *makes a move for the box but* CURT *waves her hand away.*)

CURT. No, I don't think you better try that, Art. (*Pause*). Tell me, Art. Why don't you want to smoke any marijuana?

ART. Why don't . . . I don't understand why you should ask me that.

CURT. Is your playin' hero for Pandora a game to cover up somethin', man?

(MAMMA *is clutching herself as if she has returned to the womb.*)

MAMMA. Oh . . . shit shit shit . . . shit . . . just today . . . just today they cut me loose . . . just today.

PANDORA (*no longer angry, placing hand on* CURT's *arm*). Easy, baby, I think he's okay.

CURT. You would!

ART. Now, look, man, I don't put down anybody for doin' what they want but just don't hassle me!

PANDORA (*hostile, to* ART). Cool it, baby, you're in some deep trouble now.

MAMMA. Oh, goddamn . . . why can't I just be plain ass Queenie Bell Mack?

CURT (*low*). What's happen'n, brother?

ART. I just don't get high . . . that's all . . .

MAMMA (*nearly screaming*). Neither does J. Edgar Hoover, sucker, but he don't come in here pretend'n to be no friend!

PANDORA (*enraged, fearful of losing control, to* MAMMA). Shut up, bitch! This is Curt and our place. We got mo' to lose than just our ass. Just shut on up!

(MAMMA *looks almost like a small girl with wide, moist eyes.*)

CURT. For the last time, Art, tell me somethin'.

ART. I just don't . . .

(PANDORA *stands and moves in front of* CURT. *The coffee table separates them from* ART, *but she leans over.*)

PANDORA (*to* CURT, *behind her*). He's all right, honey. If he were a cop he'd be smokin' stuff right along with us . . . you know that . . .

ART (*bewildered*). A cop! . . .

PANDORA (*sarcastic*). He's just a little square around the edges, Curt . . . (*Silence, then to* ART) But why, honey?

ART (*shrugging sheepishly*). I had a bad experience once behind pot, that's all.

(MAMMA *cackles until* CURT *stops her.*)

MAMMA. He had a bad experience . . . hee hee hee . . . ha ha ha . . . He had . . .

CURT (*menace*). Pan has already told you to check yourself, woman, he's still my friend.

PANDORA. What was it all about, man . . . can you tell us about it?

ART. I'd rather not . . .

CURT (*cutting*). We know you'd rather not but . . .

PANDORA (*cutting*). Now look, Art, you're not givin' us much of a break . . . we don't want to act like this but we got a lot of the future riding on what happens in the nex' few days. Why don't you tell us?

ART. I would but it don't seem that much . . .

CURT (*not so threatening*). But it is, Art!

PANDORA. C'mon, trust me. Can't you say anything? We've gone more than half- . . .

CURT. Stop rankin' him, will ya!

PANDORA. I'm only doin' it for you!

(*Silence as* CURT *and* PANDORA *stare at each other.*)

ART. Yeah, I'll talk about it . . . (CURT *sits.* PANDORA *moves around the table closer to* ART. *The cigarette has been dropped by* MAMMA *beside the box. "Delilah" plays.*) You see . . . it was about three years ago. I shipped out on a freighter . . . ya know, one of those scows that fly the Panamanian or Liberian flag but don't really belong to any country . . .

MAMMA (*in small girl's voice*). Ain't they Americans?

ART. Well, in a way. They belong to American corporations and the businessmen don't want to pay high taxes on 'em. They're pretty ratty. (PANDORA *makes a seat on the floor between the men.*) Well I went on a four-month cruise, ya know, to ports around the West Indies and then to North Africa.

MAMMA. Wow . . . that sounds gassy . . . I wish . . .

PANDORA (*cutting*). Mamma!

ART. Well I been blowin' weed since I was about twelve . . .

MAMMA (*ridicule*). Ha ha ha . . . since he was twelve . . .

(PANDORA *and* CURT *frown at her and she huddles in her seat and looks cold.*)

ART. . . . and everything was cool. I smoked it when I ran into it and never thought about it much unless someone turned me on. But in Tangier it was about as easy to get as a bottle of beer. Man, I had a ball all the while I was over there and before I left I bought a big bag. (*Showing with his hands*) This big for about five bucks. All the way back on my night watches I just smoked grass and just thought of what the guys on my corner back home would say when I would pull out a joint or two and just give it to them. Prices back East are about triple what they are here, so you can guess what it was worth . . . And all the broads I would make . . . you know how it goes . . . take a broad up to your room and smoke a little weed and if you have anything goin' for you at all, man, that's it.

PANDORA (*disgust*). Yeah, there's a lot of stupid broads in this world.

ART (*sensing the reduced tension*). And I could still sell some when my money got low and come out beautiful. I was really feeling good about that grass, Curt. Well this tub docks in Philly about 1:00 A.M. and I have to leave ship and when I get to the station I find that my train don't leave until two the next afternoon. I got my pay and my belongings, so I stash most of my bags in a locker at the station, the bag of weed is in one but I have about half a dozen joints on me. Now I know Philly a little. I know where there's an after-hour joint so I grab a cab and go over there. The place is jumpin' . . . they're havin' a fish fry, and I start in drinkin' and talkin' to girls but none of them are listen'n 'cept for seven bucks for them and three for the management for rentin' one of the upstairs rooms, and I ain't buyin' no cock . . . not in the States . . .

PANDORA. Well, I'm glad of that. I can take squares but not tricks, baby.

CURT (*to* PANDORA). You still runnin' your mouth, ain't you?

ART. So I start talkin' with some guy and he tells me of a place he knows 'cross town that's better than this one. He looks okay to me. A blood. Dressed real sharp with a little goatee and everything. I had been talkin' to him about bein' out to sea and since he don't try and con me into a crap game and is buyin' one drink for every one of mine, I don't give a damn where we go cause I got the whole night to kill.

MAMMA. Oh wow . . . I know this is the bad part . . .

PANDORA. Listen, Mamma.

MAMMA (*turning her face away*). I don't like to hear bad things.

ART. So we drinkin' bottles of beer and drivin' up Broad Street in Philly in his old wreck of a Buick and I think how it would be nice to turn on and get really loaded before we get where we're goin'. So I reach for my pocket but it's wintertime and I got on a pea jacket and sweaters and I have trouble gettin' to my pocket. And while I was lookin' I start in laughin'.

CURT. Laughin'?

ART. Yeah. I start wonderin' what would happen if this was a cop I was with and the idea was just too much. So funny. So I started in laughin'. And the guy asks me what I was laughin' at and I said I was just laughin' about him bein' a cop. And he said that he was and how did I know. (*Two-beat pause*) I don't know how I got out of that car or away from him. But soon after I was pukin' my guts up, and I threw those joints into a sewer and they wouldn't go down 'cause snow and ice was cloggin' it up. And I was stompin' on 'em so they would go down and gettin' sick and after a while my feet were all covered with ice and snow and puke and marijuana . . . Ya know . . . I had nearly twenty bucks worth of dope frozen to the soles of my shoes.

MAMMA (*seriously*). Awww . . . no, man . . . I can't stand any more.

PANDORA (*giggling*). That's the best trip I've been on this week, Art.

ART. Nawh, really . . . baby. And the bag . . . I left it in a locker. Not the one I used but another empty one.

MAMMA. Those janitors must'a naturally been happy the next day.

ART. Yeah, they must have been but I couldn't even think of the stuff for a long time without wanting to heave up my guts.

CURT. That must'a been pretty scary, man.

(PANDORA *has reached over and gotten the cigarette and relit it.*)

PANDORA (*offering it to* ART). Now it's time to get back on the horse, cowboy.

ART (*placing hand on stomach*). I don't think I can.

MAMMA. You'll never think about that time in Philly again after the first drag, baby.

CURT. C'mon, man, you're already one of us. Do you think I'd bring you in if I thought you'd be a square?

PANDORA. Don't say that, Curt. He's not. Somethin' like what happened to him can mess up your mind about things. (*She stands over him and puffs on the cigarette. Staring at him*) Now don't think about anything . . . just look into my eyes. (*She inhales once more and gives the cigarette to* ART.) Now, here, put it in your mouth.

ART (*takes it and puts to lips*). I can do it all right but I just don't want to.

PANDORA (*staring*). Look into my eyes and inhale. Don't think about it being in your hand. (ART *inhales and looks at her.*) All the way down now and hold it.

MAMMA. Don't ever say you don't believe in witches, boy.

CURT. Cool it, Mamma!

PANDORA. Now one more drag, Art.

(ART *takes another puff and hands the reefer to* CURT. ART *has a great grin on his face.*)

ART. So that's what's in Pandora's box.

(*Lights change.*)

PANDORA (*fantasy*). Among other things, Art. Among other

things. But those have been lies you've been told about bad things comin' out of Pandora's box.

MAMMA. Most people think that a girl's box is in other places.

PANDORA. Nothin' can be found bad in there either. People only bring evil there with them. They only look for evil there. The sick . . .

ART. What do you mean by sick?

PANDORA. The come freaks, that's who. The queers who buy sex from a woman.

MAMMA (*bitterly*). Yeah, they say we're wrong but they're the queers . . . payin' for another person's body.

CURT (*in euphoria, musing*). Art, my man, we're goin'a Buffalo . . . goin' one day real soon.

PANDORA (*repulsion*). Some of them are real nice-lookin' cats. Not old with fat greasy bellies. Real nice-lookin' studs. (*Bitterly*) Those are the real queers you have ta watch. They want ta hurt women.

MAMMA. You hip ta that, baby? Those muscle cats, you know, muscle queens . . . always wantin' ta freak out on ya.

ART. And that's all that comes out of Pandora's box?

(CURT *pulls a nickel-plated revolver out of the box.*)

CURT. No. Right now this is the most important thing. There's always something new in there. (*Handing gun to* ART) Feel it, brother.

(ART *takes the gun. He is caught up in the music and with his new friends.*)

ART. It's a good one.

MAMMA. Look how it shines.

(*Lights change.*)

ART (*dreamlike*). Yeah . . . like Pandora's eyes.

(*Lights change.*)

PANDORA (*fantasy*). Nothin' bad comes out of me or from my box, baby. Nothin' bad. You can believe that. It's all in what you bring to us.

(*Lights change.*)

MAMMA. That's wha's happen'n, baby.

CURT. It's yours now, Art, as much yours as mine. Can you handle it, brother?

ART (*looking at Pandora and taking a new reefer*). If that's my job, brother.

(*The cigarette has been replaced by a new one and others are in the hands of the group;* PANDORA *drags in deeply.*)

PANDORA. Buffalo's goin'a be a gas.

(*The phone rings from the dressing room and* CURT *goes to answer. His shadow can be seen upon the wall at the top of the stairs.*)

CURT (*off*). Yeah, Deeny . . . yeah yeah yeah . . . yeah, man, . . . yeah.

MAMMA. Who ever heard of a telephone in the toilet?

PANDORA. It's in the dressing room next to the bathroom, Mamma.

MAMMA. Sho is strange . . . Hey, are you goin'a Buffalo too, fuzz wuzz?

ART. It looks that way.

PANDORA (*smiling*). I think I'll like that, Art. I think that'll be nice.

(*A knock sounds at the front door.* CURT's *shadow hangs up the phone and retreats farther into the area.*)

CURT (*off*). Pandora! Move! Goddamn it! Get a move on!

(ART *stands as* PANDORA *jumps to her feet. He has a cross expression as he looks toward the dressing room entrance.*)

ART (*to* PANDORA). Can I help you?

(PANDORA *shakes her head.*)

ART. Is there anything I can do?

PANDORA. No, I don't think anybody can do anything, especially you. (*She places the gun and the marijuana in the box and hurries up the stairs. The knock comes again.*)

MAMMA (*still seated, toward door*). Just a minute!

(ART *watches* PANDORA *enter dressing room.*)

MAMMA. You want to get the door, Art?

ART. I learned once never to open another man's door.

(PANDORA *and* CURT, *in coats, come from the dressing room;* PANDORA *has her costumes in her arms.*

MAMMA TOO TIGHT *gets up and walks downstage.*)

CURT. That fuckin' Deeny wants you to rehearse some new music before your act, Pan.

PANDORA. Sonna bitch! Always late payin' somebody and always wantin' you to work your ass off.

CURT. Is your car parked far, Art?

ART. Not too far.

MAMMA (*looking out window*). It's only Rich.

CURT. Good. He can stay here and watch the phone while we're at the club. First, we'll stop and get you some gas, Art, and then you can take us to the Strip Club.

PANDORA. Is your car big enough to get us all to the Strip Club on Western, Art?

ART. It'll even get us as far as Buffalo, Pandora.

(*They exit.* RICH *enters, turns in doorway and is seen talking to someone outside. Then he shuts door, saunters gracefully across the room, and turns the radio off. Lights dim out as he sprawls upon the couch.*)

CURTAIN

ACT II

The curtain opens showing the Strip Club, or rather the sug-gested representation of a cheap night club in the Wilshire area of Los Angeles, featuring "Bronze" stripteasers. But the effect should be directed toward the illusions of time, place, and matter. Reality is questionable here. The set should be painted in lavish phony hues except for the bare brown floor. Seeing the set the female audience should respond with: "gorgeous, lovely, marvelous, delightful," and similar banalities. The men should wonder if the habitat of whores is not indeed the same as the region of their creatures of private myth, dream, and fantasy.

A rotating color wheel, in front of the major lights, should turn constantly throughout this scene, giving an entire spectrum of altering colored shadows. Additional colored lights and spots should be used to stress mood changes and the violence of the ending scene.

A musician plays randomly at the piano. He is tall, wearing a dark suit with an open-necked dark shirt. The bartender, wiry with his head shaven clean, sweeps the floor and empties ash trays. A few customers sit and watch the musician, and, later, the group, as the show hasn't begun.

The voice which is heard at the close of this act can be that of a customer.

Two other musicians enter and climb upon the stage.

PIANO PLAYER (*joking, to* BASS PLAYER *seated at piano*). Hey, man, they lookin' for bass players all up and down the street but you cats are all bangin' out chords on out-of-tune pianos.

BASS PLAYER. What's happen'n, man? Say . . . listen to this . . . (*He plays a couple of frames.*) What about that, man . . . huh?

PIANO PLAYER. Man, like I said . . . you're a damn good bass man . . .

BASS PLAYER (*getting up*). What you say about somebody lookin' for bass men? . . . Man! Turn me on. I wouldn't be here in this trap if I knew where one of those gigs were.

DRUMMER (*seated, working up a beat*). Yeah, man, they need you like they need me.

PIANO (*wryly*). How's it feel to keep gettin' replaced by a juke box?

(BASS PLAYER *begins working with* DRUMMER. PIANO PLAYER *strikes a few chords, then lights a cigarette.*)

BASS. Hey, where's Stew and Ronny? I want to practice those new charts before Pandora gets in.

PIANO (*blowing smoke out*). They quit.

BASS (*halting*). What?

DRUMMER. Deeny wouldn't pay them this afternoon and pushed the new charts on them. They didn't want to learn new scores, not getting paid the money owed them, so they quit.

BASS. Just like that . . . they quit?

PIANO. This is our last night here, too. Deeny's in trouble with the union. No more gigs here until the hearin'.

BASS. Awww, man . . . there's always some shit with that jive-ass sucker. Is we gettin' our bread from Deeny tonight?

DRUMMER. Who knows? He don't have to pay until the last performance, and the union says stay on the gig until tonight.

BASS. We always gettin' put in some cross . . .

PIANO. Yeah, man. But juke boxes don't go on strike and Deeny knows we know it, so let's take care of business.

BASS. Man, don't tell me that . . . the broads can't dance to no juke box.

PIANO (*seriously*). Why not, man?

BASS. It just ain't done, man. No machine ain't never goin'a take a musician's play from him when it comes to providin' music for shows.

PIANO. Don't believe it, baby . . . in a couple of mo' years they'll find a way. Broads will be shakin' their cans to canned music just as good as to your playin' or mine and the customers will be payin' even higher prices . . . nobody wins, man. Least of all us. C'mon, let's hit it . . .

(*He begins playing "Delilah" as* PANDORA, MAMMA TOO TIGHT, *and* CURT *make their entrances. The girls wave at the musicians and stop at the bar, then move to a table near the bandstand.* PANDORA *places her costumes on an empty chair of a nearby table.* CURT *stands with his back to the bar.*)

PIANO. Okay. That's better . . . c'mon . . . Cook! . . .

BASS (*not enthused, to* MAMMA *who waves again*). Hey, pretty girl . . .

(ART *walks in, saunters to the cigarette machine;* CURT *joins the girls.*)

CURT. Hey, I wonder where everybody's at.

DRUMMER (*stopping, followed by others*). Hey . . . hey . . . what's the use of this fuckin' shit . . . ?

PIANO. What's happen'n now, man?

(DRUMMER *hops from stage*.)

MAMMA. Damn . . . Stew and Ronny must be late, Pan.

PANDORA (*to* BARTENDER). What happened to your boss, Deeny, Chico?

(BARTENDER *ignores her*.)

DRUMMER (*to* PIANO PLAYER). Not a thing, man . . . everything's cool . . . (*Goes to bar, to* BARTENDER) Hey, Chico. Give me a screwdriver and charge it to your boss.

BARTENDER. Deeny ain't in the charity business, baby.

(ART *sits down with his friends. One of the customers leaves*.)

PANDORA (*to* BARTENDER). Yeah, baby, give me the usual and give my friends what they want. Put it on my tab.

DRUMMER (*to* BARTENDER). You let me and Deeny worry about that, cool breeze. Give me a screwdriver like I said.

(BARTENDER *goes behind bar and begins mixing* DRUMMER's *drink*.)

BARTENDER (*sullenly, to* PANDORA). When you gonna take care of that tab, sweetcake?

PANDORA (*angry*). When your fuckin' boss pays me, mister! Now get us our drinks, please!

CURT (*to* BASS PLAYER *who stands beside instrument*). Where's Deeny?

(PIANO PLAYER *has gotten off of stage and talks to* DRUMMER *at the bar. A customer goes to jukebox and looks over the selections*.)

PIANO. What's happen'n, man? We got to make this gig . . . that's what the union says.

DRUMMER. Fuck the union.

BASS (*to* CURT) It's a mystery to me, Curt.

MAMMA (*to* BASS PLAYER). That number's a gassy one, honey. Pan's gonna work by that, ain't she?

BASS. Looks that way, Mamma, if anybody works at all tonight.

PIANO (*to* DRUMMER). Awww, man . . . you know I know how you feel . . .

DRUMMER. Well, just don't run that crap down to me. I'm just fed up. The union screws you out of your dues and the clubs fuck you every chance they get . . .

PIANO. It ain't exactly that way . . . now if . . .

MAMMA. Don't you like Pan's new number, Art?

(ART *doesn't answer. The customer drops a coin into the jukebox and punches a selection; "Something Cool" sung by June Christie is played.*)

PANDORA (*to* ART *and* MAMMA). Can't come in here one day without some shit goin' down. Where's the brass so I can rehearse?

MAMMA. They better get here soon, honey. It'll be too late after a while.

BASS (*to* PAN). Forget about it, Pan. They ain't no brass tonight.

DRUMMER (*to* PIANO PLAYER). Well I know all that, but it's no use rehearsin' without any brass and if this is our last night anyhow . . .

CURT (*rising and going to the bar*). You said this is the last night, man?

PANDORA (*to* BASS PLAYER). NO BRASS!

MAMMA (*to* ART). You hear what he said?

BASS (*putting down instrument*). Hey, fix me a C.C. and ginger ale, Chico!

(*Customer who played record goes to the bar and sits down.*)

PANDORA (*to* BARTENDER). Hey, what about our drinks, man?

BARTENDER. Okay, Pandora . . . just a minute.

CURT. Hey, fellas . . . what's goin' down?

(*The musicians tell* CURT *about the trouble as the scene plays on in center stage at the table. The conversations should overlap as they have but become increasingly rapid and confusing if necessary. After the musicians are served the* BARTENDER *takes the orders at* PANDORA'S *table as* CURT *continues to talk at the bar.)*

PANDORA. Shit . . . no brass . . . musicians quittin' . . . I ain't got no job no more.

MAMMA. Yeah. It don't look so good but perhaps Deeny can do somethin' when he comes in . . .

PANDORA. Deeny . . . shit . . . Deeny . . . all he can do! . . . *(furious, searching for words)* Why, shit, woman! Deeny can't even do numbers and shit cucumbers!

ART. Thanks for the drink, Pan.

PANDORA. Is that all you can do, man? Say thank you?

ART. No. It's not the only thing.

*(*MAMMA *gets up and goes over to the* BASS PLAYER *who drops out of the conversation between* CURT, *the other two musicians, and the* BARTENDER. *Another customer leaves, leaving only one sitting upon a stool, attempting to get the* BARTENDER'S *attention.)*

BARTENDER. Well look, man, I only work here. You better settle that with Deeny.

(Behind the bar the phone rings. The BARTENDER *answers.)*

CURT. If that's Deeny I want to talk to him.

BARTENDER. Hey, man, I'm talkin' on the phone.

DRUMMER. Let me talk to the mathafukker! *(He tries to reach across the bar.)*

BARTENDER *(backing off).* Hey, cool it! Wait!

PIANO *(grabbing* DRUMMER'S *arm).* Hold it, man!

DRUMMER. Take your fuckin' hands off me, baby!

BARTENDER. Wait, I said.

CURT. Tell Deeny I'm waitin' for him.

*(*DRUMMER *breaks away from* PIANO PLAYER *and begins around the bar.* BARTENDER *reaches under bar for a weapon.)*

BARTENDER *(shouts).* Wait!

(The scene freezes in tableau except for the BARTENDER, PANDORA, *and* CURT. *Lights go down to purples and deep shadow*

shades as an eerie spot plays upon the table. Occasionally from the shadows voices are heard.)

BARTENDER (*in shadows*). Okay, Deeny. I'll be expectin' ya.

PANDORA (*to* ART). So he's comin'.

ART. Yeah, no need to wait for very long now.

PANDORA. What else can you do, Art?

ART. What else can I do except say thank you, you mean?

PANDORA. Yeah. That's what I mean.

ART. I can wait, Pandora.

PANDORA (*jolly*). What's the good of waitin' when things have ta be done? Is that why you have to eat at Rescue Missions and get favors from friends, baby? Cause you waitin'? Tell me. What are you waitin' on, Art?

ART. Me? I'm just waitin' so I won't jump into somethin' too fast and I think you should do the same.

PANDORA. I didn't know you gave out advice too. But I wish I could take some of it. Ya see, we're already in the middle of some deep shit . . . There just ain't time to sit back and cool it, honey . . .

ART (*disregarding the ridicule in her voice, soothing*). Yes you can . . . just sit back and look around and wait a while. You don't have to do anything . . . baby, the whole world will come to you if you just sit back and be ready for it.

PANDORA (*serious*). I wish I could. But so much has to be done and we keep fallin' behind.

BARTENDER (*in shadows*). Now what can I do, man? Deeny left with Pete and he said he'd be right back and for you guys to practice with the girls.

(*One of the customers who walked out enters with a* SHOW GIRL. *She is dark and thin and pretty in a tinseled way. They stop in the shadows and whisper and the girl separates from him, enters the light, passes through and heads toward the dressing rooms in the rear. The* CUSTOMER *takes a seat at the bar. He is engulfed by shadows and becomes frozen in place like the others.*)

PANDORA (*nodding to show girl as she passes*). Hi, Cookie. I really dig that dress, baby.

ART. Things can always get worse, Pan.

PANDORA. Oh, you're one of those? How can they? Just lost my job. This was to keep me goin' until you guys turned up somethin' big and I didn't even get paid from the last two weeks so I know this just means another great big zero.

ART. What do you think will happen now?

PANDORA. I don't know . . . the job Curt's got planned can't be pulled off until three more days and in a week we got to have all our money together for the restitution and juice . . . not to mention the goin' away money. And I'm not even goin'a get paid for this gig.

ART. Haven't you got any now?

PANDORA. Just a couple of hundred but we can't go into that. Got to hold onto it. We wouldn't eat if we didn't have to. We got to hold on to every cent.

BARTENDER (*in shadows*). Do you want that scotch with anything?

(DRUMMER *momentarily breaks out of position.*)

DRUMMER. I ain't finished talkin' yet, Chico.

BARTENDER. Just a minute, man.

(MAMMA *breaks out of position and goes to* PANDORA.)

MAMMA. Lend me a dime, Pan. I got to call Shaky.

PANDORA (*fishing in her oversized purse*). You got somethin' workin', baby?

MAMMA. Yeah. Slim's gonna get somethin' from Shaky.

PANDORA. That's workin'.

(*She gives* MAMMA *a coin.* MAMMA *enters the shadows and walks to the rear of the club.* PANDORA *notices* ART *looking at her.*)

PANDORA. Forget about her. Shaky's got her up tight. All you could do is play young lover a little. You can't support her habit, Art.

ART. She can't have a habit if she's just hit the street.

PANDORA. She's got one. What do you think they came in high on? In a couple more days she'll be hooked as bad as before. Shaky'll see to that.

ART. What does she do it for?

PANDORA. What does . . . ? Awww, man . . . what kinda question is that? I thought you knew somethin', baby.

ART. I tried to ask an honest question, Pan.

PANDORA. Is it an honest question when you don't have anything to go by to compare her experience with yours?

ART. I don't know. Is it?

PANDORA. Do you know how it feels havin' somebody paw all over you every day?

ART. Well, no . . .

PANDORA. Then you don't know that she has to use that stuff to put off the reality of it happen'n?

ART. Oh, I see.

PANDORA (*bitter*). Yeah, you see. Do you see her givin' up her body every day and murdering herself every day? Is that what the world has brought to her, Art? That's all she can look forward to each day . . . killin' herself with that needle by inches. She has her fix, and maybe a bust and she has keepin' her man. She just takes her fixes to get through the day and Shaky keeps her on it so she'll need him more.

ART. That's too bad.

PANDORA. Wait a minute, Art. Don't sing no sad songs for that woman, you understand? She's not askin' for your pity. She's a real woman in some ways and she won't let you take it away from her by your pity. She'd spit on your pity.

ART (*annoyed*). And you?

(*Lights change.*)

PANDORA (*fantasy*). And me? . . . Well I ain't no whore . . . I'm just makin' this money so Curt and me can get on our feet. One day we gonna own property and maybe some businesses when we get straight . . . and out of this town.

ART. In Buffalo?

PANDORA. Maybe if we decide to stay there but I'm really an entertainer. I'll show you my act one day and Curt's got a good mind. He's a good hustler but he's givin' that up after a while. He can be anything he wants.

(*Lights change.*)

ART. What does he want?

PANDORA. He wants what I want.

ART. How do you know?

PANDORA. He tells me . . . We talk about it all the time.

ART. Can you be sure?

PANDORA. Sure?

ART. Yeah . . . like Mamma's sure she'll always get her fix and her bail paid.

PANDORA. You little smooth-faced punk . . . wha . . .

ART (*cutting*). Some guys are really lucky.

PANDORA. Kiss my ass, sucker!

ART. Curt and Shaky are really into something.

PANDORA. Yeah! Because they're men!

ART. Is that what bein' a man is, bein' lucky?

PANDORA. No. It's from gettin' what you want.

ART. And how do you get what you want, Pan?

PANDORA. You go after it.

ART. And after you have it.

PANDORA. Then maybe it's yours and you can do whatever you want with it.

ART. And what if I wanted you, Pandora?

PANDORA (*three-beat pause*). You don't have enough to give me, Art. What could you give me that would make things better for me?

ART. I'm not a giver, Pan. I'm a taker.

(*Lights go up evenly. Figures become animated and resume activities. The* BARTENDER *pours drinks and nods to grumbling musicians and to* CURT. *A customer goes to jukebox and drops coin in. "Parisian Thoroughfare" plays. The* SHOW GIRL, *in thin robe, revealing skimpy costume, walks from the rear and takes seat beside customer she entered with.* MAMMA TOO TIGHT *goes to the table and sits.*)

MAMMA (*brightly*). What you guys been talkin' bout so long?

PANDORA. Nothin' much, why?

MAMMA. Oh nothin' . . . just thought I'd ask. But the way you and old fuzz wuzz was goin' at it and lookin' at each other . . .

PANDORA. Looks can't hurt you, Mamma, but your big mouth can.

MAMMA (*fake surprise*). Pan . . . I didn't mean . . .

PANDORA. I'm sure you didn't, Mamma!

MAMMA (*now hurt*). Now listen, Pan. If you can't take a little teasin' . . . What's wrong with you? This is my first day home and you been on my ass all the time. Girl . . . you been the best friend I ever had, but lighten up.

PANDORA. Awww, Mamma . . . let's not you and me start in actin' flaky . . .

ART. Would you like a drink, Mamma?

MAMMA (*pleased*). Yeah . . . but you can't pry Chico from behind that bar.

(ART *stands and places hand upon* MAMMA's *shoulder.*)

ART. That's okay. Just sit. (*He goes to bar and stands beside* CURT *who has his back to him, drinking and brooding.*)

MAMMA (*to Pandora*). Hey, he's so nice.

PANDORA. See . . . I told you I wasn't tryin' to steal your little playmate.

MAMMA (*serious*). If I didn't know you was kiddin' I wouldn't take that, Pan.

PANDORA. You wouldn't? . . . Well, I wasn't kiddin', broad!

MAMMA (*half rising*). Hey, check yourself, girl. This is me! Remember? Mamma Too Tight. Don't you know me? Lil ole Queenie Bell Mack from Biloxi, Mississippi.

PANDORA. Okay. Sit down before you trip over yourself. I know who you are.

MAMMA (*sitting*). And I know you too, baby. Remember I

was the one who was there those times so many yesterdays ago. Remember? I was there with you holding your hand in those dark, little lonely rooms all them nights that your man was out on a job . . . Remember how we shivered together, girl? Remember how we cried together each time he got busted and sent away again . . . I'm your friend, baby . . . and you actin' like this to me?

PANDORA (*genuine*). I'm sorry, Mamma. It's just that Art. He's different. Everything seems different when he's around.

MAMMA. I think I know what you mean, Pan. I think I know . . .

(*Lights dim; color wheel still throws pastel shadows.* CURT *and* ART *stand in spot at end of bar. In the shadows there are rustles from the other people and lighted cigarettes arc through the gloom toward mouths which suck at them like spiders draining fireflies.* CURT *turns.*)

CURT. Hey, Art. Sorry to put you through all this hassle but some bad shit is goin' down, man. I'm really gettin' worried . . . If things keep breakin' bad like this . . .

ART. Don't worry about me, Curt. I'm just along for the ride. Try and get yourself together. It don't matter to me what you have to go through to get yourself straight, man. Just work it on out.

(*Spot off* ART *and* CURT. *Spot on* SHOW GIRL *and* CUSTOMER.)

CUSTOMER. How 'bout it, sugar?

SHOW GIRL. Are you kiddin', man?

CUSTOMER (*whining*) Well christ . . . twenty-five bucks . . . what's it lined with . . . gold or somethin'?

SHOW GIRL. You see those two broads over at that table?

(*Lights on* PANDORA *and* MAMMA.)

CUSTOMER. Yeah. You suggestin' that I hit on them?

SHOW GIRL. Yeah. Do that. The one in the black dress won't even speak to you unless you're ready to leave a hundred or more . . . and besides . . . she has to like your type first. The other one might consider it for fifty.

CUSTOMER. Who's the girl in the black dress?

(*Lights change.*)

SHOW GIRL. That's *Pandora*. She headlines the Revue. You have to give her twenty bucks just to get her phone number. So why don't you go hit on her?

(*Lights off. Spot on* BARTENDER.)

BARTENDER. You call yourselves artists and then you want me to bleed for you? What kinda crap is that?

DRUMMER (*in shadows*). Listen you jive-time whiskey-pourer. We are artists and I don't care what you call us or how you bleed. It's cats like you and your boss who make us all the time have to act like thugs, pimps and leeches to just make it out here in this world.

BARTENDER. So why ya tellin' me? So make it some other way?

PIANO PLAYER (*in shadows*). It's just impossible to talk to you people . . . it's just impossible to be heard any more.

(*Spot off* BARTENDER. *Spot on* CURT *and* ART.)

CURT. Yeah . . . when I first met her, Art. You should of seen her. It was in a joint somethin' like this . . .

(*Light off; spot picks up* PANDORA *standing in the door looking younger, nervous.* CURT *crosses stage to meet her as he speaks.*)

CURT (*entering light*). She was just eighteen . . . had the prettiest little pair of tits poking right out at me . . . sharp enough to put your eyes out. (*He takes* PANDORA *in his arms and kisses her violently. She resists but he is overwhelming.*)

PANDORA (*young voice*). I beg your pardon, mister.

CURT. I said that you're beautiful . . . that I want you . . . that you are mine forever . . . that it will always be this way for you, for you are mine. (*He brutally subdues her. Her hair falls across her face. Her face has that expression that prisoners' sometimes have when they are shifted without prior explanation from an old cell to an unfamiliar cell, equally as old.*)

PANDORA. Are you the man I'm to love?

CURT (*dragging her into the shadows*). Don't talk of something you'll never know anything about . . .

(*They speak from the shadows now, facing the audience.*)

PANDORA. I can't love you? I can't love if I even wanted . . . ?

CURT. You are mine . . . my flesh . . . my body . . . you are in my keeping.

PANDORA. Is it so much to ask for . . . just to be your woman?

CURT. You will do as I say . . . your flesh, your soul, your spirit is at my command . . . I possess you . . .

PANDORA. First there were others . . . now there is you . . . always the same for me . . .

(*Lights change.*)

CURT (*in shadows, walking toward* ART). Yeah . . . she was ready . . . has always been.

(*Spot on* ART. CURT *enters light.*)

ART. Pandora's a beautiful girl, Curt. You're lucky, man, to have her. I envy you.

CURT. Thanks, Art.

ART. Don't mention it, don't mention it at all.

(*Lights go down. Come up with* SHAKY *sitting at the table with* MAMMA *and* PANDORA.)

SHAKY. What's happen'n, baby?

MAMMA. Nothin' yet, Shaky. Give me time. The joint ain't even open yet.

SHAKY. Don't take too long, woman.

MAMMA. Give me time, Shaky. Why you got to come on so strong, man? You know I always take care of business. You know I got to get used to it agin. Didn't I set up that thing between you and Slim?

SHAKY. Yeah, baby. But that's my department. You take care of business on your side of the street. (*The* BASS PLAYER *comes over to the table. To* BASS PLAYER) Let's take a walk, poppa.

BASS. After you, Shake Shake.

MAMMA. I'll be here, Shaky.

SHAKY. Let's hope you're either here or there . . . okay?

MAMMA. Shaky . . . you're goin' too fast. Don't push me so hard.

SHAKY (*leaving*). Tonight, baby. One hundred stone cold dollars, baby.

(*Light on* SHOW GIRL *and* CUSTOMER.)

SHOW GIRL. They're alone. Why not now?

CUSTOMER. Okay . . . okay . . . twenty-five you get . . . after the show tonight.

(*Lights off; spot on* CURT *and* ART.)

CURT. When I saw you in action, Art, I said to myself I could really use that kid. Man, you're like a little brother to me now, man. I watch the way you act around people. You think on your feet and study them like a good gambler does. You're like me in a lot of ways. Man, we're a new breed, ya know. Renegades. Rebels. There's no rules for us . . . we make them as we break them.

ART. Sounds kind'a romantic, Curt.

CURT. And why shouldn't it? Man, this ain't a world we built so why should we try and fit in it? We have to make it over the best we can . . . and we are the ones to do it. We are, man, we are!

(*Spot on* MAMMA.)

MAMMA. I don't know why I'm this way . . . I just am. Is it because my name is different and I am different? Is it because I talk like a spade?

PANDORA (*from shadows*). Take a look at that! Just because this white broad's been hangin' out with us for a couple of years she's goin' ta blame that bad talk on us.

(*Light on table.*)

PANDORA (*to* MAMMA). When you brought your funky ass from Mississippi woman we couldn't even understand you . . . sheeet . . . we taught you how to speak if anything!

MAMMA (*out at audience*). All I know is that I'm here and that's where I'm at . . . and I'll be here until somethin' happens . . . I wish Shaky wouldn't push me so . . . I want to be good for him . . . I want him to be my man and care about me a little . . .

(ART *brings* MAMMA *her drink.* CURT *sits with him at the table.*)

CURT (*to* PANDORA). Don't look so pissed off, honey.

PANDORA. Why shouldn't I? Everything's gone wrong.

(CURT *stands and takes* PANDORA's *arm.*)

CURT. C'mere, baby. Let me talk to you. (*They walk into the shadows.*)

ART. Just saw Shaky. He didn't stay long.

MAMMA. Nawh. He's gone to take care of some business. Wants me to stay here and take care of mine.

ART. I guess that's what you should do then.

MAMMA. Should I? He's rushin' me too fast, that's what he's doin'. He knows I take a little time gettin' right inside before I can go back to work but he's pushin' me. It's Curt's and Pan's fault . . . they're desperate for money and they're pressin' Shaky.

ART. Maybe you should try and talk to him or to Curt.

MAMMA. It wouldn't do any good!

ART. It wouldn't? If you were my girl I'd listen to what you had to say.

MAMMA. Oh, man, knock off the bullshit!

ART. But I would, really.

MAMMA (*hesitant*). You would? I bet you're full of shit.

ART. Sure I would. I look young but I know what you need . . . and I know what you want.

MAMMA (*giggling*). You do? (*Peering over her glass*) What do I need and want, fuzz wuzz?

ART. Understanding.

MAMMA. What?

ART (*soft*). Understanding.

MAMMA. Sheeet . . .

ART (*softer*). Understanding.

(*Lights down; spot on* CURT *and* PANDORA.)

PANDORA. I'm gettin' fed up with this shit, Curt. We seem to be goin' backwards, not forward.

CURT. I know that, baby. But things will get straightened out. You know it has to. When the job . . .

PANDORA (*cutting*). The job! Yeah . . . it better be somethin', Curt, or you're in some big trouble . . . We're both in some big trouble . . . what'd I do without you?

CURT. If anything happens, baby . . . let Art take care of things . . .

PANDORA. Art?

CURT. Yeah.

PANDORA (*afraid*). But I'm your woman, remember?

CURT. He's like a little brother to me. I've already spoken to him about it . . . you can get a real gig in a show or somethin' and share an apartment with him. He'll look out for you while I'm away. Go up to Frisco and wait for me . . . Art's got a head and he can look after things until I get out . . . then things will be okay again. But that's if the worst happens and we don't get the juice money . . .

PANDORA (*struck*). You think that much of him, Curt?

CURT. I told you he's like my brother, baby. I've been waitin' a long time for a real cat to come along . . . we're on our way now . . .

(*Lights lower; spot on table as* SHAKY *enters.*)

SHAKY (*to* ART). Hey, what you say your name was?

ART (*smiling, holding out his hand*). It's Art, Shaky, you know I met . . .

SHAKY (*cutting*). Yeah, I know . . . what you doin' takin' up my ole lady's time?

(BASS PLAYER *enters.*)

ART. I was only sittin' here and bought her a drink. She rode over in my car with Curt and Pan.

SHAKY. That's what I mean, man . . . takin' up her time.

MAMMA. Shaky . . . stop it! He wasn't doin' nothin' . . . he's a friend of Curt's and . . .

SHAKY. Shut up!

MAMMA. You don't understand . . .

(*He slaps her.* ART *grabs his arm and pushes him sprawling across a chair.* SHAKY *regains his balance and begins to lunge but is caught by* CURT.)

CURT. Hey, cool it, man! What's goin' on?

SHAKY. This little punk friend of yours doesn't like what I do with my woman.

BASS PLAYER. Why don't you forget it, Shaky. If it had been me I would of done the same thing. Forget it. It ain't worth it.

MAMMA (*scared*). He don't understand.

SHAKY. You'll see what I understand when we get home, bitch!

ART (*putting out his hand*). I'm sorry, man. It was my fault. I had . . .

(SHAKY *knocks* ART's *hand aside and turns, being led toward the door by the musician.*)

SHAKY (*to* ART). I'll see you later.

CURT. Hey, Shaky. C'mere, man. It don't mean nothin'.

(*They exit.* PANDORA *takes a seat.* CURT *goes to the bar and answers the questions of the musicians and the* BARTENDER. *The* SHOW GIRL *goes to the rear of the club and the* CUSTOMER *orders another drink.*)

MAMMA. He just don't understand . . . he can't understand and he can't give me any understanding . . .

PANDORA. Who don't understand, Mamma?

MAMMA. Shaky . . . he just don't understand . . . he should try and understand me more.

PANDORA. Girl, you so stoned you're not makin' any sense. He understands, Mamma. He understands you perfectly.

MAMMA. He can't, Pan. He can't or I wouldn't feel this way about him now.

ART. Maybe you're changin'.

PANDORA. Oh, man, you're full of it!

ART. You're cynical but not that hard, Pandora.

PANDORA. Man, I've seen it all. I don't have to be hard . . .
I just use what I know.

ART. Have you seen everything, Pan?

PANDORA. Yes!

ART. Then you've seen me before?

PANDORA (*staring*). Yeah . . . I've seen you before. There's a
you standin' on every corner with his hands in his pockets and
his fly half unzipped . . . there's a you in every drunk tank in
every city . . . there's a you sniffin' around moochin' drinks and
kissin' ass and thinkin' he's a make-out artist. Yeah . . . I've
seen you before, punk!

MAMMA. He just don't understand . . .

ART. No, you've never seen me before, Pandora. I'm goin'a
tell you something.

PANDORA (*sarcastic*). What are you goin'a tell me, Art?

ART. That I'm goin'a change your life.

PANDORA. *What?*

(*Lights go up with a startling flash.* DEENY *and the* BOUNCER,
Pete, *enter.* DEENY, *in black glasses, sports an ascot and a cum-
merbund under his sport coat. In the thin dress she entered in,
the* SHOW GIRL *walks from the rear and takes a seat beside the*
CUSTOMER. MAMMA TOO TIGHT *stands and* CURT *nearly bowls
over a customer on his way to meet* DEENY *in center stage in
front of* PANDORA'S *table.* PANDORA *jumps to her feet beside*
MAMMA, *followed by* ART.)

CURT. Deeny!

(*The* BASS PLAYER *enters, and the* DRUMMER *and* PIANO PLAY-
ER *hurry over. Behind the bar the* BARTENDER *stands tensed;
the* BASS PLAYER *climbs upon the stage and begins zippering his
bass fiddle into its cloth bag.*)

DEENY. Keep it, Curt! I don't want to hear it. I just come
from the union and I've taken all the crap I'm gonna . . . the
show's closed.

(*Chorus of yells.*)

CURT. Deeny, what you take us for?

PANDORA. Hey, man . . . let's go in the back and talk . . .

DRUMMER (*pushing his way around the* PIANO PLAYER). Yeah, Deeny, I want to talk to you!

DEENY. I just don't want to hear it from any of you. Okay? . . . Okay! Now everybody . . . this club is closin'. Ya hear? Everybody out inside of ten minutes . . . understand? This is my property. Get off it inside of ten minutes or I'm callin' the cops . . . your things and you out . . . hit the street . . . that means everybody!

(*Another chorus of yells from nearly everyone. The customers hurry out the exit and the* SHOW GIRL *joins the group.*)

BASS PLAYER (*to other musicians*). Hey, fellas, I'm splittin' . . . what about you?

(MAMMA *turns and goes over to him.*)

DRUMMER. Man, what about my pay?

DEENY. Take your bitchin' to the union, fellah. They instigated this hassle.

PANDORA. We don't know nothin' bout no union, Deeny . . .

DEENY (*sarcastic*). I know you don't, sugar. But you girls should get organized . . . try to get paid hourly and get off the quota system and you'd . . .

CURT. Watch your mouth, mathafukker!

BOUNCER. You'd better watch yours!

DEENY (*to* BARTENDER). Hey, Chico, call the cops! You just can't reason with some jerks! Call them now!

(*The* BARTENDER *dials.*)

PANDORA (*to* CURT). What we gonna do, baby . . . ?

CURT. Quiet!

PANDORA. But your case, honey . . .

BARTENDER (*on phone*). Yeah . . . there's trouble at the Strip Club on Western . . . yeah . . .

(DEENY *tries to push his way past but* CURT *blocks him. The* BOUNCER *moves to shove* CURT *out of the way but* ART *steps in as the four confront each other, and the girls back off. The* PIANO PLAYER *has coaxed the* DRUMMER *to join the* BASS PLAYER

upon the stage, packing away his equipment. At a run, the
SHOW GIRL *rushes to the rear of the club as the* BARTENDER *hangs
up the phone. As the other musicians pack up, the* PIANO PLAY-
ER *comes back to the group.)*

PIANO. Deeny, you just can't do this. This ain't right about
us. We stuck by you for below scale wages, riskin' our own
necks with the union to keep you in business, until you got on
your feet. And still we never got paid on time. Now I hear you
gonna put some names in here and clean up on the rep we
made for you.

BOUNCER. Shut up, mister. You're not supposed to be here
right now, remember?

PANDORA (*furious*). You owe me for two and a half weeks,
man!

DEENY (*trying to get by again*). Sorry, baby. Come around
some time and maybe we can work out somethin'.

CURT. I know why you doin' this, Deeny. Don't pull that
union shit on me! You want all the girls to work for you . . .
on the block like tramps for ten and fifteen dollars a trick. Pan,
Mamma and all the other broads. I'd die before I'd let you
put my woman on the street for ten tricks a day. Why you got
to be so fuckin' greedy, man? You ain't right! You already got
six girls now.

BOUNCER. Just say he has taste and discrimination, Curt. You
know he wants your old lady because . . .

DEENY (*cutting*). Shut up all of you! And are you goin' to get
out of my way?

MAMMA (*from bandstand*). Deeny. Who you think you are?

DEENY (*to* MAMMA). You know who I am, you stupid country
cunt. And if you want to stay on the streets and keep that
junkie ole man of yours cool, just keep your mouth out of this!
That way you won't get your legs broke and . . .

CURT (*cutting*). I know why you doin' this, Deeny.

(SHAKY *enters. The* SHOW GIRL *rushes from the rear with
costumes in arms and exits, speaking to no one.*)

SHAKY. Did I hear somebody say they gonna break Mamma's legs?

(*There is general bedlam with shouts and near screaming.*)

DRUMMER (*exiting*). I'm goin' ta take this farther than to the union, Deeny!

BOUNCER. You can take it to your mother, punk!

(DRUMMER *drops equipment and lunges toward* BOUNCER *but* PIANO PLAYER *grabs him and holds.* BASS PLAYER *helps.*)

BASS PLAYER (*exiting with* DRUMMER). Hey, Deeny, you're wrong! You're dead wrong, man!

PIANO (*to* CURT *and* PANDORA). Cool it. Let's all split. This ain't nothin' but a big bust. (*It becomes suddenly quiet and the* BARTENDER, *a club in hand, comes around the bar and stands behind* CURT *and* ART. SHAKY *stands to the side of* DEENY *and the* BOUNCER. MAMMA *is on the bandstand, wide-eyed, and* PANDORA *is downstage glowering at her enemies. Leaving*) I'll see you guys. (*Seeing* SHAKY) Hey, man. It ain't worth it.

SHAKY. I'll get in touch with you, okay?

PIANO. C'mon, man. I don't like what I see.

SHAKY. Make it! Be a good friend and make it.

(PIANO PLAYER *exits. It is even more quiet. Very low, from somewhere outside, the theme is heard as each group eyes the other and tenses.*)

PANDORA (*spitting it out, violent as unexpected spit spattering a face*). Fuck you, Deeny! Fuck you! Fuck you! *Fuck you!*

DEENY (*frenzied*). You little trampy bitch . . . you . . .

(CURT *smashes him in the mouth as he reaches for* PANDORA. DEENY *falls back beside the table, grabs a glass and hurls it into* CURT'S *face, shattering it.* CURT *launches himself upon him and pummels* DEENY *to the floor. Meanwhile, the* BOUNCER *and* ART *fight in center stage.* SHAKY *is struck almost immediately from behind by the* BARTENDER'S *club.* ART, *seeing the* BARTENDER *advancing on* CURT'S *rear, breaks away and desperately kicks out at the* BARTENDER. *With a screech he doubles over and grabs his groin. The* BOUNCER *seizes* ART *from behind, about the throat, in an armlock, and begins strangling him.* PANDORA, *who has taken off her shoes after kicking* DEENY *several times as* CURT *beats him upon the floor, attacks the* BOUNCER *from behind and repeatedly strikes him about the head with her shoe heels. The* BOUNCER *loosens his grip on* ART *and grabs* PANDORA *and punches her. She falls.* ART, *gasping, reaches down for the* BARTENDER'S *dropped club, picks it up and turns and beats the* BOUNCER *to the floor. All the while* MAMMA TOO TIGHT *screams. With face bloodied from splintered glass,* CURT *has beaten* DEENY *into unconsciousness and staggers over and pulls* PANDORA *up. Sirens, screeches, and slamming car doors are heard from outside. Shouts.)*

CURT (*towing Pandora*). C'mon, Art! Pull yourself together. The cops are here.

(ART *staggers over to* SHAKY *and tries to lift him but he is too weak.* MAMMA, *crying and screaming, jumps from the bandstand and pulls at* SHAKY.)

CURT (*heading for the rear*). He's too heavy, Art. Leave him. Grab Mamma and let's get out the back way. Move! C'mon, man, move!

(*Dazed, but following orders,* ART *grabs* MAMMA'S *arms and struggles with her.*)

MAMMA (*resisting*). No! No! I can't leave him like that!

CURT (*exiting*). Bring her, Art. Out the back way to the car.

MAMMA (*being dragged out by* ART). My first day out . . . my first day . . .

(*They exit and immediately the stage blackens, then the rumble of running feet.*)

VOICE. CHRIST! (*More heavy running, then stop.*) Hey, call a couple of ambulances . . . Emergency!

CURTAIN

ACT III

Scene I

Time: Three days later. Afternoon.
Scene: CURT's *apartment. He and* RICH *play chess as in Act I. The bed is lowered and* MAMMA TOO TIGHT *sleeps with the covers pulled up to her chin as if she is cold. The radio is off and the California sunshine glistens in the clean room. The room looks sterile, unlived-in and motel-like without the lighting of the first act.*

CURT *wears two band-aids upon his face, one upon his forehead, the other on the bridge of his nose.*

CURT (*bored*). It'll be mate in two moves, Rich. Do you want to play it out?

RICH. Nawh, man. I ain't up to it.

CURT (*sitting back*). The last three day have just taken everything out of me, man.

RICH. Yeah. They been pretty rough. (CURT *stands, stretches, and walks across the stage.*) Hey, man. Is there any more beer?

CURT. Nawh. Pan and Art's bringing some in with them when they come.

RICH (*muttering*). Yeah . . . when they get here.

CURT (*noticing* RICH's *tone*). What did you say, man?

RICH. Oh. Nothin', man.

CURT (*sharply*). You're a liar . . . I heard what you said!

RICH (*sullen*). I ain't goin'a be many more of them liars, Curt.

CURT (*gesturing*). Awww, man. Forget it . . . you know how I feel with Deeny in a coma from his concussion for the past three days and me not knowin' if he's goin' ta press charges finally or die.

RICH. Yeah, man. I'm a bit edgy myself. Forget about what I said.

(CURT *returns to the couch and sprawls back.*)

CURT. But I'd like to know what you meant by it, Rich.

RICH (*seeing no way out*). Now, Curt. You and I been friends since we were young punks stealin' hub caps and tires together, right? Remember that time you, me and the guys gang-banged that Pachuco broad? . . . And the Dog Town boys came up and we had that big rumble and they killed Sparky?

CURT (*sensing something coming*). How can I forget it . . . I served my first stretch behind it for stabbin' that Mexican kid, Manuel.

RICH. Yeah. That was a good time ago and Manuel ain't no kid no more . . .

CURT. Yeah. But, tell me. What do you have to say, good buddy?

RICH (*pausing, then serious*). It's about this guy Art and Pandora, man.

CURT. What do you mean, man?

RICH. Man . . . I don't mean there's anything goin' on yet . . . but each afternoon he's taken Pandora out for the past three days they been gettin' back later . . . and . . .

CURT. And what, Rich?

RICH. And the way she looks at him, Curt.

CURT (*disgusted and angry*). Awww, man . . . I thought I knew you better.

RICH. Well I told you that I didn't think that they were doin' anything really.

CURT. But, what? That he drives her up to Sunset Strip to keep her dates with the big tricks . . . you know how much dough she brings back, man?

RICH (*resolutely*). Yeah, man. Sometimes over a hundred dollars for one trick.

CURT. So you can't hurry those people for that kinda bread, man.

RICH (*trying to be understood*). But I wasn't talkin' about the tricks, Curt. I don't think they're holdin' back any money on you.

CURT. Then what are you talkin' 'bout?

RICH. About that little jive-ass square gettin' next to your woman, that's what!

CURT. Now listen, Rich. We're friends and all that but that little jive-ass square as you call him is just like a brother to me . . . and we been in some tighter things than you and me will ever be in.

RICH (*obviously hurt*). Well, forget it!

CURT. No, let's not forget it. You're accusing my wife of jivin' around on me. You know that Pan's the straightest broad you'll ever find. That's why I married her. You know if we couldn't have gotten another man that she would have gone on the job and been as good as most men. She and I are a team. What could she gain by messin' 'round on me with my ace buddy?

RICH. Forget it, I said.

CURT. Nawh, Rich. I don't want to. I know what's really buggin' you. Ever since Shaky got busted at the Club and they found all that smack on him you been buggin' Mamma to be your woman 'cause you know that with Shaky's record he won't be hittin' the streets again for at least ten years. But you're wrong on two counts cause we're bailin' out Shaky tonight and takin' him with us and Mamma don't want you cause she wants Art but he don't go for her.

RICH (*getting to his feet*). I'll see you, man. Between your broad and that cat you can't think any more! (CURT *reaches for* RICH'S *shirt front;* RICH *throws his hands off.*) Take it easy, Curt. You already won a close one this week. And your guardian angel ain't round to sneak-punch people.

(CURT *stares at him and steps back.*)

MAMMA (*from bed*). Hey, what's all that shoutin' about?

CURT. Nothin', baby. Rich and I are just crackin' jokes.

MAMMA (*sitting up*). Curt, I wonder if . . .

CURT. No, Mamma. You can't have no fix. Remember what I told you? You don't turn no tricks in town cause you're hot behind Shaky's bust so you don't need any heroin, right? You're on holiday and besides, you're full of codeine now . . . that's enough . . .

MAMMA. But I would be good if I could get some. I wouldn't worry about Shaky so much and I'd feel . . .

CURT. You just come out of the joint clean, Mamma. You don't need anything but to keep cool.

MAMMA (*pouting*). But I got the sixteen hundred dollars that Shaky had stashed at our pad. I could buy it okay, Curt.

CURT. Forget it. That money is with the other bread. We all takin' a trip with that. Besides . . . Shaky had over two thousand bucks worth of stuff in the pad and we sellin' it tonight so we can bail him out so he can leave with us . . .

(MAMMA *jumps out of bed in a thin gown.*)

MAMMA (*delighted*). You are? Then he'll be home soon?

CURT. Yeah. Then we all make it before Deeny comes out of his coma or croaks. Now get back in bed before Rich grabs you!

MAMMA (*playful*). Rich, you better not. Shaky will be home soon.

RICH (*teasing*). Sheeet, woman. I don't care about old ass Shaky. C'mon, baby, why don't you get yourself a young stud?

MAMMA (*getting in bed*). When I get one it won't be you.

RICH (*serious*). Then who?

CURT (*mutters*). I told Art and Pan that we need the car this evening to drop off the stuff. After that it'll be time to get ready for the job.

RICH (*bitterly, to* MAMMA). So he's got to you, too.

MAMMA. Nobody's got to me. What'chou talkin' 'bout, Rich? Art's been stayin' over to Shaky and my place for the last couple of nights while I stayed here. How can he get . . .

RICH (*cutting*). How did you know I was talkin' about Art?

MAMMA. Cause you got Art on the brain, that's why!

CURT. I thought we dropped that, Rich.

RICH (*to* MAMMA). If you're goin'a get somebody young . . . get a man . . . not some little book-readin' faggot . . .

MAMMA (*red-faced, to* RICH). Oh, go fuck yourself, man! (*She covers her head.*)

RICH. Okay, man. We got a lot to do tonight, so I'll lay off.

(*Through the back curtain the outside kitchen door can be seen opening. Dusk is come and* ART *enters first with a large bag;* PANDORA *follows, closes the door, and purposely bumps against him as she passes. She wears dark glasses, her pants, and boots.*)

ART. Hey, you almost made me drop this! Where should I put it?

(PANDORA *enters front room smiling.*)

PANDORA. Hi, honey. Hello, Rich. (*She walks over to* CURT, *kisses him, and places money in his hand.*)

CURT. Hey, pretty baby. (*He pulls her to him, gives her an extended kiss, and breaks it, looking over* PANDORA'S *shoulders at* RICH *who looks away.*)

CURT. Everything okay?

PANDORA. Smooth as Silky Sullivan.

(*In the kitchen* ART *is taking items from the bag.* CURT *hands back the money to* PANDORA.)

CURT. Here, Pan, put this in the box with the rest.

PANDORA. Okay. (*She walks past bed and looks down.*) What's wrong with Mamma?

CURT. Rich's been tryin' to love her up.

RICH. She won't go for my program, baby.

PANDORA (*entering the kitchen*). That's too bad . . . you better cultivate some charm, Rich.

RICH. Yeah, that's what's happen'n. I'm not one of the lucky ones . . . some people don't need it.

PANDORA (*going to* ART). Let me take in the beer, Art. You put the frozen food in the refrigerator and the canned things in the cupboard.

(ART *pulls her to him and kisses her.*)

PANDORA (*taking breath*). Hand me the glasses, will ya?

(*They kiss again, she responding this time, then she pushes him away and begins fixing beer for* CURT *and* RICH.)

CURT. Hey, Mamma. You want any beer?

MAMMA (*under the cover*). No, no.

(PANDORA *serves* CURT *and* RICH, *then climbs the stairs and enters the dressing room.* ART *comes out of the kitchen.*)

RICH. How you feel, Art?

ART. Okay. Hollywood's an interesting place. First job I ever had just drivin' somebody around.

CURT. Hope it's your last, Art. With this job tonight and my cut from sellin' Shaky's heroin we'll be just about in. Might even go into business back East.

ART. Yeah? I hope so.

CURT. We already got almost twenty-four hundred with Shaky's money we found at his place and the bread we've been able to hustle the last few days. After tonight we'll be set.

RICH. Yeah. After tonight you'll be set.

CURT (*looking at* RICH). It's too bad you won't come with us, Rich. But your share will fix you up out here okay.

RICH. Fix me up? Ha ha . . . I'll probably shoot that up in smack inside of several months . . . but if I make it I'll probably be lookin' you up in two more years when my probation's up. No use ruin'n a good thing. When I cut this town loose I want to be clean. I just hope all goes well with you.

ART (*smiling*). Why shouldn't it?

CURT. Yeah, Rich, why shouldn't it?

RICH. Funny things happen to funny-style people, ya know.

CURT. Yeah. Too bad you won't be comin' along . . . we need a clown in our show.

(RICH *watches* ART *studying the chess game.*)

RICH. Do you see anything I missed, good buddy?

ART. Oh. I don't know.

RICH. You know I seldom beat Curt. Why don't you play him?

ART (*still looking at board*). Maybe I will when we find time.

CURT. What would you have done from there, Art?

ART. It's according to what side I'm on.

CURT. You have the black. White's going to mate you in two moves.

ART. He is?

RICH. Yeah. He is.

(ART *reaches over and picks up the black king.*)

ART. Most kings need a queen to be most powerful but others do the best they can. (*He places the king upon another square.*) That's what I'd do, Rich.

CURT (*perceiving*). Yeah. I see . . . I see . . .

RICH. Say, why'd you move there? . . . He can't move now . . . he can't put himself in check . . .

ART (*as* RICH *stares at him*). Yeah, Rich?

CURT (*matter-of-factly*). A stalemate.

RICH (*muttering*). I should of seen that. (*To* ART) How did you . . . why . . .

ART. When you play the game you look for any break you can make.

CURT. We should play sometime, Art.

ART. I'm looking forward to it, Curt. But you name the time.

CURT (*standing*). I'll do that. Hey, Pandora! We got to go! (PANDORA *comes to the top of the stairs. She has changed into a simple dress.*)

PANDORA. We goin' some place?

CURT. I got to drop Shaky's stuff off and go down to the bail bondsman and the lawyer. I want you to drive. C'mon, Rich. Pan will sit in the car down the street in the next block and you and me will walk up the street talkin' about baseball, understand? On the corner of Adams and Crenshaw we'll meet a man and hit a grand slam.

RICH. Yeah, I hope so, brother.

CURT. It's trip time from here on in, baby.

PANDORA (*excited*). Wait until I get my coat.

CURT (*in good humor*). Let's go, woman. It's eighty degrees outside and we might be the hottest thing in L.A. but it just ain't that warm. Let's go, now. See you, Art. (*Going to* ART) Oh, I almost forgot the car keys.

ART (*handing him the keys*). See you guys.

CURT (*hands keys to* PANDORA). You'll watch the phone, okay?

ART. Sure, good buddy, I'll see to the phone.

CURT. If Mamma wakes up and wants a fix don't give in to her.

ART. I'll try not to.

CURT (*serious*). I mean it, Art.

ART (*smiling*). I'm dead serious, man.

PANDORA. See you later, Art.

ART. See you later, Pan. Good-bye, Curt. Good-bye, Rich.

(*The trio exit and* ART *goes to the radio and switches it on. It plays the theme as he enters the kitchen and gets himself a beer. He comes from the kitchen drinking from the bottle and climbs the bathroom stairs. His shadow is seen lifting and then dialing. His voice is muffled by the music and by his whisper; nothing is understood. After the shadow hangs up,* ART *returns to the living room and descends the stairs. He sits upon the bed and shakes* MAMMA TOO TIGHT.)

MAMMA (*being shaken*). Huh? I don't want any beer. (ART *shakes her once more. She uncovers her head.*) Oh, Art. It's you. Where's everybody? (*He doesn't answer, looks at her. Evening comes and the room blackens.*) I'm glad you woke me. I always like to talk to you but I guess I bug you since you don't say too much to me. Why ain't you sayin' nothin' now? (*Three-beat pause.*)

ART (*laughing*). Ha ha ha . . . ha ha . . . Ma-ma Too Tight! . . . ha ha ha . . .

MAMMA. You said it! Sometimes you have such a nice look on your face and now . . . you look different . . . (*Pause*) like you so happy you could scream . . . You never looked at me like this before, Art, never. (*In total blackness as the music plays*) You said Shaky wouldn't be back? . . . You won't? . . . I don't care as long as you don't go away . . . You know . . . you understand me. It's like you can look inside my head . . . Oh how did you know? Just a little bit? More? You say I can have a fix any time I want? . . . Oh! . . . You understand me, don't cha? Don't let Curt know . . . you say don't worry about Curt . . . don't care what anybody thinks or says except you? (*Silence, pause*) Oh I feel so good now . . . I didn't know but I was hoping . . . I didn't know, honey . . . Oh, Art! . . . Ahhhh . . . now I can feel you oozing out of me . . . and I'm glad so glad . . . it's good . . .

ACT III

Scene II

PANDORA *leans against the kitchen door as the lights go up. The atmosphere of the first act is recreated by the lights and music. The bed has been put up and* ART *sits upon the couch.* PANDORA *has been crying and what can be seen of her face around her dark glasses appears shocked.*

She walks to the center of the room and faces ART.

PANDORA. Art . . . Art . . . they got them. They got Curt and Rich . . . with all that stuff on them. The cops were waitin' on them. They busted them with all those narcotics . . . we'll never see them again.

ART (*rising*). We're hot, Pandora. We got to get out of town.

PANDORA. They got 'em, don't you hear me, Art? What can we do?

ART. Nothin' . . . we got to make it before Curt or Rich break and the cops are kickin' that door in.

PANDORA. You said nothin'? But we . . . what do you mean? We got to do somethin'! (*Crying*) We can't just let it happen to them . . . we got to do somethin' like Curt would do if it was one of us . . . Art! Art! Don't just stand there! Do . . . (*He slaps her viciously, knocking off her glasses, exposing her blackened eyes.*)

ART (*commanding*). Get a hold on yourself, Pandora. You've had a bad experience. (*She holds her face and looks dazed.*) Now listen to me. Mamma has gone over to her place to pack and as soon as she gets back we're all leaving.

PANDORA (*dazed*). Mamma is packin'? . . . Did Curt tell her to pack?

ART. You know he didn't. Now as soon as she gets here I want us to be packed, okay?

PANDORA. But . . . Art . . . packed . . . where we goin'?

ART. To Buffalo, baby. Where else?

PANDORA. To Buffalo?

ART. That's what I said. Now go up in your dressing room and get your suit case . . . (*A knock comes from the front door.*) That's Mamma already . . . we're runnin' late, woman. C'mon, get a move on. (*He shoves her.*) Move! Get a move on, Pandora! (*She stumbles over the first step, catches her balance and begins climbing.* ART *looks after her.*) Oh . . . Pandora . . . (*She turns and looks vacantly at him.*) Don't forget your box!

(*As she turns and climbs the last steps* ART *saunters to the radio as the knock sounds again. Instantaneously, as he switches the radio off, the stage is thrown in complete blackness.*)

THE END

Family Meeting

A Play in One Act

WILLIAM WELLINGTON MACKEY

Cast of Characters

FATHER LOVE: *A very proud and successful Negro capitalist. He was born and shall die in the great land, America.*

MOTHER LOVE: *His precious wife.*

BROTHER LOVE: *His precious son.*

PRECIOUS LOVE: *His precious daughter.*

LILLIE OF THE FLOWERS: *His precious maid.*

FOUR TO EIGHT MIDDLE-AGED LADIES: *The precious sorority sisters of Mother Love. Old bags, really, who are unworthy of further description.*

A COLORED BOY OF THIRTEEN

TWO TO FOUR WOMEN DRESSED IN WHITE

A YOUNG MAN DRESSED IN WHITE

THE TIME: Yesterday and today

THE PLACE: Heavenly Heights, U.S.A.

AUTHOR'S NOTES

Staging

There need only be a suggestion of elegant furnishings. I envision painted abstract caricatures depicting various pieces of furnishings either suspended or hanging from the flies. A spiral stairway which appears to be extended up into the flies is the focal point of the set.

A bier is located at upstage center. Its coloring is blood red. The body of a very black Negro woman who is hideously obese lies on the bier. Her hair is extremely bushy and wild-looking. It is pure white. The woman, who is very dead, appears to have lived for a million years.

The Characters

We are dealing, I believe, with exaggerated caricatures. The characters are frightfully Southern in manner. It is suggested that the two PRECIOUS LOVES *be dressed in very gay, sprightly looking outfits. A little-girl simpleness must be achieved if these roles are to come across correctly.*

FATHER LOVE'S *and the two* BROTHER LOVES' *appearances should further add to the absurdity of the "funny house" situation which evolves as the play develops.* FATHER LOVE *is probably fiftyish and is probably overbearing and endowed with a somewhat snobbish effrontery. The* TWO BROTHER LOVES *are in their middle or late twenties and are simply the sons (or son, as the case may be) of their father.*

MOTHER LOVE'S *first entrance down the spiral stairway should indeed be an almost blinding experience for the audience. She is probably attired in an unusually loud-colored, extraordinarily flamboyant-looking outfit. Her every move, her every mannerism to the nth degree is that of a grand duchess.*

Note: In Act I, the roles of PRECIOUS LOVE *and* BROTHER LOVE *should be played by Negroes.* LILLIE OF THE FLOWERS *during this act is played by a white actress. In Act II the roles reverse.*

PRECIOUS LOVE of *Act I (the Negro actress) assumes the role of* LILLIE OF THE FLOWERS. LILLIE OF THE FLOWERS of *Act I (the white actress) assumes the role of* PRECIOUS LOVE. BROTHER LOVE *in Act II (first sequence only) is played by a white actor.* MOTHER LOVE *is played by a Negro actress and* FATHER LOVE *by a white actor.* MISS P. P. *is played by a very fat, very black Negro woman. The other sorority sisters are played by white actresses. In the final scene, the Negro and white* BROTHER LOVES *play the scene as one.*

Re: Final Scene. The Apotheosis

A true montage effect suggested. Quick and precise collection of scenes; sequential enticement of movement and speech —almost precision choreography. Possibly the use of visual projections during the monologue of the BROTHERS, *projecting the best pictorial images that may be pulled from the text for good effect, i.e., the funeral processions down Washington's Pennsylvania Avenue of both F.D.R. and J.F.K., the bombing of Hiroshima, the 1963 march on Washington, and such lines as sit-ins, stand-ins, etc.*

Indeed, for the final scene, a staccato effect; full percussive catharsis—total collage staged to the nth degree of perfection.

ACT ONE

Part One

Darkness for a second or so. Enter music—the melody to a minuet. Lights enter PRECIOUS LOVE *dancing about in a minuet routine. Lillie adjusting something on the bier.*

LILLIE. Good morning, Miss Precious.

PRECIOUS LOVE. Good morning, Lillie, dear Lillie of the Flowers. Isn't it a loverly day?

LILLIE (*a slight pause, and somewhat hesitantly*). You dance divinely, Miss Precious.

PRECIOUS LOVE. Yes I do, don't I, I'm sure.

LILLIE (*curtseying*). Oh my, indeed you do, Miss Precious. Indeed you do, like an angel, like one of God's own angels, you do.

PRECIOUS LOVE (*curtseying*). Why thank you, Lillie. I do thank you ever so kindly for your sweet compliment.

LILLIE. Miss Precious Love! Now don't you go curtseying me none. Shucks, I's only Lillie the maid. Your mother'd have a plum fit if she saw you bowing down to me. Now you stop that foolishness and go on with your dancing lessons.

PRECIOUS LOVE. Lillie you are a dear; a dear darling angel.

LILLIE. No I ain't either. I's only Lillie. Better not let your mama hear you talking that kin'a talk.

PRECIOUS LOVE. But Lillie . . .

LILLIE. Now you just hush now. Don't you vex me none. I's only Lillie, the maid. And you for shorenuf is Miss Precious Love. I knows my place and you should know yours too; least by now you should.

PRECIOUS LOVE. I suppose you're right, of course. Though sometimes it rightly seems just as silly as all hell, it does. I mean it really does. Seems just as silly as all pure hell, it does sometimes. It really does.

LILLIE. Miss Precious Love!

PRECIOUS LOVE. Oh my goodness gracious. I said a bad word, didn't I? Tee hee hee . . .

LILLIE. Glory sands alive! If your mama's anywhere near listening breath . . .

PRECIOUS LOVE. Precious sakes! You don't have to tell me about it if you don't want to. (*Teasingly*) Besides . . . I'm gonna let you in on a lil ole secret, Lillie, dear Lillie of the Flowers. Want me to tell you what I know, what I done just gone and done all by my lil ole precious self?

LILLIE. *Glory Jesus above!*

PRECIOUS LOVE. I did! I did! Yes I did too. I've seen it all with my own lil ole precious eyes, I did. And I heard it all

with my own two lil ole precious ears, I did! Yes I did! And
Lillie, I swear to Sweet God Above, I shorenuf ain't never
seen or heard nothing like it in all of my lil ole precious seventeen years, I haven't. Ohhhh, Lillie, it was just the most exciting experience I have ever encountered in all of my precious
seventeen years, it was. It really was! Why them ole nasty dirty
niggers over there in Goodbread Alley are just exactly like
Mother Love and Father Love say they are, they really are! And
Lillie, they actually really do smell too! Ohhhhh it was just
so exciting, Lillie. It really was! Lillie, you just have to; if you
really love me at all, you just have to let me come and visit you
some precious Sunday. You just have to! Why I ain't never
seen nothing so mysterious and exciting as them old dirty
ordinary niggers in all of my precious seventeen years, I haven't.
Promise . . . you promise, Lillie?

LILLIE. Now I don't know bout that, Miss Precious. Seems
like that's asking for shorenuf trouble. (*Slight pause*) No, Miss
Precious. No Mam! Your daddy ain't gonna kill me. And your
mama ain't gonna be spreading the word round to all these
other precious people up here in Heavenly Heights and cause
me not to git my steady employment. No Mam! That'd be
trouble for shore, Miss Precious. If I had anything to do with
tainting those precious ears and those lil old precious eyes of
your precious self, ain't no telling what would happen to me.

PRECIOUS LOVE (*babyishly*). But Lillie, it ain't fair. It ain't
fair at all. I want to see Goodbread Alley.

LILLIE (*snappingly*). Thought you said you'd seen it. Thought
you said you been there. I done caught you in one, ain't I?
Done caught you in one.

PRECIOUS LOVE. But I . . . I . . .

LILLIE (*angered*). Where you learn them bad words from?
You ain't been to no Goodbread Alley. Where you learn them
alley words from?

PRECIOUS LOVE. I . . . I . . . No, I was just fibbing. I haven't
been to no Goodbread Alley. Shucks! I thought I could fool

you, Lillie. I was just fibbing. (*Like a little baby*) I'm sorry, Lillie, I'm sorry. (*She sniffles.*)

LILLIE (*moving and comforting the girl*). Now don't cry none, Miss Precious. Hurts my heart to see those precious tears falling like that.

PRECIOUS LOVE. But I do awful-like want to see for myself, Lillie. I honest-to-goodness do. Cross my heart, I do. Just don't seem fair not to ever be able to see what those poor colored people are like. Miss Blessingful at school says that just as sure as all us precious children sitting there in her classroom, one of these days, we're all going to have to be sitting in the same room with those people; and maybe even eating in the same room with them, Lillie; even living with them. Can you imagine that? Ain't that something, Lillie?

LILLIE. Honey child, that's one thing you and your precious self needn't ever fear. God give a special blessing a long, long time ago to you folks up here in Heavenly Heights. Not that I rightly know what it was, or anybody does for a fact. Yes mam! Long, long ago, he planted that seed, and he says: "Now these people is gotta be different from these people." And he says, "And there's a reason. There's a reason. People just gotta be different."

PRECIOUS LOVE. But . . . But I didn't ask to be born, Lillie. It ain't my fault I was blessed to be born in Heavenly Heights.

LILLIE. Well, the sun don't ask to shine and the rain don't ask to fall, either.

PRECIOUS LOVE. Lillie . . .

LILLIE. Yes, Miss Precious Love.

PRECIOUS LOVE. You don't suppose . . . Well, you don't suppose that . . .

LILLIE. What is it, Miss Precious Love?

PRECIOUS LOVE. Well that ole nasty Billie Joe Hankerson over in Goodbread Alley told me that . . .

LILLIE (*shocked*). Miss Precious Love! What are you doing talking to that lil ole nasty Billie Joe Hankerson?

PRECIOUS LOVE. Oh, I ain't done no talking to him, Lillie. It's him. He's always a'talking to me. He's always picking on me all the time.

LILLIE. Well you just stay away from him. He ain't nothin' but old common nigger trash. Even worse than me, thinking of what part of the Alley he's from.

PRECIOUS LOVE. I still wants to tell you what he says, Lillie. Listen. He says that . . .

LILLIE (*placing her hands to her ears*). Can't be worth listening to.

PRECIOUS LOVE. Lillie, please. It's important. I got to know something. 'Cause I'm rightly confused and upset about what Billy Joe Hankerson said to me, with his disgusting self.

LILLIE. Well what did that old nasty Billie Joe Hankerson, with his disgusting self, say to you honey?

PRECIOUS LOVE. Well . . . He said that God . . . Lillie, he said that God—

LILLIE. Lord! What in glory's name that old nasty nigger done said to my baby?

PRECIOUS LOVE. He said that God ain't rightly as white as precious ivory. He said that God ain't necessarily as preciously fair and golden ivory as the color of my precious self. Lillie, he said . . . (*Frightfully*) He said that precious God above is just as black as he is, Lillie. Ain't true is it, Lillie? Ain't true, is it? God ain't black, Lillie, is he? God ain't black! Not precious God the Father. (*Shouting*) God ain't black! He ain't black! He ain't black! Is he Lillie?

LILLIE (*tenderly*). Honey, come here to Lillie.

PRECIOUS LOVE. But he ain't black, is he Lillie? God can't be black, Lillie. He can't be black. That'd make everything about almost everything wrong. He ain't black, is he Lillie?

LILLIE. Honey, you shorenuf putting your Lillie on the spot. I don't know what God is like. Nobody know that. Ain't nobody yet seen the face of God. Ain't nobody yet touched him or really rocked in his bosom the way the Bible says it is.

PRECIOUS LOVE. But is he black, Lillie? Is he black like that dirty ole Billie Joe Hankerson? Or is he . . . (*Hesitantly*) Is he ever precious white and ivory . . . like the color of my precious self?

LILLIE. Miss Precious—God is just God. He's what you believe He is.

PRECIOUS LOVE. But, Lillie . . .

LILLIE. No. No Miss Precious. I guess you is right. No, He . . . God ain't nasty. And he ain't dirty, either.

PRECIOUS LOVE. Like that old Billie Joe Hankerson?

LILLIE. Like that old Billie Joe Hankerson.

PRECIOUS LOVE (*embracing* LILLIE). Oh, Lillie! You are so good. I love you. I love you. I love you.

LILLIE. And your Lillie loves you, little darling.

PRECIOUS LOVE (*again babyishly*). Lillie . . . Do me a sweet lil ole favor, please.

LILLIE. Anything your precious lil heart desires, Miss Precious.

PRECIOUS LOVE. I have got the silliest ole desire for some of that precious gumbo you've been cooking in there. Would you be a dear and fix me up a lil ole serving of it? I am positively frightfully starved.

LILLIE. Well Lillie had better do something bout that, hadn't she? (*Leaving*) Ain't gonna just stand round here and see her precious angel starve now, is she? (*She exits.*)

PRECIOUS LOVE (*as* LILLIE *is leaving*). Oh Lillie . . . Dear Lillie of the Flowers! You are so sweet to lil ole undeserving me. (*The music from the minuet enters again.* PRECIOUS LOVE *begins the dance routine again. Again, perhaps a minute or so of the dancing.* PRECIOUS LOVE *then glides very gracefully towards the bier and stops there. The music continues.*) Did you hear, Grandmother? Did you hear? God ain't black! God ain't black! Ain't it just wonderful, grandmother? Ain't it just wonderful? (*A loud crash is heard offstage.* PRECIOUS LOVE *stares frightfully and speaks toward the direction of the sound. Down music.*

Calling frightfully) Father . . . Father . . . Father Love . . . Is anything wrong?

FATHER LOVE (*offstage, hauntingly*). No. No dear. Nothing is wrong. Everything is in order. I . . . I was asleep. Asleep. No. Nothing is wrong with the world today. I was asleep. Must have been dreaming. Yes—dreaming. An accident. I was asleep.

PRECIOUS LOVE. Father . . . Father Love . . . Are you sure? Is everything all right? (*A second of quiet.*) Poor Father. Poor Father Love. (*She begins dance routine again. Up music, full and voluminous. A full minute of the dancing. The telephone rings.* PRECIOUS LOVE *dances toward the telephone and answers. Down music. Like all precious Southern Belles*) Heavenly Heights Manor—One, One, One. Precious Love speaking.

FATHER LOVE (*offstage*). If that is for me, I'm not in today.

(*The music stops.*)

PRECIOUS LOVE. Oh hello, Dr. Successman. However are you doing? Well isn't that just loverly. I do declare. And how is Mrs. Successman, these loverly days? Oh really, she is? Well I do declare. Isn't that just loverly. I shall certainly tell Mother Love. She will be positively delighted to attend, I'm sure. No. No sir. I am so sorry, but Father Love isn't in as of yet. I can't imagine what has detained him. He should be in shortly, I'm sure. The family is scheduled to attend the baccalaureate this afternoon. We never miss going, you know. Yes, I understand he is supposed to be the speaker. He is so divine, isn't he? Such an eloquent speaker. I do look forward to hearing him again. I beg your pardon. Why Dr. Successman! You ought to be ashamed of yourself. Tee hee . . . Well maybe he is and maybe he isn't. Mother Love doesn't allow us to cater to rumors, you know. (*She laughs again.*) Perhaps so. Perhaps so. I agree, I'm sure. Well, we all do have our moments, don't we, we do. All right then. I shall be more than delighted to do just that, I shall. As soon as he arrives, I'll give him your message, I'm sure. Bye now. (*To Father Love*) That was Dr. Successman.

FATHER LOVE (*offstage, hauntingly*). What did he have to say?

PRECIOUS LOVE. Nothing.

FATHER LOVE (*offstage*). What did he want?

PRECIOUS LOVE. Nothing, I'm sure. Perhaps you will call him when you arrive.

FATHER LOVE (*offstage*). I shall call him when I arrive. (*A pause*) Precious . . . Precious Love . . .

PRECIOUS LOVE. Yes, Father Love.

FATHER LOVE (*offstage*). Perhaps you had better remind me when I arrive. I may forget.

(BROTHER LOVE *appears at the top of the stairway. He moves halfway down the stairs and stops. He remains unseen by* PRECIOUS LOVE.)

PRECIOUS LOVE. I shall certainly will do just that, Father Love, I shall.

FATHER LOVE. Promise?

PRECIOUS LOVE. I promise, I do.

FATHER LOVE. Cross your heart and hope to die?

PRECIOUS LOVE (*doing it*). Cross my heart and hope to die.

FATHER LOVE. Like dear Grandmother Love?

PRECIOUS LOVE (*crossing her heart again*). Cross my heart and hope to die.

FATHER LOVE. You're a good daughter. A fine, fine . . . A good daughter. A good . . .

(BROTHER LOVE *springs across the railing of the stairway into the main level of the stage mimicking very loudly the sound of a whinnying jackass. Music continues, but down.*)

BROTHER LOVE. Hee haw, hee haw . . .

PRECIOUS LOVE (*overlapping, screaming*). Ayeeeeeeeeee! Ayeeeeeee!

BROTHER LOVE (*overlapping, roaring*). Ha ha ha ha ha ha ha . . . .

PRECIOUS LOVE (*infuriated*). Damn-it-to-hell all, Brother Love. Don't you do that to me. What is ever the matter with you? You plum crazy or something?

(*Up music.*)

FATHER LOVE (*offstage, somewhat disturbed*). Precious . . . Precious Love!

PRECIOUS LOVE (*clutching to her heart as if out of breath*). My precious self is all right, Father Love. It's just your crazy son out here acting like some clowning nigger! Sneaking up on me and scaring the living daylights outta me precious self.

FATHER LOVE. I was afraid. You had crossed your . . .

PRECIOUS LOVE (*still angered*). I'm exhaustedly all right now, Father Love. You go on back and get your precious rest.

FATHER LOVE. Very well. I need . . . to rest.

PRECIOUS LOVE. Promise?

FATHER LOVE. I promise.

(*The music begins to fade.*)

PRECIOUS LOVE. Cross your heart and hope to die? (*Music fading out.*) Cross my heart and hope to die . . . (*The music stops. Very bitterly*) Now just look what you done gone and done. You done upset Father Love. Ain't you ashamed of yourself?

BROTHER LOVE (*teasingly and imitating* PRECIOUS LOVE). You done gone and upset Father Love. Ain't you ashamed of yourself?

PRECIOUS LOVE (*somewhat disgusted*). Brother Love, I have for all of these precious seventeen years of my livelihood on this precious earth tried to understand how you could have possibly ever been so preciously deserving to be a member of this precious family.

BROTHER LOVE (*outrightly clowning*). Well Precious Love, I tell you. It was like this. It was a long cold night and all. And Father Love just couldn't stand it for another minute. And so he just tiptoed on down to Mother Love's room, and patted her on the behind, and whispered ever sweetly in those precious ears . . . (*Now, rather Amos and Andyishly*) "Honey, I'm sorry. I know this is Tuesday and that us upper-class folks cohabitate only on Monday, Wednesday, and Friday . . . But like honey love, I know this is off-schedule and all . . . But sweet love, I just got the hots tonight, I does. And I just got to have a lil bit, if you and your precious self don't mind . . . (*A slight pause*) "Goddammit! Move over Woman!"

PRECIOUS LOVE. Brother Love! You are acting like some common nigger now. This, this Alley Talk! I will not let my precious ears be subgeecated for another precious minute to such crude and savage jungalism!

BROTHER LOVE. Ha ha ha ha ha . . . Little Sister. Little Precious Love . . . Haven't you learned yet? Don't you know? (*Slight pause*) No. I guess not. (*Slight pause. In a more serious vein*) And to think . . . All those precious seventeen years too. (*Moving toward the coffin. The music enters again.*) But you will. Yessiree you will. Ole Granny did. (*He is now standing by the head of the bier.*) Yessiree she did. Bless her sweet lil ole concubining soul. (*He directly addresses the bier.*) Granny! Grandmother Love! It was rough, wasn't it?

(*Up music.*)

PRECIOUS LOVE (*frightfully*). Brother Love! You should be ashamed of yourself. Addressing the dead in such an unholy manner. Now you just stop that now! Sure as you're standing there, God Almighty's gonna strike you down with a bolt of lightning so powerful . . . so powerful . . .

BROTHER LOVE (*continuing, rather maudlin*). Yes . . . Here within lies the genesis of mankind; histories, counterpoints, a thousand civilizations; rectal flowerings and births of a thousand nightmares. (*Slight pause*) Beginnings and endings; nonsensical ambivalences . . . (*Pause*) Mother earth, a trillion tomorrows, for nothing ends that begins.

PRECIOUS LOVE (*even more frightened*). My sands alive! Brother Love, what on earth are you ever talking about?

BROTHER LOVE (*in the same mood*). God. Seeds of time . . . the earth, life, death. (*Pause*) *Anything*. Take your pick. (*He takes a deep breath.*) And . . . *nothing*. Nothing is everything. Anything is nothing. Nothing is anything. Right Granny? (*Speaks to the bier again*) You gotta burn, girl. Yessiree, you gotta burn. Don't give a damn if they held a thousand pistols at your skull. You shouldn't have done it. (*Bitterly*) There are Heavenly Heights all over this goddamn world now because of bitches like you. *Mother whores!* Damn pity. Rottenness goddamn shame of the world.

PRECIOUS LOVE. Now you just hush that kinna talk. You ain't got no right mocking Precious Grandmother like that. No right at all. And don't think you ain't mocking your ownself, either. If you don't hush talking this vile talk into my precious ears, I am going to call Mother Love downstairs this very minute.

BROTHER LOVE (*pondering*). Yes, I had better, hadn't I? Behave, that is, in the customary manner more properly befitting our rather caecilian ancestral heritage.

PRECIOUS LOVE (*puzzled*). What? (*They stare at each other for a long second; and then as if finally understanding,* PRECIOUS LOVE *speaks.*) Why, Brother Love! I do declare! I really do declare!

BROTHER LOVE (*smiling, a slight pause*). Here. (*Extending his hand*) Dance with me, Precious Love. Dance with me. (*He snaps his fingers and simultaneously the pompous and grand beat of the music of a waltz enters.*) Dance with Brother Love (*Precious Love curtseys.*) Dance with Brother Love. (*He bows.*) Mother Love could never understand the action on this level at any rate. So it doesn't really matter despite the circumstances. Nothing really matters at any rate. And besides, it is twelve o'clock. (*He bows again.*)

PRECIOUS LOVE (*happily*). Yes . . . It is twelve o'clock. (*She curtseys again.* BROTHER LOVE *takes* PRECIOUS LOVE *and they merrily waltz about the room. Overlapping as they dance.*)

BROTHER LOVE. Twelve o'clock it is. Twelve o'clock at Heavenly Manor. One, One, One. Time for the afternoon. Beeeeeeeee Mmmmmmmm . . .

PRECIOUS LOVE (*happily*). Brother Love! I do beg your pardon.

BROTHER LOVE. And I yours, dear sister. (*Louder and in the direction of the bier*) AND YOURS TOO, GRANNY. (*Still louder and towards offstage*) Your pardon too, Father Love. (*And still louder toward the top of the stairway*) And of course, I do beg your pardon, dear, dear Precious Mother Love. To all of you: A pardon for everything. For the breath of foul air that binds us together! For life and its hideous aftermaths and afterthoughts! For yesterday's miseries and today's happy sadness! For the trillion smelly farts that tomorrow will bring! Tomorrow . . . Tomorrow . . . Tomorrow . . .

PRECIOUS LOVE (*elated*). Oh this is fun! This is fun! Are you going to do it? Are you going to do it?

BROTHER LOVE. Well . . . only for you, of course. Only for you. (*He releases* PRECIOUS LOVE *and bows.*)

PRECIOUS LOVE (*enthralled*). Oh goody! Oh goody! (BROTHER LOVE *moves near the stairway and begins mimicking rather profusely a punch-drunk boxer. The speech is purposely exaggerated. The music continues.*)

BROTHER LOVE. Oh yes . . . the afternoon B.M. I am my mother's keeper. We must remember the *schedule. Aukaudin* tu this guyh, Dahtau Successman. Well nawh come on, lisn youse guyhs. Ahmm tryin tuh talk some sense tuh youse guhys. Nayh anybody whose got any sense atahl; who wants tuh keep emself in good fisical coindision gonna take a B.M. three toines a day; when youse wake up in the moining, thas when youse rise and shine; and then youse take anuther round twelve a'cluck like the ole lady's doing now; and then ONE MORE in before youse tuck in tuh bed at night. Now lisn youse guyhs, lisn! I knows! Hell! I got the best trainer in this here camp. (*Points toward the top of the stairs*) And this here broad *always knows* what's best fer you, cause this broad is *Mother dear.* And there ain't nothing like *Mother dears.* Right, Miss Precious?

PRECIOUS LOVE (*clapping her hands*). Well I'm sure that I just have to agree, I'm sure.

BROTHER LOVE.* So fer the betterment of yer fisique and yer whole self, be sure and git in them three B.M.'s a day, and always on SCHEDUALEE. (*The word schedule is exaggerated.*)

PRECIOUS LOVE (*still clapping*). Hurrah for our leader! Hurrah! Hurrah! On with the movement. (*The "a" in Hurrah is pronounced as "a" in May or Day.*)

BROTHER LOVE* (*vindictively*). On with the movement! Before the dush . . . The movement! We must have movement! A hot steaming shower, orders to the maid . . . (*Pause, and then very sadly*) Lillie . . . Dear lillie of the flowers. Orders! Orders! And then the movement! We must have movements!

PRECIOUS LOVE (*still clapping, but now somewhat sadly.*) Hurrah for the movement! Hurrah! Hurrah!

BROTHER LOVE.* Hurrah for the movement! Orders for the day. A cooling refreshing hour resting comfortably, blissfully there! On top of the world, the commode, the drain. Down, down, down it comes. There is peace. The movement commences. There is silence. There is peace.

PRECIOUS LOVE. Hurrah for the movement! Hurrah! Hurrah!

BROTHER LOVE. There is *peace. There is peace.*

PRECIOUS LOVE (*sadly*). Mandy Luther King of Spades, I salute you. (*She curtseys.*)

BROTHER LOVE (*puzzled*). Who dat?

PRECIOUS LOVE (*equally as puzzled*). I don't know. Don't you?

BROTHER LOVE. There is something strikingly familiar about the meter.

PRECIOUS LOVE. Napoleon, do you suppose?

BROTHER LOVE. Could be. Something or other at least.

PRECIOUS LOVE. It's probably important.

BROTHER LOVE. Probably. Perhaps so. But does it really matter? In time we'll remember if it's important. Takes time for everything you know.

* Brother Love's lines in these three speeches spoken as if he were reciting a television commercial.

PRECIOUS LOVE. Takes time.

BROTHER LOVE. Takes time.

PRECIOUS LOVE. I suppose you're right.

(*There is a long pause. They stare at each other.*)

BROTHER LOVE. I suppose we could do the thing again.

PRECIOUS LOVE. I suppose.

(BROTHER LOVE *moves toward* PRECIOUS LOVE. *He bows. She curtseys. After a second or so, he snaps his fingers and the music goes up. And again they dance about the room. The lights begin to dim.*)

DARKNESS

ACT ONE

PART TWO

Scene 1

THE SCENE: The same. The play continues as if there has been no break between scenes.

Music enter; lights up, and PRECIOUS LOVE *and* BROTHER LOVE *still dancing about.*

MOTHER LOVE (*calling from offstage*). Precious . . . Precious . . . Precious Love . . . Are you still practicing?

PRECIOUS LOVE (*still dancing with* BROTHER LOVE). Yes Mother Love. My precious self is still practicing, I'm sure.

MOTHER LOVE (*a clock is heard being wound*). Very good girl. You still have a few minutes of practice time remaining.

BROTHER LOVE (*jokingly*). Home sweet home! (*He sings to the beat of the music.*) "There's no place like home for the holidays . . ." Clutz! Damn!

PRECIOUS LOVE (*teasingly*). Well! I do ever declare, Brother Love. Clutz! My, my, my. I do ever declare! What those Yankee schools won't do for you precious Southern Boys. I do declare!

FATHER LOVE (*entering*). *Clutz? Clutz?* What is wrong? What is wrong with the world today? Is the precious world coming to an end?

BROTHER LOVE (*jokingly*). Only as close as Brother Dante managed to get, Father Love.

FATHER LOVE. Is that a fact? Hmph! Well, I do declare. How about that. How about that.

PRECIOUS LOVE (*moving and kissing* FATHER LOVE). Miss Blessingful did, as I recall, speak ever so highly of the *devine Comedia.*

FATHER LOVE. Is that right? Is that a fact? Well, well, well.

BROTHER LOVE. Fare thee well, Grandmother. Father thee well (*to the coffin*).

PRECIOUS LOVE. Oh yes indeed. A most interesting and enlightening symposium.

FATHER LOVE. No doubt, I'm sure. (*Pondering*) Strange though. I'm sure the journey was a rewarding one. We all have our journeys . . . our retributions . . . . our dreams.

PRECIOUS LOVE. How was baccalaureate, Father Love?

FATHER LOVE. Baccalaureatish, dear. Baccalaureatish. Same old rigamarole. Everything on schedule. Speeches, tears, glorified tributes, dressed-up gobbledygook. Master Degreed and PhDeed Precious Colored People parading in all their glory. The Pope on the day of Ascension.

MOTHER LOVE (*calling*). Father Love . . . Father Love . . . Is that you, dear?

FATHER LOVE (*hesitantly*). Yes, Mother Love, dear. It is I. I have arrived.

MOTHER LOVE (*still calling*). Father Love . . . Are you there? Have you arrived, dear?

FATHER LOVE (*a little louder*). I have arrived, Mother Love, dear. I am home . . . (*Not quite as loud*) Home . . . Sweet home.

MOTHER LOVE. Very well. I shall be down shortly. Tell Precious Love that she may stop practicing now. (*Simultaneously,* FATHER LOVE, BROTHER LOVE, *and* PRECIOUS LOVE, *look at their watches and then at each other smiling.*) I'll be down in a minute or so. Please see to it that Brother Love has arrived by the time I come down. Family meeting, remember?

FATHER LOVE. Yes, Mother Love, dear.

BROTHER LOVE. Yes, Mother Love. I have arrived.

PRECIOUS LOVE. Yes, Mother Love.

MOTHER LOVE. Very good then. Everything is in order. I'll be right down.

BROTHER LOVE. And what is this all about, Father Love? Family meeting . . .

PRECIOUS LOVE. I thought all the arrangements were complete, I'm sure, I thought they were.

BROTHER LOVE (*sudden exasperation*). Are we bankrupt again?

PRECIOUS LOVE. Oh goody!

FATHER LOVE. Don't be impetuous, the two of you. We're going to have a little family meeting, that's all. There is no crisis, no great problem. Your mother and I have already taken measures about the little incident.

PRECIOUS LOVE (*pondering*). Hmmmmm . . . Little incident, little incident, incident . . . Hmmmmm. (*Very quickly*) Father Love! Oh my gracious Lord, No!

BROTHER LOVE (*sprightly*). Hopeful's pregnant again?

FATHER LOVE. I didn't say that. You said that.

MOTHER LOVE (*appearing at the top of the stairs*). Oh Father Love, dahhlinggg, don't play tiddle-le-winks with the children. Of course she's pregnant, dahhling. What else could it be? (MOTHER LOVE *moves grandly down the stairway.*)

BROTHER LOVE (*to the bier*). Well, Granny . . . Here we go again.

MOTHER LOVE. And how was Baccalaureate, dear?

FATHER LOVE. Baccalaureatish, dear.

MOTHER LOVE. Wonderful. Wonderful! And your address, how did it go?

FATHER LOVE. The usual response: mild, appropriate, receptive as usual. Dear, let's get on with this, shall we. We must be getting ready for the funeral, remember?

BROTHER LOVE. Is it necessary to go through this routine again? Thirteen times! Thirteen times in three years we've been through the same routine. Good Lord! Call Dr. Successman.

MOTHER LOVE (*somewhat aggravated*). Brother Love, will you please be quiet and listen, stupid son of mine. The matter has been attended to. Dr. Successman has been informed. In fact, well, Hopeful is at his office now. See . . . See . . . If you'd only wait and not jump to conclusions about things, you'd understand.

BROTHER LOVE (*sarcastically*). Yes, I know. Understand that everything is in order. Understand that we're right on schedule.

MOTHER LOVE. Understand that you have a family. Everyone isn't as fortunate as you, Brother Love; to have a family that share and resolve their problems as a unit, as we do.

BROTHER LOVE. Mother Love, you are vague . . . very very vague. (*Slight pause*) But what does it matter. An abortion's an abortion. Hmph. And life goes on.

MOTHER LOVE (*tearfully*). Yes dear, another abortion. It hurts me to my heart to have to say this again. But your sister . . . your sister, Hopeful, has disgraced us again.

FATHER LOVE. There, there, dear. Try to bear the pain. These things do happen occasionally, and to the best of families. Children are expected to make a few mistakes. Our children are no exception.

MOTHER LOVE. But that's not true, Father Love. Mistakes! Mistakes! Every time Hopeful does this to us, it's a catastrophe. These things are not supposed to happen to better families. Certainly never before in this family. Nowhere in my family tree is there an inkling of such behavior and catastrophe.

BROTHER LOVE (*adjusting something on the bier*). Hear that, Grandmother?

PRECIOUS LOVE (*as if to be helpful*). We understand, Mother Love. We do know how fortunate we are. We understand the importance of these delicate matters. (*The little girl again*) I certainly know how blessed I am to have a precious family that loves me, I do.

MOTHER LOVE (*near tears*). Oh, Hopeful, Hopeful, Hopeful! That daughter of mine. If she'd only listen. If she only had your attitude, Precious Love. Your father and I understand how it is with young people, in these modern times, we do. Seven years! Seven Years of Columbia's Child Psychology wasted! Wasted on that foolish ungrateful child. If she'd only listen. I've told her. I've told that girl time and time again, as only a precious mother who loves her precious daughter would do, I have. If she'd only listen. Then . . . Then, these little incidents, these catastrophes would never happen.

PRECIOUS LOVE (*quickly taking out her purse*). See, Mother Love. See, Father Love. I remember. I remember. I carry my materials with me everywhere. I always remember what you've told me. You can never be too careful in this wicked, wicked world. There are vileful evil spirits everywhere.

FATHER LOVE. Yes and we're right proud of you, Precious Love. Right proud of you. One would think that you were the oldest, at times.

MOTHER LOVE (*crying now, very melodramatic*). Oh what are we ever going to do? What are we ever going to do?

BROTHER LOVE. Well for one thing, we need to stop having these family meetings. That's for sure. We should let Hopeful have this baby.

PRECIOUS LOVE. But Brother Love. Hopeful is entirely too awful young to have a baby. Why . . . Why she'd have to get married.

BROTHER LOVE. Well whose baby is it, Hopeful's or ours?

MOTHER LOVE (*with nervous exasperation*). Brother Love! Father Love, am I hearing correctly? Do you hear our son? After all that we've done for him, he has the unmitigated gall to suggest that, that I become a grandmother before any of my precious children are even grown. (*She starts to cry again.*)

FATHER LOVE (*comforting*). There, there, dear. There, there. He's only a child.

MOTHER LOVE. Why, why, what would I be able to say at sorority meetings? Why, my own baby, my precious little daughter who was a debutante. (*Frightfully*) Oh my God! They'd discontinue my membership.

FATHER LOVE. There, there dear. Try to bear the pain. Everything will be all right, I'm sure.

MOTHER LOVE (*almost hysterical*). But, But . . . Can you imagine me at the convention next year? "Oh yes, Mrs. *Happy Hollow*, didn't you know? I'm a grandmother. Yesssssss . . . a Grandmother! Hopeful is married. She's been married for more than a year now. That dear, dear, daughter of mine. She just went off and eloped and didn't even let us know. Isn't that just too cute? These modern children are just always so full of surprises, aren't they? My son-in-law? Oh he's just the nicest young man. A gay young blade if I've ever seen one. His name? (*Very nervously*) Henry . . . Yes, Henry, Henry something or other. Or is it Joe? Or Amos? Or is it . . . Is it . . . (*She starts to cry again.*)

PRECIOUS LOVE (*comforting* MOTHER LOVE). Father Love, does Hopeful know? Does she know who he is?

FATHER LOVE. I'm not sure. Your mother and I called Sinners at the University last evening. He mentioned that Hopeful has been seen in the company of a young man there quite often as of late. Let me see now. His name was . . . It was . . . Henry something or other. Yes, Henry. That's it. Henry Joseph Hankerson!

PRECIOUS LOVE (*surprised*). Henry Joseph Hankerson!

BROTHER LOVE. You're joking of course. Whoever heard of anyone with a name like that?

MOTHER LOVE. Oh! My gracious alive! How ordinary sounding.

PRECIOUS LOVE. Joseph? How biblical. Henry Joseph Hankerson. That's cute. Is he a darkie, Father Love? The name sounds rather Africana.

FATHER LOVE. Can't be sure. Can't be sure. Sinners mentioned that he was originally from Miami, Florida.

PRECIOUS LOVE (*elated*). Miami, Florida! You mean Miami Beach, Florida?

BROTHER LOVE. Don't be ridiculous, Precious Love. There aren't any Heavenly Heights at that place.

MOTHER LOVE. Don't stop there, Father Love. Tell all! Tell them the rest.

FATHER LOVE. Well I don't rightly think that the other part's that important, dear.

MOTHER LOVE (*snappingly*). Tell them! Goddamn it! Tell them! They may as well know what's in store for them if we don't do something about this matter.

FATHER LOVE (*somewhat reluctantly*). Well it seems as if this Henry Joseph Hankerson is, well, is just a NOBODY! JUST A NOBODY! I understand that he's related to the Hankersons from round these parts, the Hankersons over in Goodbread Alley.

PRECIOUS LOVE (*frightfully*). Billie Joseph Hankerson.

MOTHER LOVE (*overlapping*). Goodbread Alley! Ugghh! Precious Love, you can't imagine the kind of people, you can't imagine the kind of people that live over there. They're . . . They're animals! Savages!

PRECIOUS LOVE (*just above a whisper*). Billie Joe Hankerson.

FATHER LOVE. And, who, Precious Love, is Billie Joe Hankerson?

PRECIOUS LOVE. He . . . He's one of them old dirty nasty niggers over there in Goodbread Alley. He's always teasing me and calling me awful names, and saying vile terrible things into my precious ears.

MOTHER LOVE (*horrified*). What kinds of things, Precious Love?

PRECIOUS LOVE. Real, real, dirty, nasty, vileful things, Mother Love. Real, awful, terrible things; terrible things like *hell, damn, sonuvabitch,* Mother . . .

BROTHER LOVE (*overlapping, roaring*). Ha ha ha ha ha . . .

MOTHER LOVE. Oh my precious, precious little baby. (*She embraces* PRECIOUS LOVE.) Your precious ears have been tainted by vileness. My precious, precious baby.

FATHER LOVE (*infuriated*). The blackheart must be punished. He must be dealt with immediately. How dare he taint the precious ears of my precious daughter. How dare he! Damn nigger!

BROTHER LOVE (*still laughing*). Her precious ears have been tainted permanently.

FATHER LOVE (*scornfully*). Brother Love! Acquit yourself of this unbrotherly behavior or leave the room immediately.

BROTHER LOVE. I'm sorry, Father Love. (*Whispering towards the bier*) Like Hell I am, eh, Granny?

FATHER LOVE. What did you just say?

BROTHER LOVE (*catching himself*). I . . . I said, I said . . . Like hell will Henry Joseph Hankerson be afforded the honor of affiance with the likes of my precious fair sister, Hopeful. Like hell will the blackheart do such, as would well be the case, if the matter is not attended to at once! It is not the time for the bloods to become one. (*Slight pause*) And besides, I understand that they stink.

PRECIOUS LOVE (*crying now*). And . . . And, Father Love, and precious family of mine, that old nasty Billie Joe Hankerson told me, he told me . . .

FATHER LOVE (*like a knight in shining armor*). What else did that old nasty dirty Billie Joe Hankerson tell you, precious daughter?

PRECIOUS LOVE. He told me, precious family of mine, that, that God Almighty and powerful above was, was a black God! (MOTHER LOVE *screams.*) He said that God was as black as he was and as black as all them people over there in Goodbread Alley.

MOTHER LOVE (*bursting, almost to the point of hysteria*). Enough! Enough! I can't take it! I can't take it! I can't take it! Give me strength! Father Love! I suggest that we vote immediately! Before the very foundation to this holy and precious establishment crumbles away to precious nothingness!

FATHER LOVE. I agree, Mother Love. I agree! (*Slight pause*) And this is no dream. Then is it unanimous? Say aye, if it is so, precious family.

MOTHER LOVE. Aye.

PRECIOUS LOVE (*tearfully*). Aye.

BROTHER LOVE (*somewhat hesitantly*). Aye.

MOTHER LOVE. And you, Father Love?

FATHER LOVE (*moving toward the bier*). Grandmother Love and I vote . . . vote, aye.

MOTHER LOVE. Poor Grandmother. Poor, poor, Grandmother.

PRECIOUS LOVE. Dear, dear Grandmother.

BROTHER LOVE. A mighty fortress is our . . .

LILLIE (*entering*). Mrs. Love . . . Madam . . .

MOTHER LOVE (*tearfully*). Yes, Lillie.

LILLIE. The ladies from your sorority are entering the driveway.

MOTHER LOVE. Oh dear, dear, dear. They're here. I'll have to hurry. (*She starts to leave—and stops.*) Father Love . . . THE MATTER IS SETTLED?

FATHER LOVE. Yes, dear. The matter is settled.

MOTHER LOVE (*approaching the stairway*). Very well then. And please, Father Love, try not to be impertinent to P.P. and the girls. They're only trying to be helpful.

FATHER LOVE. I won't, dear.

MOTHER LOVE. Lillie . . . Have the ladies come in. Give me a moment or so to change before you send them up.

BROTHER LOVE. Mother Love, you're having them come up? Why up rather than down . . . here?

MOTHER LOVE. Brother Love, we are in mourning, remember? How would it look for us to receive people who have come to comfort me, down here?

BROTHER LOVE. Yes, but I still don't . . . But what does it matter, really? What does it matter?

MOTHER LOVE. Yes, you're quite right, I'm sure. (*Affirmatively*) Your Grandmother is dead, Son. She is resting in Abraham's bosom at this very moment. We are in mourning, remember? We are in mourning. Come, Precious Love.

(*The two women exit up the stairway.*)

FATHER LOVE (*leaving*). Your mother says that we are in mourning, son. Please . . . Try to understand that we are in mourning. (*He exits.*)

(*The sorority sisters enter. There are from two to four women at the most. They are gaudily made up. Cheap fur pieces and excessive jewelry add to the absurdity of their appearance.*)

MISS P. P. (*in a high falsetto*). Brother Love! Girls, will you just look at Brother Love. I do declare this precious child has certainly grown. I have been hearing great things about you, Brother Love. When are we going to get a peek at this novelette we hear you've been writing?

BROTHER LOVE. Oh it's nothing, Miss P. P., nothing at all. Just throwing around some ideas on paper. Mother Love shouldn't have mentioned it yet. It's really nothing.

MISS P. P. Ohhhhhh, now don't be so modest with us, Brother Love. Remember, I taught you English Literature. I taught you English Literature. I know your talents, boy, I do. I know your abilities. Girls, I have always said that this young man was exceptionally talented. I have always said so, I have. Isn't that right, Brother Love?

BROTHER LOVE. Yes, Miss P. P. Yes mam. Still . . . What I'm doing amounts to little or nothing, really. Ideas mainly. Ideas that have yet to be . . .

MISS P. P. Well I'm sure that we will just not listen to any of that kind of talk, will we, girls? And before we leave, you had better read some of this lil ole novelette to us, or I swear to God that we'll just never forgive you, will we girls?

BROTHER LOVE. Well . . . Maybe a few lines. But it's really nothing, ladies; really nothing.

PRECIOUS LOVE (*appears at the top of the stairs*). Miss P. P. Ladies . . . Mother will see you now.

(*Almost ritualistically, the mood of the women shifts to one of sadness.* MISS P. P. *begins to cry. The other women, as if cued, take handkerchiefs out and sniffle.*)

MISS P. P. Precious Love . . . Dear, dear Precious Love. How is the dear?

PRECIOUS LOVE. She's taking it well, I'm sure, Miss P. P. Won't you ladies please come up now?

(*The ladies solemnly file up the stairway. The lights begin to fade and focus on* BROTHER LOVE *who has moved beside the coffin. Off stage the women are heard singing.*)

WOMEN (*offstage*). The hymn (*To the melody of "America the Beautiful"*).

> Sorority . . . Sorority,
> The Sisters in the bond.
> Sorority . . . Sorority,
> The bond so big and strong.
> Sorority . . . Sorority,
> And we shall move along.
> Sorority . . . Sorority,
> We'll even stand the bomb.

(*The song is repeated a second time.*)

BROTHER LOVE (*overlapping, during the second chorus; to the bier*). Hear those bitches. Hear them, Granny. Listen to them. "Sorority, the sisters in the bond; the bond so big and strong; they'll even stand the bomb." Isn't that absurd? Stupid fools. Fighting to hold on to a dream. Some dream. Some dream. (*A pause*) Oh I wish . . . I wish . . . (*Angrily*) You old cold bitch! (*He spits onto the bier.*) Why didn't you die? Goddamn you! I hate you! Why didn't you die? Why didn't you die? Why didn't you die?

(*The lights begin to fade out. The singing of the sorority sisters is now overlapped and drowned out by other voices singing the old Negro spiritual, "I've Been Buked."* BROTHER LOVE *backs away and exits. Only the bier is seen until the complete blackout.*)

I've been buked and I've been scorned.
Yes, I've been buked and I've been scorned,
    children.
I've been buked and I've been scorned.
I've been talked about sho as you born.
There is trouble all over this world.
There is trouble all over this world,
    children.
There is trouble all over this world.
There is trouble all over this world.
Ain't gwine lay my ligion down.
Yes, ain't gwine lay my ligion down,
    children.
Ain't gwine lay my ligion down
Ain't gwine lay my ligion down.

DARKNESS

ACT ONE

PART TWO

Scene 2

    The stage is dark for only a moment or so between the division of scenes.

    What is most important, for staging this scene, is that the mystic quality of a dream be established. We are concerned with a sequence of sensations, images, thoughts, etc. passing through a sleeping person's mind.

Author's suggestions about staging: (1) A white spot (dimmed a bit) on the BOY *who is located at downstage right. (2)* BROTHER LOVE *(white) off to the right side of the bier. He recites the dialogue of the narrator. A blue spot is on him. (3)* BROTHER LOVE *(Negro) off to the left side of the bier. He is almost unseen. A purple spot is on him. (4) The sorority sisters are seated in chairs at center stage. They face the bier with their backs to the audience.*

NARRATOR *(passionately)*. An open field stretched for miles about. Red clay hills in the distance. An early morning breeze —central Georgia. A colored boy of thirteen standing upright— a mule grazing nearby. A blood-red sun blazing overhead. An occasional rumble-like sound from above.

THE BOY. Lord have mercy! It's gonna rain. *(Pause)* Well ain't that one. The devil and his wife shorenuf must be fighting now with the sun up there a'blazing like that. *(To the mule)* Jinny—guess we'd better git going now or we'll shorenuf drown, gal.

NARRATOR. A crackling of thunder—and the boy looking hesitantly in various directions; and then kneeling and picking up a wrapped package. The boy unties the package. A revolver is revealed. The boy faces the animal and points the weapon in its direction.

THE BOY *(jokingly)*. Shoot, Jinny! I ain't gonna kill you, girl. I shore wouldn't git no gun to run off and kill no dumb jackass. You don't think I'd take and shoot you, do you, girl? *With this gun?* Lord, no, Jesus! Mama'd kill me for shore if I went off and did something as stupid as that. Hmph! Sides—done all we could to git her to let me keep the damn thing. So you needn't worry none, girl. You just sit there and keep still now so I can git the feel of this thing.

NARRATOR. The boy raises the gun as if preparing to fire it.

THE BOY. Now see . . . See, Jinny. All you got to know about this thing is that you ain't suppose to pull this here click here unless you really want to kill something. See . . .

NARRATOR. It begins to rain. The boy lowers the weapon and then raises it again. The animal moves about. The boy abruptly, but proudly, paces off thirteen steps, shouting aloud the numbers in cadence. He stops and brings the weapon to his side. He ponders to himself for a moment and raises the gun again—pointing it toward the beast.

A piercing bursting eruption from above. And the boy moving away from the beast in fear.

THE BOY (*frightfully*). Lord, Jesus! I ain't got no business being such a scaredy cat. I'm thirteen years old today. Pa says I's a man today. He says Ahm almost a man today.

NARRATOR. The sound of thunder again. Spasmodic ejaculations from the sky above—entering and subsiding. A branch from a tree falling to the ground. And the animal moving about frightfully in meaningless directions. And the boy—terrified and falling onto the ground. And the crackling outburst of a beast in pain. And the sound of the rain seemingly amplified a thousand times over. (*Pause*) And the boy—horrified, and grabbing ahold of his arms; examining them closely, as if they were torn away from his body . . . and then tenderly squeezing his fingers and hands between his legs for a long second. (*Pause*) And the boy placing the damp hand that held the weapon into his mouth, as if to warm it; to stop the pain.

And the surmounting cries of the beast—the beast in pain. And the boy staring sadly at the animal . . . a sickening sight. The boy, looking, wanting not to believe . . . And the boy finally overcome to the state of vomit at the sight of the very red blood, pouring away from the dying body; fast—very fast, and then settling into a pool of murky red liquid; the blood of life, being sucked away into the bowels of a very black and uneasy earth. (*The second verse of the Negro spiritual enters and overlaps the remaining action.*)

There is trouble all over this world.
Yes, there is trouble all over this world,
   children.
There is trouble all over this world.
There is trouble all over this world.

NARRATOR (*continuing, overlapping*). And the boy panics. He takes a handful of black wet earth and frantically attempts to insert it into the animal's wound. (*Pause*) And then . . . a final cry from the animal. The beast dies. (*The lights begin to fade. Continuing*) And the boy slowly rising with the gun in the hand that destroyed the beast.

THE BOY (*sadly*). Oh, Lord! Damn! Damn! Damn!

NARRATOR. And the boy firing the weapon; emptying it of its entrails into the animal's body, and then slowly walking toward the tree. He kneels there, at the foot of the tree and hurriedly buries the weapon.

And the rain and the thunder and the cries of the boy become one.

THE BOY (*cryingly*). Mama . . . Mama . . . Mama . . .

DARKNESS

(*A quick count and then back to main set and final scene.*)

ACT ONE

PART TWO

Scene 3

APOTHEOSIS

Lights up. The sorority sisters are now congregated together. They listen in delight as BROTHER LOVE (*both Negro and White* BROTHER LOVES *play as one*) *recites to them a brief synopsis of the novel he is writing.*

It must be established through direction and acting that the vignette of the colored boy killing the mule has been a part of

BROTHER LOVE's *monologue. The first lines of the monologue should begin during the change of scenes.*

This final scene requires a staccato effect; full percussive-like carthartic resolution.

BROTHER LOVE BLACK (*abruptly, resoundingly*). And so this slow purge towards meeting the reality . . . the life . . . explodes into painful understandings and knowledges as the boy emerges into adolescence. For then, the reality of the life can no longer be kept hidden behind the veil of the dream which has been the very essence of his existence up to this point.

(*The change of scenes is complete. The sorority sisters listen, entranced by the eloquence of the brothers who are now one.*)

BROTHER LOVE WHITE. And . . . my protagonist, dear ladies, is thrown, his eyes wide open, plum smack damn into the middle of the forties. And . . . And . . . well I haven't given him a name yet, mind you. So let's just call him . . . Clutz; yeah . . . Clutz! Let's just call him Clutz. Clutz it is! And so Clutz lives . . .

BROTHER LOVE BLACK. He suffers . . .

BROTHER LOVE WHITE. He dreams . . . Imagine if you will, Miss P. P., Clutz is in an elementary school. The school bell starts a'ringing like all hell that day. Something very terrible has happened. Sirens are blasting away all over the city every which-a-way. Cars on the streets are honking their horns something mighty frightful. Remember . . . Clutz is just a lil olè child now. And that poor boy is as scared as all pure hell. And that poor boy says to himself, "My God! Has the world gone plum crazy?"

BROTHER LOVE BLACK. But then . . . just as quick as all the confusion had started, everything is all quiet again. Quiet like a hush-a-bye lullaby. The world just stops completely still. And you can't even hear the sweet sound of a baby sucking away at his mammy's nipple. The whole world is silent. Stilled faces . . . glazed eyes seem to devour that boy as he makes his way home. Home to his mama—his sweet mama. A nation is mourning. A nation eulogizes with ramifications of love and honor and respect for *that man . . . that man* who had just a while ago stole his way to the sweet bosom of Abraham. When the boy gets home, his mama makes some sense of all the confusion for him. She says to him those words in such a terrifying way until he knows for sure that he ain't gonna ever forget them words for as long as he lives on God's sweet earth. With all them tears falling down that woman's face, she says to him: "Honey, git down on your knees and pray! Mr. Roosevelt is dead! Mr. Roosevelt is dead!"

BROTHER LOVE WHITE. And Clutz mourns for his first hero. (*Slight pause*) How emotional the times are during that poor boy's childhood, Miss P. P.

BROTHER LOVE BLACK. TERRIFYING!

BROTHER LOVE WHITE. And there was that other time. Yes, that day too. And Clutz's mama crying and carrying on all over again. When was it—before that man died, or was it after he died? It was something awfully mysterious about this bomb; this great big old powerful bomb that is set off somewhere and kills thousands and thousands of people . . .

BROTHER LOVE BLACK. Slant-eyed yellow people!

(PRECIOUS LOVE *appears. The white* PRECIOUS LOVE. *She stands and listens.*)

BROTHER LOVE WHITE. "Those dirty Japs! Those damn dirty Japs!" Miss P. P., this is all them poor helpless children heard everywhere during those times. "Those goddamn Jap sonsavbitches! Good for them! They were warned! They were warned!"

BROTHER LOVE BLACK (*sarcastically*). The American Dream is saved again.

BROTHER LOVE WHITE. Yes, my brother! Yes! Yes! Yes! That dream is saved again. (*Slight pause*) And this is when that child gets his first hearing about this dream.

BROTHER LOVE BLACK. Yes . . . but again—Clutz's mama crying again. "Lord, when is my mama gonna stop crying?" that boy says. But then he finds out the woman's crying because she's happy. The boy's daddy is coming home. The boy's daddy is on his way home; coming clear across all that water to his sweet wife and child. Coming home to his home sweet home.

BROTHER LOVE WHITE. But when his daddy gets home, he's acting differently from the way he acted before he went across that ocean to fight those dirty, those dirty Japs. He's acting mighty, mighty strange now. Clutz ain't never seen his daddy act like he acted now. Something mighty terrible must have happened to that man while he was over there in that war. Something terrible had hurt that boy's daddy. Took Clutz a long time before he figured out what had happened to that man. It all started that morning when his mama told him that his daddy had been called practically outta his senses by some white men cause his daddy had refused to sit in the colored seats on the city bus.

BROTHER LOVE BLACK. Lord oh Lord, Clutz's daddy, that man! Everybody in the neighborhood called him the craziest man. But he wouldn't stop. No, he just wouldn't stop. He got beat and kicked around so much up to the time Clutz was in high school, until that big pretty man that had come back from that war wasn't nothing but a cringy bag of bones. Yeah . . . Clutz's daddy shorenuf wasn't a man no more. But he just kept on fighting and causing trouble until a 38-caliber bullet found its way clear through his cringy boney skull one dark Saturday night. (MOTHER LOVE *appears.*) And then the craziest thing happened, Miss P. P.

BROTHER LOVE WHITE. The damnest craziest thing! In no time at all, back across the waters went a couple of Clutz's cousins to some godforsaken place called Korea. (*Slight pause*) And neither of them ever came back. They never came back. Though he was only a child, Clutz couldn't help but think to himself . . .

BROTHER LOVE BLACK. "This ain't right! This ain't right at

all! Seems like those poor boys just ain't never got a chance to live. They ain't never got a chance to live."

BROTHER LOVE WHITE. But by then, the boy was finally beginning to understand what everything was all about. Now Miss P. P., that boy certainly did love America, his country . . . They, his country, America—they had seen to that. But the Dream? The Dream? My country 'tis of thee and all that, that . . . crap? Well none of it seemed to have had any kind of meaning to him any more. No goddamn meaning at all. (*With nervous exasperation*) Yet . . . Yet, his teachers at school were beginning to act very peculiar about something. There was something very strange going on; something that had to do with this dream . . . Again! All over again. Something about that goddamn dream! (*The last lines antagonize the sorority sisters. They begin to fidget and move about.*) What a mess of a world to be living in!

BROTHER LOVE BLACK. A goddamn funny house!

BOTH BROTHER LOVES. A mess of mass chaotic confusion leading here and there and absolutely no goddamn where!

(MOTHER LOVE *gives with a sharp, piercing scream. She then starts to moan, as if she were experiencing labor pains. This business of hers will overlap the monologue to* CURTAIN. PRECIOUS LOVE *at this point begins to laugh. Her laughter and giggling produces a rather sickening sound. It becomes evident at this point that she is near madness. The music from the minuet enters again. Occasionally,* PRECIOUS LOVE *enters into the ballet routine which began the play.*)

BROTHER LOVE BLACK (*overlapping*). But then . . . then . . . a lull; a quiet hush-a-bye baby lullaby.

(*The sorority sisters are now crying. They make occasional outbursts and screams which depict intense inner suffering and turmoil.* FATHER LOVE *enters at this point. He goes to the bier and kneels before the body and clasps his hands together in prayer. We vaguely hear him reciting the child's prayer.*)

FATHER LOVE (*just above whisper, overlapping*). "Now I lay

me down to sleep, I pray thee Lord my soul to keep. If I should die before I wake, I pray thee Lord my soul to take." (*He continues to end of play.*)

BROTHER LOVE BLACK. My God! What was happening now?

BROTHER LOVE WHITE. Had the world gone plum crazy again?

BROTHER LOVE BLACK (*resoundingly*). Goddammit! Clutz had had it!

BROTHER LOVE WHITE (*with fervor*). He was damn tired of being a boy!

BROTHER LOVE BLACK. Despite the fact that certain species of people had other ideas in mind.

BROTHER LOVE WHITE. He remembered his daddy!

BOTH BROTHER LOVES. He was tired of being a boy child! (*Slight pause, then sadly*) Boy child.

(FATHER LOVE's *chanting,* MOTHER LOVE's *moaning, and* PRECIOUS LOVE's *dancing about and laughter continue to overlap the monologue. The sorority sisters are now walking aimlessly about the room. They are beginning to undress.*)

BROTHER LOVE BLACK. And then Miss P. P. . . . (*Slight pause*) Miss P. P.

BROTHER LOVE WHITE. Miss P. P. . . .

BROTHER LOVE BLACK. Miss P. P. . . .

BROTHER LOVE WHITE. Miss P. P. . . .

BROTHER LOVE BLACK. Miss P. P. . . .

BOTH BROTHER LOVES (*screamingly*). Miss P. Peeeeeeeeeeee . . . (MISS *P. P. screams frightfully. She then enters into a rather catatonic state of uneasy quivering and jerking-like bodily movements.*) Then, Miss P. P. You know what happened? What happened after that. You know goddamn well, you do!

(MISS P. P. *screams again. The other sorority sisters scream. They too now enter into catatonic bodily movements. Now enter the sounds of ringing chimes. The following series of lines to accompaniment of an effect full, voluminous, staccato. Almost equivalent to that of a constant drum roll.*)

BROTHER LOVE WHITE. Sit-ins . . . .

BROTHER LOVE BLACK. Stand-ins . . .

BROTHER LOVE WHITE. Walk-ins . . .

BROTHER LOVE BLACK. Wade-ins . . .

BROTHER LOVE WHITE. A bald-headed madman slamming away his shoes on a table.

BROTHER LOVE BLACK. A bearded beatnik and other hairy apes a'comin' down the mountains.

BROTHER LOVE WHITE. Hands across the sea . . .

BROTHER LOVE BLACK. My country tis of thee . . .

BROTHER LOVE WHITE. Sit-ins . . .

BROTHER LOVE BLACK. Stand-ins . . .

BROTHER LOVE WHITE. Walk-ins . . .

BROTHER LOVE BLACK. Ride-ins . . .

BROTHER LOVE WHITE. God bless the Pope.

BROTHER LOVE BLACK. May he rest in peace.

BROTHER LOVE WHITE. The nation must move forward with vigahhh . . .

BROTHER LOVE BLACK. Vigahhhhhhhhh . . .

BROTHER LOVE WHITE. Vigahhhhhhhh . . .

BROTHER LOVE BLACK. God bless America and all that jazz.

BROTHER LOVE WHITE (*singing*). "There is trouble all over this world . . ."

BROTHER LOVE BLACK (*singing*). "We shall overcome. We shall overcome . . ."

BROTHER LOVE WHITE. Bullshit!

BROTHER LOVE BLACK. Bullshit! Amen! Turn thy cheek, fool! Don't mind the dogs. They're only animals. They're just playing.

BROTHER LOVE WHITE. Bullshit! I'm getting tired of this crap! (*Resoundingly*) Forward with vigahhhhhhhh . . .

BROTHER LOVE BLACK (*religiously, like an old Southern Baptist preacher*). With vigahhhhhhhhhhhh . . .

BROTHER LOVE WHITE. Burning flesh!

BROTHER LOVE BLACK. A heifer!

BROTHER LOVE WHITE. Hands across the sea.

BROTHER LOVE BLACK (*joyfully*). And we just march along.

BOTH BROTHER LOVES. March on, darkies . . . March, darkies, march!

BROTHER LOVE WHITE. On to the promised land of nowhere!

BROTHER LOVE BLACK. And that big, fat, big-mouthed black pretty woman leads us on in song.

BROTHER LOVE WHITE (*singing*). "I've been buked and I've been scorned. I've been buked and I've been scorned . . ."

BROTHER LOVE BLACK (*cantoring*). "There is trouble all over this world . . . There is trouble all over this world . . ."

BROTHER LOVE WHITE (*now cantoring, as if answering the cries*). "What does it mean . . . Where is it leading us . . ."

BOTH BROTHER LOVES (*snappingly, directly to audience*). Nowhere! My brothers! Here and there and absolutely no goddamn where! (*After a pause*) And then . . . Prayer!

BROTHER LOVE WHITE. Prayer from your leader.

BROTHER LOVE BLACK. Prayer from that man.

BOTH BROTHER LOVES (*chantingly*). I have a dream . . .

THE OTHER CHARACTERS. Aaaaaaaamen, brother!

BOTH BROTHER LOVES. I have a dream . . .

THE OTHER CHARACTERS. Aaaaaaaamen, brother!

BOTH BROTHER LOVES. I have a dream . . .

THE OTHER CHARACTERS. Aaaaaaaamen, brother!

BOTH BROTHER LOVES (*with joyful passion*). Requimmmmmm-mm . . .

(*The other characters stop their movements. There is a full minute of quiet. Only the ringing chimes are heard.* LILLIE OF THE FLOWERS, *played by the Negro* PRECIOUS LOVE, *enters. Two other women escort the sorority sisters off the stage. One of them will return and take* PRECIOUS LOVE *away.* PRECIOUS LOVE *hums the melody to the minuet as she is leaving. A man who is also dressed in white will enter and take* FATHER LOVE *away. He returns and escorts the two* BROTHER LOVES *off the stage after their monologue is completed.*)

(*Following monologue overlapping the business.*)

BOTH BROTHER LOVES. The heifer is still bleeding.
Passion! Beautiful pain. A hush-a-bye baby lullaby.
The nation, my country tis of thee, is silent again.
The world is stilled.
Another man is dead.
Another hero has stole his way to the bosom of Abraham.
Another man is dead.
For a moment—a pitiful handful of seconds . . .
Hands across the sea . . . and the world is silent.
There is peace . . . There is peace . . . There is peace . . .
There is peace . . . There is peace . . .

(*The last lines are repeated as the* BROTHERS *are taken off the stage.* LILLIE OF THE FLOWERS *gestures towards* MOTHER LOVE. LILLIE *is smiling.*)

MOTHER LOVE (*frightfully*). I won't go! I will not go back there! I won't go without Hopeful Damn-it-to-hell-all! I won't go without Hopeful! You can't make me go. (LILLIE *moves towards* MOTHER LOVE.) You black nigger! Take your black hands off of me! I won't go! I won't go! I will not go back there! (LILLIE *takes her away. Lamentfully, as she is taken away*) Hoooooooooooooooopeeeeeeefulllllll . . . Where is Hopeful? Where is Hopeful? Hooooooooopeeeeeeefulllll . . .

(*A dim light beams on the bier for a long second before fading. The clanking sounds of iron doors being closed are heard.*)

DARKNESS

CURTAIN

Notes on Contributors

ED BULLINS, formerly of San Francisco, where he was associated with the Black Arts Theatre, now lives in New York City. He edits *Black Theatre* magazine and is resident playwright at the New Lafayette Theatre, which produced his three-act play *In the Wine Time* and, more recently, *Goin' a Buffalo*.

A number of Mr. Bullins' plays have been produced off-Broadway and have been received with critical enthusiasm. *The Electronic Nigger, Clara's Old Man,* and *Son, Come Home* were produced in 1968 by the American Place Theatre. In 1969 his play *The Gentleman Caller* was one of four by black playwrights produced under the title *Black Quartet*. Another Bullins play, *The Pig Pen,* was produced off-Broadway in the spring of 1970.

A talented creative writer, Mr. Bullins is also an able spokesman for the revolutionary theater, and his provocative essays have appeared in several publications.

PAUL CARTER HARRISON was born and reared in New York City. His childhood was spent in Harlem, but he moved to "the artistic ghetto" of Greenwich Village in his early teens. In 1961 he went to Europe, taking up residence in Amsterdam. During this time, he produced and directed his works for stage, television, and film and published two one-act plays, *Pavane for a Dead-pan Minstrel* and *The Experimental Leader*. Both plays have since been produced in America and have enjoyed critical—if not financial— success.

Two other one-act plays produced in Europe and America are *Pawns* and *Tophat*. Mr. Harrison also published two books in the Netherlands, *The Modern Drama Footnote* (a collection of essays on various approaches to modern theater) and *A Rebel's Dialogue* (based on *The Experimental Leader*). His first novel, *One Anonymous Mourning,* is to be published by Doubleday. He currently teaches playwriting at Howard University in Washington, D.C.

ADRIENNE KENNEDY, the daughter of a school teacher and social worker, was born in 1931 in Pittsburgh and grew up in Cleveland, Ohio. After high school she attended Ohio State University but found the social structure there during the fifties "so opposed to Negroes" that she hardly did any academic work and started writing at twenty. She has written two novels, as well as stories and poems. Her plays include *Funnyhouse of a Negro* (1962), *The Owl Answers* (1963), *A Lesson in Dead Language* (1964), *A Rat's Mass* (1965), and *A Beast's Story* (1966).

The Owl Answers was produced for the first time at the White Barn Theater in Westport, Connecticut, sponsored by Eva LeGallienne, Ralph Alswang, and Lucille Lortel. The play was directed by Michael Kahn. *A Rat's Mass* was performed by the Theater Company of Boston in April, 1966. Her play *Funnyhouse of a Negro* won an Obie Distinguished Play Award in 1964.

Miss Kennedy's play *In His Own Write,* an adaptation of John

Lennon's book, was presented by the National Theatre in London. *A Beast's Story* was produced by the New York Shakespeare Festival Public Theatre. Miss Kennedy is presently living in New York City.

WILLIAM WELLINGTON MACKEY is from Louisiana and attended Southern University in Baton Rouge. After graduation in 1958 he taught high school in Miami, Florida. With money earned during summers as a waiter and bellhop in the Catskills—a job Cab Calloway helped him land—he entered the University of Minnesota, where he earned a master's degree.

While working as a recreational therapist at the Colorado State Hospital in Pueblo, Mr. Mackey completed his first full-length play, *Behold! Cometh the Vanderkellans*, begun when he was a graduate student at Minnesota. The play, "an attack on the black bourgeoisie" done in avant-garde manner, was performed by the Eden Workshop, the Negro theater group in Denver, in 1965. *Cometh the Vanderkellans*, which is particularly satiric of a Negro college president and his family, has attracted a great deal of attention.

Mr. Mackey's one-act play *Requiem for Brother X, A Homage to Malcolm X* has been presented at various experimental theaters and universities around the country and had a twelve-week run at Chicago's Hull House Parkway Theater in 1968. His musical *Billy Noname*, written in collaboration with the London composer Johnny Brandon, has been produced off-Broadway.

DOUGLAS TURNER WARD was born on a plantation at Burnside, Louisiana, and grew up in New Orleans. In 1948 he came to New York and worked as a journalist for three years. To learn the actor's craft as an aid in his ambition to become a playwright, he enrolled in Paul Mann's Actors' Workshop. From this grew a successful acting career. He made his debut at off-Broadway's highly esteemed Circle in the Square in *The Iceman Cometh*. Next he was featured in the New York City

Center production of *Lost in the Stars*, under the direction of Jose Quintero. He then won the position of understudy to Sidney Poitier in *A Raisin in the Sun* and assumed this leading role opposite Claudia McNeil during the ten-month national tour of the play. On Broadway he has also been seen in *One Flew Over the Cuckoo's Nest* with Kirk Douglas, and with Jean Simmons and Raf Vallone in the pre-Broadway tour of *Rich Little Rich Girl*. Off-Broadway he gained critical acclaim in *The Blacks* and *Blood Knot*, playing the latter in Chicago and Washington as well. His Shakespearean credits include *Coriolanus* for the New York Shakespeare Festival. On television, Mr. Ward has been seen on many of the leading network shows, including *East Side, West Side, The DuPont Show of the Month*, and *The Edge of Night*, and as co-star of a television special on CBS's *Look Up and Live*.

Mr. Ward's first produced plays, *Happy Ending* and *Day of Absence*, were presented at the St. Mark's Playhouse with Mr. Ward acting in one of the major roles. The satiric double bill, which won praise from critics and audiences alike, received the Vernon Rice Drama Award and the Obie Award in 1966, and had a run of well over a year.